# GRASS ROOTS

# GRASS ROOTS

## How Ordinary People
## Are Changing America

Tom Adams

A Citadel Press Book
Published by Carol Publishing Group

A Citadel Press Book
Published by Carol Publishing Group
Citadel Press is a registered trademark of Carol
  Communications, Inc.

Editorial Offices: 600 Madison Avenue, New York, N.Y. 10022
Sales & Distribution Offices: 120 Enterprise Avenue,
  Secaucus, N.J. 07094
In Canada: Musson Book Company, a division of General Publishing
  Company, Ltd., Don Mills, Ontario M3B 2T6

Queries regarding rights and permissions should be addressed to
  Carol Publishing Group, 600 Madison Avenue, New York, N.Y. 10022

Carol Publishing Group books are available at special discounts for bulk purchases, for sales promotions, fund raising, or educational purposes. Special editions can be created to specifications. For details contact: Special Sales Department, Carol Publishing Group, 120 Enterprise Avenue, Secaucus, N.J. 07094

Manufactured in the United States of America

10  9  8  7  6  5  4  3  2  1

**Library of Congress Cataloging-in-Publication Data**

Adams, William Thomas, 1929-
     Grass roots : how ordinary people are changing America / by
Tom Adams.
          p.  cm.
     Includes bibliographical references and index.
     ISBN 0-8065-1246-6 --ISBN 0-8065-1232-6 (pbk.)
          1. Social movements--United States. 2. Pressure groups--
United States. 3. Political participation--United States. I. Title.
HN65.A62   1991
303.484'0973--dc20                              91-20309

*To Mother and my son, Philip*

# Contents

# Acknowledgments

Scores of people gave information, guidance, and support as I wrote this book about ordinary people who exercise their right in America to seek redress of a grievance.

From the beginning, Daniel Levy, my editor at Citadel Press, eagerly embraced the idea for this book and encouraged me to explore and record these powerful social movements. And Steven Schragis, the publisher, enthusiastically approved of my approach.

George Greenfield of Lecture Literary Management encouraged me to develop this book and arrange presentations to audiences concerned with these issues.I obtained invaluable information about grass roots activism from many sources. Through personal interviews with key grass roots leaders and scholars, important insights were gained. I am indebted to the following for their observations: Lois Marie Biggs, Keith Schuchard, Bobby Muller, Ingrid Newkirk, Susan Rich, Elliot Katz, Randy Hayes, Larry Kramer, Randy Shilts, Paul Allen, Tom Huntington, Pat and Jack Baird, Terry Rakolta, Eve Pell, Doris Aiken, George Gerbner, Howard and Marion Higman, and Joan Brann.

In addition to interviews, I sent questionnaires and an early draft of the book to grass roots activists to gain insights, reactions, and materials. Special thanks go to those who quickly responded in writing: Shirley Graves, Will Collette, Jane Kelso, Joan Brann, Pat and Jack Baird, Doris Aiken, Randy Hayes, Scott Tucker, Jean McMillen, Ingrid Newkirk, and Nancy Ricci.

Sensitive internal documents of corporations and government agencies that oppose grass roots efforts were given to me by People for the Ethical Treatment of Animals (PETA), Americans for Responsible Television (ART), Rainforest Action Network, In Defense of Animals, and Citizens' Clearinghouse for Hazardous Waste. Confidential documents were leaked by sympathetic corporate and government staff to these grass roots groups.

My son, Phillip, assisted me in understanding and analyzing the role of the media. Kathryn Armstrong gave me ideas and encouragement. Rosa Grundig, Stephanie O'Haver, and Eric Meyer provided technical and editorial services during the manuscript's production.

Finally, I applaud ordinary people who initiate, join, and participate in grass roots democracy.

# GRASS ROOTS

# Introduction

Whatever the future may hold in store, it cannot de-
prive the Americans of their climate, their inland seas,
their great rivers, or the fertility of their soil. Bad laws,
revolutions, and anarchy cannot destroy their taste for
well-being or that spirit of enterprise which seems the
characteristic feature of their race; nor could such
things utterly extinguish the lights of knowledge guiding them.[1]

Alexis de Tocqueville,
*Democracy in America* (1835)

A failed prophecy? A challenge?

This observations was written by the French historian
who traveled to the United States in the early 1830s while
on an official Versailles mission to study the American
penal system. He became intrigued with the young host
nation's democracy and its principles of liberty. If this
learned traveler returned to America in 1991, he would
find a country beyond belief—rich and prosperous people
commanding vast material resources, adjacent to others
in poverty, decay, and despair. He could tour high-tech
factories, elegant office buildings, and beautiful parks
and dine in fine restaurants before attending some
superb opera production. Americans' taste for well-being
would surround him, and their products of enterprise
would more than satisfy. After the initial excitement,
however, less tantalizing views would intrude, and if he

3

sat with his hosts and ordinary people, he would discover a troubled land in the midst of an endangered
planet. Alexis de Tocqueville might listen in silence—
and in awe.

Uneasy hosts would talk about acid rain with its slow
destruction of civil war monuments at Gettysburg and
global warming predicted by some scientists who fear the
earth's atmosphere is becoming like a greenhouse. He
might read a scholarly environmental report prepared by
the National Academy of Sciences depicting a nation
dumping millions of tons of fertilizer, herbicides,
pesticides, and fungicides into its already overworked
soil. He would be alarmed by a national television nightly
news segment showing medical and other toxic waste
washing upon once pristine beaches and shores. If he
walked into the streets from his hotel, the toxic substances in the air would block the sun in the sky, while a
stroll to a nearby river would reveal that pollutants had
killed fish and poisoned the waters. Before retiring, de
Tocqueville might remember his prophecy and consider
these deprivations: Why have they fouled their own nest?

The following morning, reading the *New York Times*,
he would be struck by stories about devastating problems—acquired immunodeficiency syndrome (AIDS),
crack-addicted babies, racial tensions, child abuse, an
intoxicated driver killing three school-age children, Vietnam veterans seeking medical care for disabilities in-
duced by Agent Orange, and a host of other social and
personal problems festering within American communities in spite of the fact that many enjoy the benefits of a
robust economy. An article in *National Geographic*
would point out that, as a nation, the United States uses
forty-five barrels of oil per person each year, in contrast
to five each for the people in China and India. Further, he
would learn that there is only $500 per capita gross
national product for the nearly 2 billion Chinese and

Indians, but an average of $17,500 for 250 million Americans. Flying back to Paris on the Concorde, he would undoubtedly wonder: What went wrong? What does the future hold in store for this once great land? Will their taste for well-being, their spirit of enterprise, and the lights of knowledge that guide them suffice? Can they and their fellow inhabitants of this earth solve such an array of perplexing problems, survive, and prosper?

The unraveling has been long in the making. However, its acceleration can be traced to the advent of World War II, a war that changed the world forever. With the Allied victory, the United States assumed world leadership, a position tempting to a nation that was abruptly jerked from pacifism to war, from economic depression to heretofore unknown affluence, from ordinary industrial know-how to the most advanced technology and means of production, from terra firma to space, from regional cultures to a national ethic, from radio to television and computers, and from undereducated masses to enlightenment and professionalism.

During and after World War II, a new mastery of scientific knowledge enabled corporate America, with government assistance, to launch a petrochemical empire and revolutionize communications through television and, later, computers. A frantic automobile industry raced to meet the growing restlessness of a large, newly mobile population, and cities sent endless suburbs sprawling across the landscape. The chemical industry, in consort with the United States Department of Agriculture (USDA), dramatically changed farming practices, and Americans produced abundant crops, livestock, and poultry—enough to feed their own people as well as a large party of the world's hungry. Corporate America's hegemony, in partnership with the United States government, replaced the once powerful European colonial powers and took control of trade, production of many

new goods, political influence, monetary policies, entertainment, popular culture, and, most significantly,
much of the world's natural resources. Yankee know-how
and initiative dazzled the world for almost forty years
until a revitalized Japan and resurrected Western Europe began challenging this supremacy. Along the way, a
cold war with the Soviet Union honed America's zest for
competition in the world's marketplaces of political control, goods, and ideologies. Being the leader in nuclear
matters became a full-time preoccupation for both
nations.

The giant federal bureaucracy that had been started
during the Great Depression burgeoned during and after
the war, and attempts to halt its growth and influence
have largely failed. The counterparts of numerous federal
agencies fill the fifty state capitals and filter down to
county and local governments. Governing the nation has
become a major industry.

Americans consume as much as is placed before them
and want more during these heady days of buying cars,
toys, vacations, condominiums, athletic equipment, designer clothing, second homes, swimming pools, alcohol
and drugs, recreational vehicles, electronic gadgets,
computers, and a host of disposable convenience products. Few want to turn back, give it up, conserve.

However, with unprecedented progress have come
unimaginable problems, and they grow more serious
every day. The belief that we live in a boundless world
having inexhaustible resources is slowly being replaced
by the sobering recognition that its inhabitants must
conserve or face extinction.

### Early Warnings: Grass Roots Response

Gray clouds began to appear on the horizon, literally,
in the form of smog over Los Angeles in the 1940s. The

popular media trivialized the sickly, yellow haze blurring the beauty of a wondrous valley and ocean until it settled in to cause respiratory problems. Once its cruel chemistry was discovered, humor turned to concern. The anxious American public was, however, assured that the problem would be solved and believed the promises of elected leadership, scientists, and government agencies for a decade or more until the problem worsened and spread to other cities. Angelenos and others have learned to cope with ozone alerts, health warnings, and dying trees.

In 1962, Rachel Carson presented her controversial book, *Silent Spring*, in which she spelled out the dangers of persistent pesticides, especially DDT.[2] Her cogent warnings and accurate predictions were met with scorn, ad hominem barbs, and scientific refutation. Some bureaucrats, scientists, and chemical manufacturers dismissed her as an hysterical spinster, pronouncing her warnings as tantamount to promoting world hunger.[3]

Reports on the civil rights struggle filled the media in the early 1960s, at the same time as the Kennedy administration was launching the New Frontier. Later, the Johnson administration's Great Society was set in motion to close the gap between the haves and the have-nots caused by the lack of economic opportunity for the poor, and to address civil rights violations. Meanwhile the war in Vietnam and campus protests became the subjects of daily television coverage.

Gradually, after a long silence, people began to question a host of perceived, shared social and personal wrongs. They began to challenge those in charge, demanding answers and solutions to their accusations and grievances: minorities were violated and sidelined; the war in Vietnam was illegal; women were treated unequally; war was not a sane method of settling international conflicts; the production of nuclear weapons threatened world survival; Third World countries were being deprived of their rights to self-determination and economic development; and the environment was being degraded, assaulted, and plundered. Citizens of all ages began to speak out, and some were surprised when their voices were heard over the roar of protesting crowds and riot police.

This book is about ordinary people, the rank and file, who start and lead movements, working in concert to change things. It will not examine such mass struggles as the movements for civil rights, women's rights, or a nuclear freeze, nor will it dwell on the Vietnam war protests. Those have been and continue to be analyzed by scores of writers. Rather, this book turns to more recent grass roots groups—some massive, some small. It tells their stories of changing America through succeeding, little by little, in altering social norms, righting egregious wrongs, modifying or even halting deleterious practices, changing or passing laws and ordinances, and enforcing existing laws. These movements intend to bring down the walls of inaction and duplicity. Ordinary people are learning to empower themselves in a society controlled by government officials, corporate executives, academic patrons, and media bosses, for whom grass roots leaders use a variety of pejorative name tags: the establishment, city hall, the man, suits, the system.

Although phrases such as *healthy skepticism*—even *cynicism*—are used by public opinion analysts to describe a sometimes helpless public in the face of those in power, don't count the people down and out! Often they mistrust elected officials. Public passivity and apathy are twin emotions that give those in control a false sense of comfort. During the 1988 presidential election, fewer than half the eligible voters cast ballots, and an even greater number did not bother to register. But those who act are getting results and are attracting more people each day. Perhaps some people have found a direct way to transcend voting as a means of making their voices heard.

I wrote this book to inspire ordinary people to participate in the affairs of their neighborhood, city, state, and nation. In spite of what the poor voter turnout of 1988 might suggest, activism is on the rise. Millions of Americans are doing more than raising a family, working, watching television, attending sports and entertainment events, hanging out, taking drugs and drinking, or barely surviving.

By their nature, grass roots groups emerge to challenge individuals, corporations, government agencies, academia, or a combination of these when people discover they share a grievance. In their search for redress, they have encountered unresponsive, negative public agencies, self-severing private businesses, or recalcitrant individuals and groups. The answer for them is to select specific issues and find like-minded others.

Since Earth Day 1970, a growing environmental movement has continued to attract millions of Americans of all ages who are concerned about chlorofluorocarbons (CFSs) depleting the ozone layer, about persistent pesticides killing wildlife and poisoning humans, and about endangered species, old growth in the national forest, the Everglades, wildlife refuges, wetlands, and prairies.

The animal rights movement is both more complex and more controversial than some others. The movement has two primary thrusts: first, reducing or eliminating the use of animals in laboratory experiments, and second, changing or eliminating factory farms that mass-produce livestock, poultry, and dairy products. It cuts to the heart of people's relationships to their fellow inhabitants of the globe. Animal rights activists raise ethical and moral questions as they seek, among many other issues, a new definition of humans' relationship to animals.

Only an informed and active citizenry can restore equilibrium when those entrusted fail. Besides seeking to inspire political participation, this book examines why and how grass roots groups start, what their members want, how they accomplish the tasks, and who opposes them.

## The Beginnings

For each different movement, a unique story unfolds. Although the genesis of such groups vary, the classic grass roots movement is sparked by a local incident and then builds.

Thirteen-year-old Cari Lightner was killed on May 3, 1980, in Sacramento, while walking in a bike lane, by a hit-and-run driver under the influence of alcohol, who only two days earlier had been released from jail for another hit-and-run accident. The man's police record showed three prior arrests and convictions for driving under the influence of alcohol.

A guilty plea to vehicular manslaughter was allowed, through plea bargaining, and the driver who killed Cari Lightner got off with a two-year prison sentence. According to court records, the judge considered the man's alcoholism a mitigating factor, and the convicted man went to a halfway house instead of prison. He was released in less than a year and was eligible to obtain a reinstated driver's license.

Initially devastated by grief, Candy Lightner, the girl's mother, later reacted with anger toward a judicial system that did little to protect the public from the threat of drunk drivers. Gathering the facts and gaining support for her one-woman crusade, she founded one of the most effective grass roots movements in this nation's history: Mothers Against Drunk Driving (MADD). Ten years later, though, the organization is embroiled in controversy within its ranks.

Positive results of MADD's operation could not, of course, have been seen immediately. Even in its tenth year, there were still over 25,000 traffic fatalities, which exceeded the number of murder victims. The number of drunken driver-related fatalities, however, decreases each year, in part thanks to MADD's efforts to change the criminal justice system and the social norms surrounding drinking and driving. More than one million Americans support the activities of this grass roots group.

A second type of grass roots movement begins at the top, with seeds scattered by experts and ordinary people responding. That's how Mothers and Others for Pesticide Limits originated in 1988. The organization grew out of a grass roots response to the alarming disclosures of the results of a two-year study by the Natural Resources Defense Council—"Intolerable Risk: Pesticides in our Children's Food."

When ordinary people learn that their grievance is shared but correction unlikely unless they act in consort, they often pick up the challenge. Health, safety, and survival issues dominate, followed closely by economic and moral concerns. People organize and act, some in nation- or world-wide movements of hundreds or thousands of supporters and members, some in small local groups comprising scarcely more than a score of faithful. While some become not-for-profit, tax-exempt groups with national offices and local chapters, others shun all organizational trappings and form loosely connected, autonomous local groups. How they organize is examined in chapter 1.

## Grass Roots Tactics

What works and why? Because Grass roots groups generally operate without knowing much about other groups, they are often unaware of specific tactics or common goals. The striking fact is that they share a great deal. In general, tactics follow a continuum from traditional social action to nonviolent, civil disobedience to direct, violent action. Some groups have perfected strategies, trained their members, and attracted consistent media attention. Peaceful, deliberate sit-ins, with members anticipating arrest and awaiting it as a planned outcome, have, for instance, been used by animal rights activists and environmentalists alike.

Rallies, demonstrations, and street theater have been executed adroitly by members of both the Rainforest Action Network and ACT UP (AIDS Coalition to Unleash Power). Letter-writing campaigns and petition drives are also used to demonstrate support for a cause, and court watches in which mothers attend the trials of defendants involved in drunken driver cases are intended to pressure the judiciary. Boycotts have empowered grass roots groups and have become one of the most successful tactics to obtain change. By depriving the company of income—its bottom line—and damaging its public relations, the Rainforest Action Network persuaded Burger King to discontinue using beef from cattle raised where the Central American rain forests once stood. A new campaign to switch from disposable to cloth diapers is gaining momentum as the public learns about the danger of human waste in landfills and the extended length of time plastic diapers remain in the soil before breaking down.

In some states, the plebiscite has become a valuable tactic for grass roots groups. In California, Proposition 13 (the property tax rollback), Proposition 65 (requiring warnings regarding carcinogenic substances in products), and Proposition 103 (the voter revolt over automobile and home insurance rates) have won the sanction of voters. Grass roots groups, often with help from established public interest groups, developed these initiatives, took them to the voters, and gained approval. Implementing them has been difficult because of industry and state government opposition, however.

Litigation against corporate and government polluters or agencies entrusted with the protection of the environment is commonplace, especially by some environmental groups. The Fund for Animals successfully stopped the hunting of black bears in California in August 1989 by obtaining a court ruling that prohibited the state Department of Fish and Game from issuing hunting permits. In granting the plaintiff's plea, the court asked for an environmental impact statement.[4] In 1987, the Natural Resources Defense Council won a suit that requires Bethlehem Steel to donate $1 million to local environmental groups to help clean up the Chesapeake Bay and to comply with its own waste discharge permit at its plant on the Bay.[5]

Direct, violent action has been used as well. Earth First! members have engaged in ecotage, a form of monkey-wrenching, by disabling logging equipment and spiking trees in old growth forests (the practice of driving metal spikes into trees to keep them from being logged). Waging other kinds of battles, abortion opponents have bombed abortion clinics, and animal rights activists have raided animal research laboratories, destroying equipment and liberating animals. These and many more tactics are examined in chapter 2.

## The Opposition: Its Tactics

Those who are the target of or oppose a grass roots action do not ordinarily retreat; rather, they employ a

range of counteractions. Because corporations and government agencies are neither weak nor without resources and perseverance, they often attempt to ignore,
disrupt, infiltrate, and overwhelm. The National Institutes of Health and the USDA have tried to discredit
grass roots causes through public relations campaigns.
University researchers and academic departments receive support from corporations and government grants
in presenting their side of an issue. The linkages among
government agencies, corporations, and academia are
obvious in many cases because time and again they are
joined as codefendants in litigation brought by a group.

When a community group organizes to defeat a plan to
place a toxic waste incinerator in its community, the
waste management company may sue the local group,
blame it for the loss of employment,and ridicule its "not-
in-my-backyard" (NIMBY) stance. The state environmental protection office may approve the location for the
planned incinerator and employ university researchers
to prove its safety. Similar local skirmishes are taking
place in hundreds of communities over sites for toxic
waste disposal.[6]

The bottom line for corporations as well as small
businesses is return on investment, and corporate officers
are judged by performance in the economic arena, not by
their social and humanitarian accomplishments. Corporate resources and tactics to defeat organizations endan-
gering growth and profits are discussed in chapter 3.

## Media: The Trade-Offs

The media, especially nationally produced television
news and large urban daily newspapers, wield much
power in the portrayal of each grass roots movement to
the general public. They can sanction, trivialize, distort,

or ignore it. Local media play essentially the same role in smaller communities. The media are everywhere, and if a grass roots group does not understand how they function and how they can be handled, results can be harsh and negative. For example, when media officials decide that a moment has gone too far, they frame it with labels: animal activists are called "antiscience"; opponents of toxic waste sites in their community are marginalized by being termed NIMBY; and Earth First! members become "eco-radicals."

The media set the national news agenda and decide what's news. Grass roots groups want public awareness, sometimes even if the risk is great that their actions will be distorted by reporters. Getting in the public's eye can be a two-edged sword: Letting people know that the spotted owl is a threatened species is important, but the discovery that saving the species means putting loggers out of work can backfire. In August 1989, a headline in the *San Francisco Examiner* reported "Loggers Win, Owl Loses in U.S. Court." Environmentalists claim that this issue is far more complex than local jobs versus saving a threatened species.

In their assumed role as balancers of issues and ideas, the media place both sides within narrow confines and rarely examine a conflict in depth. (There are exceptions, such as the extensive and thorough coverage of the *Exxon Valdez* oil spill.) But grass roots groups are public, and they want their messages heard, their tactics noticed, and their results recorded. Justice Oliver Wendell Holmes assessed this need well with his observation that the best test of ideas is in the free market.

Grass roots groups are not subject to outside media coverage alone—they can and often do produce their own communications to reach members, supporters, and the public. Newsletters, magazines, pamphlets, studies, phone trees, meetings, and training sessions are only a few ways for a group to spread its message and inform its following. Some new recruits receive training: The Citizen's Clearinghouse for Hazardous Wastes trains community groups in grass roots activism, while People for the Ethical Treatment of Animals (PETA) provides Animals Rights 101 to newcomers. Having a media and communications arm is vital. Members of grass roots groups have learned quickly that they must know as much as possible about their subject. To be ignorant of the details places them at great disadvantage when they speak with the opposition, the media, and in public. They learn to become the experts in their cause.

Because the media play a crucial role during the course of a grass roots movement, chapter 4 is devoted to them.

## Inside the Organization

Smooth sailing is rare for grass roots groups, whether in external forays with their opponents or within the organizations themselves, at either the local or national level. Internal problems are likely, particularly because most leaders and members have not been schooled in organization dynamics and because group members have no history of working together. But there is a certain vitality present when people gather to forge change, and if this collective energy does not explode within the organization, success can follow. This book examines some of the most common and serious organizational concerns.

When the group gets the spotlight (or a floodlight if the cause is of major concern to the public), leaders lose their anonymity and may suddenly acquire celebrity status. Jealousy may ensue, and personality conflicts can drain energy and focus from the group's intent. With a largely voluntary local group, tensions invariably arise.

Setting goals and sticking to them are essential guiding principles. Some groups take on far too many issues and lose sight of the original mission. Some have learned valuable lessons about goal setting and dividing chores.

Financing the effort, particularly if the movement becomes national, with local chapters, is never easy. Some groups have learned to live within austere budgets and forego activities and tactics that are costly and time-consuming. Others have collapsed under the financial burden. Hence, how to become and remain solvent is discussed in the book as well.

Reaching out to attract new members and supporters is imperative because a movement needs numbers to impress as well as hands to do the work. While most grass roots groups discussed in this book are composed of white, middle-class, well-educated persons, some have struck a responsive chord in minority and low-income communities. In some movements, women dominate the membership and lead the efforts. Demographic composition often defines the movement's thrust.

Turf battles within the organization as well as with competing groups outside are frequent and can be time-consuming and counterproductive. For example, within the environment talk movement, grass roots and public interest groups proliferate. The book discusses whether this practice is valuable, distracting, or duplicative.

Building a bureaucracy with national, regional, state, and local offices has been the fate of some grass roots movements, and with it comes the usual problems of any large, decentralized organization. Caring for the organization may take as much time as addressing the perceived wrong. Some successful groups emphasize local autonomy over national control and appear to prosper.

Knowing when to declare victory and dismantle the organization is important. Groups may decide to hang on after they have accomplished their mission. Generally, they should disband. However, eternal vigilance is necessary because sometimes initial accomplishments are lost and must be reclaimed. Experience with the Superfund's failure to accomplish the safe removal of toxic waste proves that axiom. At times, local groups must remain to continue the pressure.

These organizational concerns and others are examined in chapter 5.

## Looking Back

America's history is replete with popular movements initiated by zealots impatient with what they believed to be an imperfection in a nation that once encouraged dissent and individualism more than it does today. Two powerful grass roots movements changed the nation in the 1800s: the abolitionists and prohibitionists. William Lloyd Garrison and John Brown were charismatic abolitionist leaders, while Carry Nation led the prohibition forces during the movement's most volatile period. Reaching their respective goals took longer than many of today's efforts: more than a hundred years for prohibition to become law and thirty-five years to abolish slavery. Antecedents of current grass roots tactics in using the media and dealing with the opposition are found in these two movements. Both changed laws, social customs, the economy, political behavior, and the nation's heritage, and were instigated by ordinary people—not government officials, elected representatives, or corporate leaders. Nonviolent civil disobedience had its origins in the nineteenth century and was applied by abolitionists as well as temperance followers. Both groups also used violent means to accomplish their goal. A civil war ended slavery, and saloons were smashed to gain prohibition. Today's grass roots members may identify with the tactics, determination, and accomplishments of their earlier vanguard.

The abolition of slavery and the prohibition of spirit beverages were defined by their groups as moral issues, and the young nation searched its conscience for answers.

## The Challenge

Grass roots movements flourish in America because ordinary people utilize the very essences of a democratic society—the rights to protest, and to seek redress of a grievance, freedoms of speech and assembly, a free press, and a representative government. Our political setting allows and encourages a participatory society, although some forces, as this book will document, seek to discourage activism. As long as these freedoms exist and ordinary people believe they have the power to press for peaceful social change when they feel wronged, our nation will remain strong and perhaps cleanse itself. By knowing about grass roots efforts, how they work, their opposition and its tactics, and the vast array of their accomplishments, I hope readers will be challenged to get involved if they feel impelled to act when a grievance occurs.[7]

The cardinal points for an effective grass roots organization are outlined in chapter 6.

Human beings are the only species with a history. Whether they have a future is not obvious. The answer will lie in the prospects for popular movements, with firm roots among all sectors of the population, dedicated to values that are suppressed or driven to the margins within existing social and political order: community, solidarity, concern for a fragile environment that will have to sustain future generations, creative work under voluntary control, independent thought and true democratic participation in varied aspects of life.[8]

Noam Chomsky,
*Necessary Illusions*, 1989

# 1

# The Beginnings

A shared wrong smolders. A spark ignites. Ordinary people take the first step. A national organization releases a report. A longstanding grievance arouses the public conscience. A grass roots movement begins.

The following accounts briefly examine the origins of four important but widely differing grass roots movements. Why did they begin? How were they organized? What was their fate?[1]

### Love Canal

Hot, humid air hung in the house late at night where a young boy coughed as he lay on a damp sheet. In the next room, his mother thrashed about in bed, trying to block out the familiar, painful sounds she repeatedly heard each night. Finally she walked in the dark to her son's room, knelt by the bed, and stroked his sweaty forehead to comfort him. His frequent illnesses worried Lois Gibbs. Why was Michael always sick, she wondered? When the air was thick and humid in Love Canal in upstate New York, the smell of chemicals seemed more

21

oppressive. She worried about her son and vowed to take him to their doctor again.

Several days later, in June 1978, Lois read a series of articles in the *Gazette*, the local paper, about Love Canal. The digging of the six- to seven-mile canal had begun in 1892 to connect the upper and lower Niagara River, but the task was abandoned during hard times, and the open ditch was sold in 1920 and used as a dump. Hooker Chemical Company, the local subsidiary of Occidental Petroleum, completely filled the canal with its chemical waste. In 1953, they covered it with dirt and sold it to the Niagara Falls City Board of Education for one dollar, with the stipulation that, should anyone incur physical harm or death because of the buried waste, Hooker would not be responsible. An elementary school was built in 1955 on the south corner of the covered canal. This was the school that Michael Gibbs attended. As his mother read the newspaper article about the chemicals in the landfill, she considered the potential link between her son's fragile health, the site of his school, and the chemical contamination.

After learning as much as she could about Love Canal and the chemicals buried in it, Lois decided to ask the school officials to transfer her son, hoping that his illnesses would subside once he no longer spent time directly on Love Canal. The superintendent requested that two letters from doctors be supplied to verify the illnesses. However, when they were produced, he refused the transfer request. Angered by his decision, Lois decided to get a petition to close the school because of the health hazard to the children. She learned that people had complained about the canal for years but had taken no further action. She would. A shy and conservative person, without any background in community action, Gibbs drew up a petition to take to her neighbors. With the encouragement of one of her best friends, she hesitantly began with a knock on the first door and found not only admittance but a neighbor also greatly worried about his family's health. Bolstered by the petition's acceptance, she proceeded, though she still expected to have doors slammed in her face and to hear epithets such as crazy, hysterical, busybody. None came; only congratulations on her courage. Her shoe leather epidemiology was working, and she learned about her neighbors' illnesses, miscarriages, birth defects, fear, anger, and helplessness.

A few weeks after the petition was presented to them, the New York State Department of Health held a meeting at the elementary school on Love Canal to announce that they would conduct a health and environmental study of the area. Those attending were shocked to hear that they were to refrain from eating vegetables grown in their gardens and that a device would be provided them to check the air in their homes. The information confused and alarmed many and, within days, word about the meeting spread throughout the town. Lois and a newly recruited friend continued to circulate the petition to ever more receptive neighbors whose homes were adjacent to the canal. Parents complained about additional problems: their children's feet burned when they played in the school playground; basements contained sludge leaking into the walls; trees died; animals were constantly sick; and the odor was unbearable on hot and humid days. Those who lived on Ninety-ninth Street, directly adjacent to the canal, recorded the most persistent and serious health problems.

Within weeks, the petition drive became political. Lois contacted U.S. senator Daniel Patrick Moynihan. The mayor was upset over the bad publicity for Niagara Falls. Hooker Chemical denied any responsibility, citing the clause in the deed of sale. The health department stalled and gave data about air sampling that confused the parents. They again issued warnings to discontinue eating from the gardens and to keep out of basements. The department suggested blood tests for residents living on certain streets.

Finally, the state health department called for a meeting in August—in Albany, three hundred miles from Love Canal. Some suspected the distant state capital had been selected to ensure a low turnout. However, Lois, her husband, and Debbie Cerrillo, her co-petition gatherer, traveled to Albany with 161 signatures. The meeting, attended by members of the press, was dramatic. The health commissioner once again read a statement urging residents to discontinue eating food from their gardens and announcing that the Ninety-Ninth Street Elementary School would be closed while the chemicals were drained from the canal. Children were to avoid the school playground, and families were urged not to go into their basements. Lois and the others had heard these warnings before. Then the commissioners stated that there was a danger to the health of pregnant women and children under two years of age and that they should evacuate the area. Lois was enraged and protested vigorously. After a heated discussion, officials of the department offered to be in Love Canal for a meeting the following day if Lois could get people to attend. She assured them of a packed house.

Upon the trio's return to Love Canal, they found angry people milling in the streets, anxious to hear from Lois. Approaching the crowd, she realized they had heard about the suggested evacuation from a radio news report. As best she could, without ever having spoken to a group before, she recounted the day's meeting in Albany. Anger exploded with each comment. She announced that the health department officials would be in their community the next day to discuss the matter with those interested. They did not need urging; they shouted their intention to attend.

With officials sitting on the stage in the elementary school auditorium, a packed house dealt with sweltering heat, humidity, and their collective rage. Before the commissioner completed reading his order, the crowd's impatience erupted. They wanted answers. Were their lives in jeopardy? What about the three-year-olds? Who would pay for the move? Did they intend to break up families? How long would the evacuation last? Where was the governor? Television, radio, and newspaper crews were everywhere. The confusion was great, and no one felt secure. The meeting was adjourned around midnight, after the officials had agreed to move the entire families of pregnant women and those with children under two years of age.

Several days later, the residents met and decided, upon an attorney's advice, to form the Love Canal Homeowners Association. Four goals were set: (1) to get the residents within the Love Canal area who wanted out evacuated and relocated, especially during the reconstruction and repair of the canal; (2) to deal with falling real estate values; (3) to get the canal drained properly; and (4) to have air sampling and soil and water testing conducted throughout the whole community.

A string of federal and state bureaucrats started streaming into Love Canal to assess the situation. An official from the Federal Disaster Assistance Administration (FDAA) toured the area. Governor Hugh Carey arrived on August 7 and announced at a public meeting that the state would purchase the first and second rings of homes around the canal and that those families would be relocated. He also assured those living outside the two rings that a health study of their area would be conducted. While most were pleased and calmed, pregnant women and their families knew that these decisions might have come too late for them. Fear held the community in its grip: fear that their health was in danger and that economic disaster awaited them. Still, the residents left the meeting feeling somewhat relieved by the governor's offers.

During the following months, Love Canal residents met one obstacle after another and learned much about the workings of their government agencies—local, state, and federal. The state began to renege on the promise to purchase some of the homes. It set up a task force to help with the relocation of some of the families but asked private agencies to pay to place them in motels. Confusion reigned and distrust grew. Each time the residents believed they had a commitment from an official, they discovered a change in plans. When the health department came in September 1978 to conduct a health survey, the residents helped collect the data. When the department decided to deny relocation, based on their own survey findings, residents were notified by form letter. They were told the canal presented no imminent danger of exploding from the chemicals or the weapons dumped by the United States Army. In the meantime, plans to drain and reconstruct the canal were underway.

The homeowners' association conducted its own survey, but the findings were discredited by health department officials and university researchers because the housewives conducting it were said to have a vested interest in the outcome. Lois remarked to a friend, "If anything is naive, it is to believe that government officials and politicians will do what they say they will do."[2]

Increasingly, Love Canal residents became concerned over the draining at the site because they learned about some of the known carcinogenic chemicals reportedly found: dioxin and benzene. Exposing the residents to these and a host of other unknown chemicals seemed reckless, and members of the homeowners' association decided to picket the construction site and to block traffic. Journalists and television crews were there from the beginning, reporting on the civil disobedience. On the second day, Lois was arrested for the first time in her life for stopping a bus at the Ninety-Ninth Street school. For six weeks, the story was kept in the news by the pickets.

During Christmas, Lois's son, Michael, developed convulsions in addition to his chronic respiratory problems, ear infection, and possible bladder disorder.

In order to keep the story in the spotlight, Love Canal mothers made baby- and adult-size coffins and delivered them to the governor's office. One reporter asked Lois, "Why don't you just move?" She was staggered by the lack of understanding. The truth was that they lacked the resources, yet were frightened to stay. No one would buy the houses. Where and how could they go?

When the state reported that dioxin had been found in the canal in concentrations of 176 parts per billion, the residents held a protest rally. They chanted, "Thanks to New York State, death is our fate. We don't want to die— listen to our cry. We want out." They carried effigies of state officials and burned them in a parking lot.

Lois and Beverly Paigen, biologist, were invited to testify at hearings on toxic waste in Washington, D.C., before then-Congressman Albert Gore. Ralph Nader came to Niagara Falls to give a speech and to learn more about Love Canal. The American Broadcasting Company (ABC) developed a documentary entitled "The Killing Ground." The notoriety helped, but the health problems continued and reconstruction at the canal proceeded. More meetings were held and Lois undertook numerous trips to Albany, but the situation dragged on and on.

The final breakthrough came in May 1980 when an Environmental Protection Agency (EPA) representative called on a Friday to alert Lois that its chromosome study on thirty-six Love Canal residents had been completed. He wanted Lois to have the families available Saturday morning at eight to learn the results individually. The hasty scheduling was necessary because the findings had been leaked to the press, and the EPA wanted the families to hear the results directly. Lois agreed and reached most of those concerned. Word of this serious event spread rapidly, and television and other media crews were waiting when Lois arrived at the home-owners' association office the next morning to gather the residents and arrange for private sessions with the Washington officials.

The residents waited quietly for their turn to learn if they were among the eleven residents testing positive for broken chromosomes of a rare type. According to the leaked news report, this damage signaled an increased risk of miscarriage, stillbirth, birth defects, cancer, or genetic mutations that could affect generations to come. As each family was told the news, the mood became more somber. By noon the job was done, and a press conference was held by the EPA to announce the findings formally. They hit the town like a bomb.

On the following Monday morning, a crowd of residents and reporters gathered. The citizens were enraged anew by a newspaper headline: "White House Blocks Love Canal Evacuations." Some poured gasoline on the lawn to form the letters EPA, then lit it, and watched it burn as the crowd cheered. Lois realized that the crowd of more than one hundred was hostile and could erupt at any moment. They wanted answers about the study. The police arrived with threats to arrest demonstrators. Lois called the EPA and asked whether anyone from the agency would come to speak with the demonstrators. When the EPA representatives appeared, the protestors threatened to take them hostage until all the people of

Love Canal who wanted out were given a chance to get out. "We have them!" they shouted. "Let's see how they like being trapped!" Afraid of the consequences if the EPA officials stepped outside and faced the angry residents, Lois kept them in her office. She decided to call the White House to explain the situation. When she mentioned that two EPA staffers were being held hostage by Love Canal residents, the message was heard. She told the crowd that she had called the White House and urged them to be calm. They cheered and finally agreed. Back in her office she waited in vain, together with the EPA officials, for word from Washington.

Instead, the Federal Bureau of Investigation called and gave Lois seven minutes to release the EPA officials. After a series of promises and negotiations, the hostages were released and the crowd dispersed, unaware of the FBI involvement or the time limit for the hostage release given to Lois. She was afraid they might riot if told the truth. They agreed to let the hostages go when Lois told them she had given Washington, D.C., until Wednesday noon to consent to the relocation and had threatened further trouble if Washington refused.

When the Wednesday noon deadline approached, a large crowd of residents and news media crews gathered to learn the decision. At 12:05 P.M., a press receptionist at the EPA read a press release announcing that 810 families in the Love Canal community would be temporarily evacuated from their homes. They could leave immediately, and the costs for lodging would be handled by the FDAA. The media crews photographed a crowd roaring in triumph. Victory was theirs—the ordinary people of Love Canal. They had persevered against great odds and defeated a host of bureaucrats and a giant chemical company.

Lois received a call from the "Phil Donahue Show," asking her and a number of residents to appear for a discussion of this grass roots phenomenon. Following a successful media event with Donahue, the residents went to the Democratic National Convention in New York to put pressure on President Jimmy Carter to release the money for permanent relocation. Eventually, they gained that long-sought promise: the money for permanent relocation was awarded in the late fall of 1980.[3]

A classic example of a grass roots movement, the Love Canal story began at the neighborhood level because a courageous mother wanted a healthy community for her child. When her progress was thwarted, many lent their support. The struggle with numerous bureaucracies, a corporate giant, and an unresponsive state university is quite typical of what these movements are faced with.

This local struggle helped push a national problem into the floodlight: millions of people live near toxic and other hazardous waste sites. This story empowers them. Lois Gibbs went to Washington, D.C., in 1982 to establish the Citizen's Clearinghouse for Hazardous Wastes, a national alliance for environmental justice to assist thousands of other concerned groups in communities across America. Tactics employed, obstacles encountered, and results achieved are presented in subsequent chapters.


### Parents in Action

The evening birthday party for an eager thirteen-year-old girl began routinely enough as her fifty invited guests arrived with gifts and joined the party in a spacious backyard. The parents anticipated an energetic young crowd, dancing to rock music, enjoying hamburgers and soft drinks, and discussing summer vacations, but the events that were to unfold in the large, festively decorated backyard would shock them. By nine o'clock, few children had eaten the hamburgers or tasted the soft drinks. The music blared, but few danced. Instead, the crowd, ages ten to nineteen, broke off into small groups and wandered into shrubbery or the deep recesses of a darkened yard.

From the window of their upstairs bedroom, the parents gazed down on the scene. When they saw lights flicker in the dark, they were troubled that the children might be smoking cigarettes and ignoring the food and music. That older, uninvited teens came and went at random also caught their attention.

Later in the evening, when the mother went into the kitchen to replenish the party food, she encountered several disoriented kids and realized immediately that they were intoxicated. The party was halted. The older children were sent home, and the parents of the younger guests were called and asked to retrieve them. Later that evening, the birthday girl's parents searched the yard and found wine and beer bottles, marijuana joints, roach clips, and rolling papers. Their worst suspicions were confirmed. After a long talk with their daughter, they acquired a list of guests. They knew many personally, but some names were unfamiliar to them. They talked late into the night, trying to decide their course of action. Should they ignore what happened? Should they punish their oldest daughter? Should they call the parents of each guest to discuss the incident? They decided that ignoring the incident was out of the question. Parents were called one by one, but the response was mixed. Some wanted to talk because they knew their kids used drugs and they wanted help. Others denied the problem or were resentful and wished to be left alone. A few blamed the host family or older teens. However, when the calls had been completed, a sizable group wanted to gather to discuss the incident. They were alarmed.

This family (unnamed at their request) in Atlanta, Georgia, launched a grass roots movement in 1976. It was unique in many ways.

At the first neighborhood meeting, thirty parents arrived, anxious and uncertain about how things would turn out. This discussion would focus on their children's behavior and perhaps their own as well. Fortunately, however, by the close of the meeting, they found themselves more united, wiser, and more resolute. One parent talked openly about her problems with her teenage son. She described how she had been rebuffed by those she thought could help: school officials denied any drug use on campus; a counselor told her not to overreact because pot was not addictive; the police said no one seemed to care; and other parents said, "Not my kid." During the frantic period of seeking help for her son, she had kept a list of young people who came to her house, who telephoned her son, and whom her son discussed. When she read the list to the group that evening, the parents were astonished upon hearing their children's names. Her list matched the party list.

That night, some of the parents vowed never to be ignorant again. They planned ways to learn about their neighborhood, their schools, the police, where drugs were purchased, and how their children obtained them. They agreed to hold a second meeting in two weeks to share their information. Most accepted the problems: their children's, their own, and the community's. Most important, they agreed to sit down with their own children to talk and listen.

Most of the parents returned for a second meeting armed with facts and anxious about their findings. The scenario described by the parent with the drug-abusing son at the first meeting was verified everywhere. Denial of the drug problem was pervasive at schools, with other adults, and with merchants. A few interviewees believed kids used drugs freely. The youngster who did not admit to using marijuana or alcohol was a striking exception. The many who did admit it excused it, saying, "Everyone does it. It's no big deal."

A teen drug culture, its slang, the paraphernalia, and the "never narc on your friend" code came alive as the parents tried to struggle with the fact that their children casually accepted drug use and resented nosy questions. The group began searching their own lives as parents: Were they too permissive, indifferent, or even estranged from their children? Did they spend too little time with the kids? Were they poor models because they drank or smoked? Some, as it turned out, used illegal drugs themselves and permitted their older children to use them in their presence. While the group began to learn about denial and unresponsive agencies outside, their main focus was on the family. They realized that if the problem of drug use by young people was to be prevented they had to take the first step—and that night they did. Most but not all parents agreed to a united effort and pledged to stick with it.

Not just rules, but also consequences of broken rules were agreed upon. While the list was short, the impact on the families of the measures to be taken over the course of two weeks would be profound. The rules were (1) each child is grounded, (2) no telephone calls can be made to or received from other kids, (3) all outings will be chaperoned by parents, and (4) no drugs or alcohol can be used by children.

In addition to the initial action, following the two-week plan, a second set of rules was imposed by some parents: (1) curfews were set, (2) no car dating was allowed, (3) chores and family responsibilities were assigned, (4) all dances and after-hour school functions were supervised, and (5) parents should join their children in activities.

With this frontal attack on the problem, the parents

adjourned and returned to their homes. In no mood to negotiate, the committed parents installed the disciplinary measures over the objections of their offspring. Close tabs were kept on the youngsters' whereabouts, and some parents spent more time with them, often to the chagrin of the watched. Some parents read their children's letters and searched their rooms for drug paraphernalia or for signs of drug use.

Merchants who sold alcohol to minors were confronted. Older teens known as users and sellers were told their illegal acts would no longer be tolerated. School authorities were visited by parents who offered to assist in supervision. Parent-Teacher Association (PTA) meetings held presentations about drug use by children, and professionals who supported responsible use and denigrated the parents' efforts were put on notice. The parents emphasized caring and spoke less about punishment.

Along with this direct confrontation, the parents offered to help older teens, single parents, and those whose children were in need of treatment. One goal was to rebuild a sense of community; another was to remove the teen drug culture. And, of course, strengthening their own families was paramount.

The children reacted with surprise at first, but resentment soon followed, with grown-ups being labeled the "Nosy Parent Association" or the "Parent Snoop Patrol." The children didn't like supervision, the curfews, or having allowances withheld and being deprived of a hair blower, cosmetics, or designer clothes. Some felt embarrassed, some gave up drugs, and some stopped selling them. A few teenagers were relieved that their parents cared enough to fight for them, and they said they once more enjoyed their families. For the most part, the youth culture survived, with fewer drugs and less alcohol and tobacco. A period of time was needed to establish the new routine for both parents and their children in this typically middle-class neighborhood of Atlanta.

The story does not end here, largely because a few parents continued to pursue the problem vigorously. That the parents alone were not the problem but that other causes contributed to youthful drug use became clear to those who suspected a deeper and darker side to the issue. They began to ask important questions: Why were drugs readily available? How were drug education programs taught at school? What did the experts say about the effects of marijuana and alcohol on children and teens? Why did some drug counselors appear to condone, excuse, or minimize pot use and subtly blame the parents for overreacting, turning against their own children, and failing to listen? Why did the media make drug use appear glamorous in films, on television, and in magazines? Why was there a large pro-drug contingent in America? Why did police react hesitantly to teen use? Why did stand-up comics make jokes about pot and coke and booze on television? Why were there no treatment programs for young people? These questions and more nagged at this band of fast-learning parents. How could it be that they alone were responsible for their children's use? After an initial examination of their own behavior as role models, the parents shifted their primary concern to influences from outside the home.

Finding answers to these baffling questions was difficult. One mother began by reading the research and medical journals in the Emory University library. She detected a consistent pattern: no one addressed the effects of illegal drugs on children; some research dismissed any dangers or deleterious effects of marijuana; and the research was contradictory and self-serving, always calling for more research. Occasionally, she found some informative writing and made copies to share with her group.

One day she wrote a long letter to Robert Dupont, the director of the National Institute on Drug Abuse (NIDA) explaining her concerns, informing him about their parent group, and documenting her dilemma about the drug problem. A month later, she received a brief reply, thanking her.

Undaunted, she wrote again. This time, her letter carried more conviction and some anger. She received another bureaucratic response, and doubted that the director had even seen her letter. She wrote once more—a harsher, longer, and more pointed letter. This routine of her sending letters and receiving noncommittal replies lasted for nearly five months. Finally, she invited the director to Atlanta to meet with the parents and their children. To her surprise, he agreed abruptly, and a date was set.

The encounter of the director of NIDA with the "Nosy Parent Association" was filled with tension, humor, conflicts, and wisdom. The parents were impressed that a distinguished federal official had come, and the children were pleased with the opportunity to debate him and their parents. The director listened and questioned them. He left with concern, but scarcely anticipated the ramifications of the evening. Upon his return to Washington, he dispatched another person to Atlanta to examine this unique community response. A decision was made to have the persistent letter writer—incidentally a university professor of English—write a book about parents, young people, and drugs. She accepted the offer.

During the following year, the members of this Atlanta community worked together to learn about each other and to hammer out an understanding.

Things changed when the author-parent delivered the keynote address at the Southeast Drug Education Conference in May 1978. The speech presented to one hundred attendees was entitled "The Family Versus the Drug

Culture." It ignited the predominantly Georgian audience, and, together with the workshops, conducted partly by parents, convinced many attendees to join the fledgling movement. The newly acquired knowledge proved credible.

An article in the *Atlanta Constitution* about the conference criticized parents for using "gestapo-like" tactics by searching their children's rooms and violating their rights of privacy. The story was picked up by a national wire service and appeared in several Sunday editions across the South. At that point, the parents' grass roots movement coalesced.

As is often the case in grass roots movements, people of like minds with shared concerns are scattered across the nation, and just one spark is needed to make them aware of each other. The first call to Atlanta came from Naples, Florida, followed by others from Tipton, Indiana, and Omaha, Nebraska. Families in those communities were struggling with their own version of the teen drug culture, their children's use, and their own agony. They understood the obstacles, and they eagerly welcomed the news that their problem was shared and they had the power to act.

In her call to action at the Parents Resource Institute for Drug Education (PRIDE) conference in May 1978, a parent said:

> We Americans have never thought of ourselves as a helpless people—why should we feel any differently about illegal drug usage? Parents may be terrified into passivity, into willful blindness, into bewildered permissiveness by the sense that drugs are something so alien, so mysterious, so overwhelming, that we, *mere* parents, cannot begin to cope with them. But drugs are not mysterious to kids. Parents should feel more confident that they can deal with them as they would with other concrete facts of life—with common sense, with

self-confidence and self-respect, with firmly articulated
and fairly enforced parental standards, and with a determined commitment not to let their children's growth
be damaged by mind-altering, mood-changing chemicals. And parents will have a lot more fun and a lot
closer sense of community if they carry this out in the
company of other parents. In a time of adolescent peer
pressure, parents need peer pressure, too.[4]

The speech was mentioned in a popular women's
magazine several months later, with a footnote that a
copy was available for those who would write to the
address listed. More than ten thousand requests were
received within two months. Parents, it became obvious,
had been waiting for this call to action. A network was in
the making.

In California, an organization called Parents Who Care
placed a full-page ad in a local newspaper to tell the
community that they cared and would do something
about preventing the drug problem. Hundreds of parents
had signed it and asked others to join them by filling out
an application at the bottom of the page. As a result,
their ranks swelled.

As to eastern cities, a town meeting was held in
Garden City, New York, to involve the citizenry. In Indiana, a letter-writing campaign was launched. One
parent was concerned about her babysitter and mobilized her group. A school official surveyed parents,
learned that drug education was a high priority, and
asked a parent to organize it. The latter, in turn, brought
in other parents. In one community, the spark was
provided by a teenager's letter to the local newspaper; in
another, it was an anti-drug abuse professional who
brought parents together in a new mood of attention and
awareness.

The main message of this grass roots beginning was
that parent power could work, both as a force to restore

the cherishing nature of the family and as a political means to counter the erosion of society caused by the use and abuse of illegal substances by American children. This movement is unique because it began from within; the problem was within: parents countered their own children's dangerous and illegal behavior. Unlike movements that are born in response to outside forces—toxic waste contamination, drunk driving, a lethal virus, ozone depletion, brutal experiments on animals, birth defects caused by Agent Orange, pesticides in children's food—this movement started when a few brave parents not only confronted their own children's dangerous acts and their own role in it, but also took action. Later, they learned that many other factors were at play in the teen drug culture: In the beginning, it was parents facing their kids, and their kids fighting back. No other grass roots movement in the history of America has had a similar origin.

Some parent networks remained in the neighborhood. Others spread into the entire community, embracing schools, parks departments, businesses, and the media. Some expanded to include state organizations, with parents and professionals working side by side. Two national organizations emerged—one a resource group, the other a membership organization.[5]

Results, problems, and the collapse of the membership organization (the National Federation of Parents for Drug Free Youth) will be discussed in chapter 5. While the organization was in its prime, ordinary people took their message to a nation harboring deep conflicts and much ambiguity about the drug problem.

### ACT UP—AIDS Coalition to Unleash Power

I have come to a terrible realization that I believe this gay community of ours has a death wish and that we are going to die because we refuse to take responsibility for our own lives.

Yes, most of all, I'm tired of you. I'm tired of the death wish of the gay community. I'm tired of our colluding in our own genocide. I'm tired of you, by your own passivity, actively participating in your own genocide.

It amazes me when I tell people they have power, and they answer me, 'Power? What power?' How can you be so conservative, dumb, blind? You know what is going on better than anybody, and yet you are silent, you constantly, consistently, and continuously sit on your collective asses and refuse to use your power."[6]

Larry Kramer, a New York playwright and novelist, issued this grim assessment to the Boston Lesbian and Gay Town Meeting in June 1987 at Faneuil Hall: provocative, angry, unrelenting. Although tired and despairing, he came to arouse his audience, and they responded.

Earlier in the year, seated at his large white desk, surrounded by books and paintings, Kramer reflected on the hundreds of friends and acquaintances who had died from AIDS (acquired immunodeficiency syndrome). In 1987 he moved about in the stricken New York gay community and saw the struggle to survive. Barely able to provide rudimentary pastoral care and aware that approved drugs had brought no breakthrough in treating AIDS, Kramer assessed his community, and it made his blood boil. He spoke about the moribund governmental response and the silence of most of the media. If those in the eye of the storm could not be moved to respond, perhaps silence equaled death. On March 10, 1987, addressing a gay and lesbian community center audience, Kramer unwittingly launched a new grass roots movement when he shouted, "How many of you here would be willing to meet again to consider direct political action?" Every hand went up. Two days later, hundreds met to establish ACT UP (AIDS Coalition

To Unleash Power). A campaign against the Food and Drug Administration (FDA) was the first order of business—a campaign to force the agency to accelerate the approval process for experimental treatment drugs and to make them available to those in need. Other actions would follow.

Within two weeks, more than two hundred men and women demonstrated on Wall Street in front of Trinity Church, where they burned an effigy of the director of the Food and Drug Administration. They held him responsible for failing to get experimental drugs to AIDS patients. In a carefully orchestrated protest, traffic was tied up before police moved in to arrest many of those engaged in their first act of nonviolent civil disobedience. Fact sheets about the FDA were distributed as the major networks' television crews covered this fledgling but raucous group. Their provocative actions did not go unnoticed either in Washington, D.C., or in other cities across the nation. ACT UP members fulfilled their charter's mandate: "diverse individuals united in anger and committed to direct action."

Larry Kramer knew that one person alone could not make a group do something it did not want to and that one voice at the head of a crowd soon loses its appeal, especially if that voice, in his own estimation, is "strong, harsh, and intrusive." Others had to share the sense of wrong and be willing to act. But he was the one to spark the action. Five years earlier, with several close friends, he had helped launch the Gay Men's Health Crisis, New York's first grass roots social service agency for those suffering from AIDS. Without government funding, dedicated people provided care with dignity and compassion to those who were dying in their community. As the agency grew and prospered, Kramer believed he saw it change not only in size but also in mission and bureaucratic structure. Estranged from the group, he started pushing for political action that had not been forthcoming from people who were consumed with pastoral duties. He wanted more.

Devoid of officers, board of directors, office, reports, and formal organization, ACT UP is different. Each Monday evening, no fewer than three hundred people crowd into a school cafeteria on West Thirteenth Street to participate in a democratic process apt to alarm any parliamentarian. For three hours, mostly young men and women, comfortable with each other and themselves, gather to speak out and throw ideas for action to this largely white and well-educated crowd. What they experience is power. Some ideas are shouted down, while others are boosted with cheers.

"Affinity groups," small and voluntarily assembled, form within the larger gathering, and they find an area in the cafeteria to convene. Groups can develop actions such as a "die-in," a brigade of volunteers putting up posters throughout a section of the city (Manhattan's Lower West Side, for instance), a training, or a "zap campaign" (an attention-getting act that attracts the media) against a government official or agency. By utilizing this strategy of breaking up into small groups, each member ends up participating in groups spreading across the city. The movement, obviously, is not for armchair activists. By evening's end, people usually depart unified, with plans to act.[7]

ACT UP meeting attendance changes, as new recruits crowd into the hall each Monday and open the session with shouts such as, "Loud and rude and strong and queer!" or "Health care is a right!" This newly found camaraderie replaces powerlessness. Money to cover the costs of materials or to pay fines is obtained by selling T-shirts and buttons with the ACT UP emblem, a pink triangle with the words SILENCE = DEATH. Contributions are received from families and supporters. Each group handles its own finances.

During its first two years, ACT UP had no problem identifying its opposition: federal bureaucracies such as the Food and Drug Administration, the National Institutes of Health, the Centers for Disease Control, university-based research, the Reagan administration, pharmaceutical companies, insurance agencies, city hall, state governments, the press, and those in the community who members think could help but do not.

When ACT UP was launched in 1987, Larry Kramer listed a set of concerns quickly embraced by its members:

- The Food and Drug Administration uses a procedure for approving a potential drug that may take seven to nine years. Most AIDS patients die in that time frame.
- Many physicians want to use drugs that have passed FDA's Phase One, the safety trial, but are blocked by agency regulations.
- AIDS sufferers with nothing to lose want to be guinea pigs but are often not selected for inclusion in clinical trials, and, further, promising new drugs are withheld.
- Giving a placebo, "an inert or innocuous substance used in a controlled experiment," is unacceptable because AIDS is terminal.
- Compassionate use of a potential drug is not allowed by the FDA.
- The federal agencies charged with halting the AIDS epidemic do not cooperate among themselves or with the French, who are also devoting sustained efforts to find a cure as well as a vaccine.[8]

Through their lively democratic process, these new grass roots activists design and execute actions to bring down these barriers and to join forces with other AIDS groups with similar intentions. They have set up pickets and held demonstrations at New York's City Hall, the White House, the *Saturday Evening Post*, the *New York Times*, and St. Patrick's Cathedral. Their voices became their power; their street theater made them known. Some threw condoms, while others lay on the street in a "die-in" and left chalk outlines of their bodies as a reminder. Groups scurried through business sections, plastering windows and walls with bloody, red hand prints. They wore clown masks to meetings to mock those who took themselves too seriously while doing nothing but talking. They turned their own rage into outrage. They bound themselves in strands of red tape to symbolize an unresponsive bureaucracy, demanding that they be noticed. Having felt like society's throwaways, outcasts, queers, and junkies, they discarded the silence.[9]

Like other grass roots groups, ACT UP activists seek media attention, and they do get it at times, mostly when their protest is dramatic and showy. When the press asks the question, "Are you hurting your own cause?" most ACT UP members do not retreat in remorse; some feel an even deeper alienation, pain, and fear. Even if the target is inappropriate or the guerrilla theater tasteless, some reason, "Why not? What else do we have to lose?"

Groups have found the "zap," a type of personal affront, particularly effective, and when a major airline announced the policy of refusing passage to AIDS sufferers, ACT UP members flooded the carrier with hundreds of bogus flight reservations. The policy was subsequently reversed.

When ACT UP members started attending scientific and medical research meetings, their presence and behavior annoyed some people. When they became disruptive, even more voices were raised against their actions. However, over time, mainstream scientists have joined them and other less volatile AIDS activists in criticizing the slow pace of clinical trials and the FDA approval process. The fury within ACT UP is not so much with the scientific efforts as it is with the bureaucratic process. Some state that ACT UP's extremes only make traditional AIDS groups appear more acceptable and moderate.[10] When one group traveled to Bethesda, Maryland, to stage a protest at the National Institutes of Health, Dr. Anthony Fauci, the director of the National Institute of Allergy and Infectious Diseases, invited members in for a discussion. Later Fauci said, "When ACT UP acts in a reasonable way, when it has a reasonable concern, it can be an effective catalyst."[11]

Ever since the epidemic began in 1981, it has received a grass roots response. People With AIDS (PWA) groups emerged in many communities to provide care and to educate a sexually active population in safe sex practices. Project Inform has gained national attention by sponsoring clandestine trials of Compound Q, a Chinese drug.

At the Sixth International Conference on AIDS, held in June 1990, Martin Delaney, the leader of Project Inform, presented a report on the clandestine trials of Compound Q. Although the findings were questioned by some scientists, Delaney's right to give the report was defended by Dr. Dan Hoth, director of the National Institute of Allergy and Infectious Disease. He said of the criticism, "It's not irresponsible to present data at a scientific meeting. I'm only concerned that patients are desperate, so I would be delighted to have our group review the data." The FDA has approved Compound Q's use in these Project Inform trials.

The Community Research Initiative (CRI) encourages physicians to make promising treatments available outside rigorous clinical experiments. In the beginning, almost the entire response to the epidemic came from the grass roots.[12]

Today, in 1991, Larry Kramer estimates that more than one hundred ACT UP or similar groups with different names are active across America. Most use the open, democratic organizational format. Their members are opinionated, argumentative, and angry. Kramer sensed the mood in the beginning, the creative tension, and he eschewed what he calls the "founding father" syndrome. However, some members of ACT UP reject Kramer's leadership and question some of his statements. When Kramer called for a "riot" at the Sixth International Conference on AIDS, some members opposed the plan as being counterproductive. Groups choose actions for themselves but work in teams.

To date, ACT UP and its counterparts have attracted mostly white gay male and lesbian members but have largely failed to reach gay people or intravenous drug users and their parents among blacks, Latinos, or other minorities in significant numbers. With AIDS rates accelerating in these latter groups, the need for outreach and inclusion is obvious.

Results and outcomes of ACT UP and other AIDS grass roots groups are presented in chapter 2. One particular event in 1989, however, will be mentioned here. Zidovudine, an antiviral drug made by Burroughs Wellcome (formerly known as AZT) was approved by the FDA as the first drug for AIDS treatment. Originally, the cost was estimated by the manufacturer to be $10,000 a year per patient. Later, it was reduced to $8,000, with the drug firm vowing to hold the line at that price. Considerable public concern was generated about the drug's high cost and the inability of many patients to pay, but Burroughs Wellcome would not budge, even in light of a study which the National Institutes of Health said indicated that the earlier a person diagnosed as HIV positive used Zidovudine, the greater the chances were to delay symptoms and the ravages of the disease. This finding alone means that the volume of business for the pharmaceutical firm would skyrocket and profits would abound. Upon the company's statement that development and manufacturing costs justified the $8,000 per patient per year cost, ACT UP members thought of a way to change their mind. They donned suits that bore fake brokerage firm identification tags and walked onto the floor of the New York Stock Exchange, where they set off miniature fog horns, unfurled a banner that read "Sell Wellcome," and chained themselves to the railing. The protesters were arrested, but, a few days later, Burroughs Wellcome announced a 20 percent reduction in the price of Zidovudine, all the while denying it was responding to outside pressure.[13] By late 1990, the cost of Zidovudine per year per person had dropped to $2,700.

During the 1990 Sixth International Conference on AIDS, held in San Francisco, ACT UP displayed a sophisticated approach to the media by delivering their daily messages to conference participants and journalists. The New York group's Treatment and Data Committee issued a detailed statement entitled *"AIDS Treatment and Research Agenda."* The report charges, "After several years of AZT and precious little else in the developed world, and after ten years of virtually *no* treatment in the third world, people afflicted with AIDS worldwide are waking to the recognition that countries with the resources to end the epidemic—chiefly the USA—have no intention of taking the necessary steps. Next year's AIDS budget is smaller than that for the space station Freedom."

ACT UP has forged new alliances during the four years it has been in operation. Their AIDS Treatment and Data Committee states:

Activists worked with NIH researchers and the FDA to design the "Parallel Track" program for systematizing expanded access to certain new therapies, and then with Bristol Meyers to design the ddl expanded access protocols; such coordination and cooperation must become the rule, rather than the exception.

The Sixth International Conference on AIDS provided a forum for ACT UP to deliver its many messages, and it did, through street theater, speeches, reports, and press briefings. At the close of the conference, ACT UP members walked with scientists and physicians in a unity march down San Francisco's Market Street. In typical fashion, their brashness was unleashed against Dr. Louis Sullivan, secretary of the Department of Health and Human Services, at the closing session, where they led a noisy demonstration that drowned out his speech. They threw wads of paper, pennies, and condoms toward the podium. Sullivan said in a subsequent press conference, "I personally resent it, and I will not work with those individuals. They have shown they are not worthy of trying to form a coalition."[14]

Larry Kramer responded, "To Dr. Sullivan, I say this: Your presence has been so negligible, and you have done so little for us, that whether you decide to work with us or not... is irrelevant."[15]

ACT UP continued to work with the National Institute of Allergy and Infectious Diseases, despite Secretary Sullivan's threat. Scott Tucker, an ACT UP leader from Philadelphia, makes the point that the group's basic tactic is to get rude and go public. "If a Quaker vigil is your speed, you won't like us," Tucker says.

ACT UP vows to continue putting pressure on government agencies and officials as they deem appropriate, and insurance companies and other pharmaceutical firms are likely targets for future group action as the cost of medical care increases. In 1990, ACT UP launched a boycott against Miller beer and Marlboro cigarettes, both products of Philip Morris, because of the corporation's financial support of North Carolina Senator Jesse Helms's reelection campaign.

In one major way, this grass roots group differs from others: its intentional absence of an organizational structure, coupled with a total reliance on a spontaneous, democratic decision-making process. It sustains itself with an enthusiastic, brash membership committed to its position that Silence equals Death.

## Mothers and Others for Pesticide Limits

These remarks signal a call to action:

> Our children are at risk because of pesticide residues in the very food that we feed them to help them to grow up healthy. It doesn't have to be this way. But solving the problem of pesticides in children's food is going to require enormous public pressure on the government and the country's agricultural interests.

In February 1989, *Intolerable Risk: Pesticides in our Children's Food* was released by the Natural Resources Defense Council (NRDC), a respected and credible environmental law organization. The report got immediate attention. Not since the publication in 1962 of *Silent Spring* has a national response been as rapid and intense, especially among mothers of preschool children.

Using government data on preschoolers' diets and the levels of pesticides actually found in produce to quantify the risk, NRDC studied only 23 of the 300 pesticides used on food, concentrating attention on fresh and processed fruits and vegetables. It concluded: "Some 6,000 preschoolers may get cancer at some point in their lifetimes because of childhood exposure to only 8 of the

66 pesticides that EPA (Environmental Protection
Agency) calls carcinogens. Some 3 million preschoolers
are being exposed to neurotoxic pesticides at levels above
those the government considers safe."[17]

A serious problem documented by the report is that the
EPA bases its limits for pesticide residues on consumption patterns of adults without taking into account those
of children. The average preschool child consumes 6
times as much fruit as the average adult, 18 times as
much apple juice and 31 times as much applesauce.

These facts and the carefully documented report might
have gone the way of other previously released, incisive
reports. Certainly, the excellent book *Malignant Neglect*,
produced by the Environmental Defense Fund ten years
earlier (1979), was neglected.[18] Although it was the first
complete, up-to-date report on known or suspected cancer-causing agents in the environment, and although it
suggested ways to control them in order to halt the
spread of cancer, few people knew about its revealing
contents and instructional choices for Americans. In the
chapter on "Children and Cancer," the author asserts
that the average human infant

> exceeds by ten times the maximum daily PCB intake
> level set by the Food and Drug Administration. Indeed,
> if human milk were marketed in interstate commerce,
> much of it would be seized and condemned by the FDA.
> Because an infant is so small as compared with an
> adult, and because an infant derives all its nourish-
> ment from milk or formula, the average baby receives a
> dietary dose of PCBs almost one hundred times greater
> than that of an adult on a body weight basis. This also
> holds true for certain pesticides.[19]

Why did one report create a grass roots movement,
while the other did not? Both were carefully prepared by
respected environmental groups. Both attempted to

spread the seeds of knowledge and concern for the nation's people to examine, but only the NRDC report stirred people to action. The answer to this question has to be seen as a valuable lesson for future grass roots movements. Prior to the NRDC's release of *Intolerable Risk: Pesticides in our Children's Food*, Meryl Streep, the well-known and highly respected actress, visited their offices to discuss her concerns about the environment—concerns that were shared by many. After the notorious summer of 1988, with toxic waste washing up on shores and beaches, and with the Mississippi River's water level so low as to make it almost unnavigable, public fear had increased. A two-year drought and the record-breaking heat of several previous summers had heightened worry about the predicted greenhouse effect. Many felt things were frighteningly amiss, and it was at a time of general public distress that a draft of the NRDC's new study was shared with Meryl Streep. She responded quickly and effectively by returning to her community to organize parents. The alarming findings reached ordinary people—and the movement Mothers and Others for Pesticide Limits was born.

Upon release of the report in February 1989, "60 Minutes," the popular CBS investigative television program, went to Falls Village, Connecticut, to cover the first public symposium on the NRDC's findings. The event was hosted by the Northwest Connecticut chapter of Mothers and Others for Pesticide Limits, the first chapter of the aspiring grass roots movement that Meryl Streep had helped organize. A nationwide television audience witnessed, on the one side, the emotional reactions of parents facing a threat to their vulnerable young children—and perhaps to all Americans—and, on the other side, the attempts by the responsible federal agencies, the FDA and the EPA, to assuage an alarmed group of ordinary citizens, environmentalists, scientists, and physicians.[20]

One chemical in particular took the spotlight: daminozide, produced and distributed by the Uniroyal Chemical Company of Connecticut under the trade name Alar. The NRDC calls Alar, applied to control the firmness, quality, and color of apples, "one of the most dangerous carcinogens now used on food."

Armed with scientific findings, concerned because she is a mother of young children, skilled as an actress, and capable of getting the media floodlight, Meryl Streep set out on a media blitz and spoke to the nation and to other mothers one-to-one about their children's risks from pesticides in their food and the intransigence of bureaucrats in Washington. As Streep made the rounds of talk shows and congressional hearings, the power of this grass roots campaign grew. On the "Phil Donahue Show," she and several other mothers explained grass roots activism. They listed the tactics of Mothers and Others for Pesticide Limits (MOPL) and its goals. People understood the process, and the response was overwhelming.

To start a local group, MOPL suggested the organizer(s) follow these steps:

- Recruit members, beginning with friends and neighbors. Stop when you reach twenty or thirty. Word-of-mouth or presentations at parent meetings get members.
- Form committees based on interests and skills, because members who participate are more likely to remain. Gather as much information on the subject as possible because informed people can stand their ground against opponents or critics.
- Concentrate on learning about local food sources, education, and organic farming to promote local alternatives to large-scale agriculture.
- Meet with supermarket officials to express concern

over pesticide residues and to promote the need for organic produce sections.

- Establish affordable membership dues to help with office expenses and publicity. Do as much of your own writing as possible; for instance, prepare press releases, fliers, statements, newsletters, and sponsor local events such as fairs, cookouts, and children's parties.
- Write your congressional representatives to support legislative reform. The NRDC urges the following:

  EPA must revise its standards for pesticides in food, using complete data on health risks of each pesticide; the Food and Drug Administration, which is responsible for enforcing EPA standards, must improve its lax monitoring program; and Congress must encourage farmers to use the well-established low pesticide farming methods.[21]

These precise steps can guide a local chapter in its grass roots activism. In addition, MOPL published a consumer book, *For Our Kids' Sake: How to Protect Your Child Against Pesticides in Food.*[22] It tells parents the facts about pesticides, how to obtain organic produce, and to whom they can write to urge reform of the pesticide laws.

The response to the MOPL campaign against Alar was swift and direct. By early May 1989, a drop in apple product sales of as much as 20 percent was announced by the Processed Apples Institutes. Across the nation, school systems and other institutions providing children food on their campuses discontinued serving apples and apple products. Parents boycotted non-organically grown apples and apple products.

At first, Uniroyal disputed the NRDC report's findings and continued to sell Alar. The EPA released a report estimating that only about 4 percent of apples were exposed to Alar, but revised it on May 13, 1989, saying that recent findings had caused it to increase that figure. It now estimated that as much as 15 percent of 1988's crop might have received Alar spray.[23]

Pressure intensified in mid-May 1989. The EPA announced steps to ban the use of the growth-regulating chemical Alar on apples and other foods but said final action was not likely for at least eighteen months. The anticipated long delay enraged consumers and environmentalists, and a press conference was called in Washington to denounce it. On May 17, a bipartisan group of senators introduced legislation to ban Alar, responding to public and scientific concern over health risks and financial losses to apple growers and apple product manufacturers. Apple growers said they would voluntarily comply with the ban.

Uniroyal made it known that it would halt the sale of Alar in the United States but would continue to supply the world market. The EPA announced an immediate ban on the use of Alar on foods. The grass roots victory was swift and stunning. In four short months, a new citizens' group, fortified by the Natural Resources Defense Council and with the help from other influential public interest groups, environmentalists, and legislators, had fundamentally shaken the chemical industry, apple growers and processors, and the federal bureaucracy.

While grass roots activists rejoiced, Alar-treated apples continued to be sold throughout the world, including America. The U.S. Department of Agriculture purchased 15 million dollars' worth of apples that might have been treated with Alar and offered them to prisons, food banks, and institutions for the retarded, and Uniroyal sold Alar to Third World countries that, in turn, sell fruits and vegetables to the United States.[24] Some, obviously, questioned these cynical actions.

In March 1990, the Environmental Protection Agency issued a final ruling on Alar, one year after its decision to ban the chemical. No Alar would be permitted in tomatoes or tomato products, milk, meat, meat by-products, eggs, and peanut meal. In addition, all fruits would have to be free of Alar by May 31, 1991. "These actions are being taken because EPA has determined that long-term dietary exposure to (Alar)... poses unacceptable risks to the general population."[25]

The Uniroyal Chemical Company complied with the ruling and ended all sales and distribution of Alar. Grass roots efforts had brought fast and complete results for those concerned about a pesticide once protected by its manufacture and a federal agency.

Unfortunately, Alar is only one of many chemicals used on foods by the nation's farmers. Each year, 430 million pounds of pesticides are sprayed on crops and into the soil, and the spray escapes into the air. Persistent worries abound, not only about eating the food but about those who harvest it. Clusters of childhood cancer cases have been found regularly in the poor farming towns of the Central Valley of California by the United Farm Workers Union. Five new cases discovered in Earlimont in 1989 have been confirmed by state health authorities, who note that the cases in this newly discovered cluster are twelve times the normal rate for a town its size. Some physicians suspect that these children are the victims of cancer-causing chemicals sprayed on grapes and other Central Valley crops. The parents of the children and the children themselves harvest these crops and consume the produce. The United Farm Workers Union members used shoe-leather epidemiology—their own brand of grass roots activism—to locate these new cases.[26]

A California Department of Health preliminary report on childhood cancer in the Central Valley, released in June 1990, stated that overall, the childhood cancer rate for the four counties is comparable to those found in California and around the nation.[27]

But those affected think otherwise. Connie Rosales, the mother of a young lymphoma victim, says: "We live in the fields. We are the field. Our immune system is constantly under attack. Cancer in children is totally abnormal. The state tries to treat it like it is a measles epidemic or something. Something that will just go away. It won't."[28]

What does the future hold for this new grass roots movement stimulated from the top by an incisive report? The Natural Resources Defense Council will continue to sponsor Mothers and Others for Pesticide Limits, with Meryl Streep serving as cochair. That a grass roots base for this movement exists is obvious. In the June 1989 issue of *Organic Gardening*, a Louis Harris poll showed that 70 percent of all consumers would buy organically grown vegetables if they were available and that more than 50 percent would be willing to pay as much as 20 percent more for them. Respondents also told the pollsters that their concern about long-term health effects was the most important factor in their decision.[29] In September 1989, five U.S. supermarket chains pledged, in an effort to shore up consumer confidence in the safety of foods, to stop selling fresh fruits and vegetables treated with cancer-causing pesticides by 1995. At the same time, spokespersons for larger chains and produce growers labeled as "misguided zealots" consumer groups who had stimulated the campaign.

Concurrently, in September 1989, the prestigious National Academy of Sciences released a report that had been five years in the making and that boosts organic farming. It concludes that carefully managed farms growing diverse crops with little or no chemicals are as productive and, at times, more profitable than those using pesticides and synthetic fertilizers. While it says

that alternative farming practices hold promise for substantial benefits, action will partly depend on the importance society places on achieving environmental goals.[30]
With the newly aroused grass roots groups' concerns
about pesticides and their children's health, fewer than
the predicted twenty to thirty years may be needed to
move farming in a new direction.

Mothers and Others for Pesticide Limits has a wide
base of support among the media and among most
environmentalists, and their cause appeals to well-educated young parents. Reaching minorities and the poor,
especially the farm workers' families, however, remains a
challenge. The group's tactics and objectives are mea-
sured and traditional, but their fulfillment portends
dramatic societal changes.

The preceding stories were about some of the people
and movements that have changed and are changing
America. Other movements discussed in this book are

Mothers Against Drunk Driving (MADD)
Remove Intoxicated Drivers (RID)
Earth First!
People for the Ethical Treatment of Animals (PETA)
Vietnam Veterans of America
Rainforest Action Network
Operation Rescue
Fairness & Accuracy in Reporting (FAIR)
Just Say No Clubs
In Defense of Animals
National Federation of Parents for Drug Free Youth
Americans for Responsible Television
Citizen's Clearinghouse for Hazardous Wastes

Two organizations, the Environmental Defense Fund
and the Natural Resources Defense Council, began as
mere grass roots efforts but have since evolved into

national environmental justice centers with regional
offices. Their actions are reported on in subsequent
chapters.

In the next chapter, tactics used by the various grass
roots groups are examined, and examples of each tactic
with anecdotal materials are presented.

# 2

# Grass Roots Tactics

Grass roots movements employ a wide range of tactics to achieve their aims—from nonviolent civil disobedience to traditional social action to violent direct action. Individual tactics are bound to be more appropriate in some situations than in others, like any broadly useful set of tools.

### Nonviolent Civil Disobedience

"Civil Disobedience," a discourse written by Henry David Thoreau in 1846, was a statement against slavery on the one hand and a call to philosophical anarchism on the other. Deeply troubled by the government's use of a poll tax to finance the proslavery war in Mexico, Thoreau refused to pay that tax and was placed in jail. Although his family paid the tax without his knowledge and he was released the following morning, Thoreau later reflected upon the incident. The result was "Civil Disobedience," and its principles have been embraced by Tolstoy, Gandhi, King, and others. Thoreau reasoned that he and not society was the better judge. His protests were peaceful; he did not advocate physical struggle against the wrong as perceived by him. He urged people to resist passively by refusing to acquiesce. He said, "I simply wish to refuse allegiance to the state, to withdraw and stand aloof from it effectually.... If governmental inequity is of such a nature that it requires you to be the agent of injustice to another, then, I say, break the law...."[1] He himself did just that and was willing to go to jail rather than strengthen slavery. By acting from principle, he fashioned the conflict between the individual and the state. Those who break the law in this personal exercise of conscience must expect the legal consequences. About civil disobedience, Tom Regan, an animal rights activist, says:

> Civil disobedience is a morally defensible strategy for encouraging social change. Its power has been demonstrated throughout history, even as recently as the peaceful change of government in the Philippines. By violating the law, the agents of civil disobedience make a public statement about an existing injustice. By accepting the possibility of punishment, they shoulder the burdens of injustice themselves. In this way, civil disobedience accepts a token of the evil imposed on those whose interests they represent.
>
> As a strategy, civil disobedience is the last, not the first, choice. Other nonviolent methods for effecting social change—discussions and boycotts, for example— must be tried first. Only after these approaches have met with unresponsiveness should civil disobedience be used.[2]

The act of civil disobedience sends a message of protest to those governing as well as to all citizens of that government. In the early 1960s, struggling for civil rights in large numbers, Americans began conducting acts of civil disobedience. In the late 1960s, students were joined by others in their protests against the Vietnam war. From its roots in New England, nonviolent civil disobedience grew, and its principles are used in the 1990s in sit-ins, die-ins, demonstrations, and guerrilla theater.

## The First Sit-In

The best-known crusader of the Temperance movement, Carry Nation, carried her message, her Bible, and her hatchet across the United States from 1900 to 1911 smashing saloons, lecturing on the evils of demon rum, corresponding from the jails where she was a prisoner, and eventually performing as an "attraction" at New York's Coney Island amusement park. The *New York Times* described her as "the Island's particular freak of the day." The *Tribune* wrote, "The Loop the Loop, the Flip Flop, the Jolly Razzle Dazzle, all the vertigo-producing machines could not compete with Carry Nation." For ten days in 1901, Carry Nation delivered fiery temperance lectures to a curious crowd assembled on the beach for sun and swimming. When the New York police arrived to arrest her for laying waste a cigar stand from which she suspected the owner dispensed alcohol, she protested: for, in her own words, she was guilty of nothing but the "destruction of malicious property." Calling the officers "purple and bloated from beer," she lay down on the sidewalk and refused to enter the police van (or Black Maria, as it was termed in those days). A policeman cracked her with a nightstick, lifted her limp body (clad in her famous black alpaca dress), and placed her in custody—thus ending the first recorded sit-in.[3] Since that day, many other acts of passive resistance have become a staple of grass roots protesters. The following anecdotes illustrate the creative use of this tactic.

## *Animals Are Dying*

During the evening of February 21, 1989, six animal rights activists climbed to the top of a crane at the construction site of the Northwest Animal Facility at the Berkeley Campus of the University of California. In the floodlight of the media, they dropped banners demanding an end to the construction project and to the use for which it was being built. The students wanted everyone to know that the animal rights movement is engaged in a struggle with the research community, placing pressure on it to seek alternatives to animal experiments. For eight days, the civil disobedience continued.

Campus police attempted to end the sit-in by isolating students and cutting off their food supply, and the university warned the young people about fines and jail sentences if they did not end the demonstration. The university placed extreme importance on the Northwest Animal Facility's achieving full accreditation of its animal care and use program and urged staff "to work against this irresponsible effort to block construction of this new building whenever possible."[4]

The six activists remained atop the crane, in the rain and cold, and without food, until the university agreed to drop all civil charges.[5] Through widespread national media attention, their message was heard. Subsequently a state appellate court ruled that the environmental review of the project had been inadequate. The university set out to conduct further environmental study as instructed by the appellate court in order to continue with the construction project.

This dramatic act of civil disobedience was planned by a grass roots group, In Defense of Animals, that was founded in 1983 by Dr. Elliot Katz, a graduate of the Cornell University School of Veterinary Medicine. "Five years ago, I founded In Defense of Animals to end the University of California's appalling abuse of animals.

Animals were dying by the hundreds of thousands of viral infections, suffocation, strangulation, encephalitis, and heat stroke. Despite the fact that veterinarians and students had been documenting these severe violations to the Animal Welfare Act, federal authorities were unwilling to step in and take action," Katz commented.[6]

## Posted: No Dumping

"We'll get arrested as often as we can," said Sally Campbell, a founder of the Allegany County Nonviolent Action Group.

"We'll throw ourselves in front of bulldozers," said Mary Gardner Smith, a day care worker from Wellsville, New York.

These reactions came from ordinary people in September 1989, when they learned that their area had been selected by the New York State Low-Level Radioactive Waste Siting Commission, which has a federal mandate to find a home for low-level nuclear waste by 1993. No other issue has created as much activism among Americans—many unaccustomed to political controversy—as the disposal of hazardous waste. In New York, people who have never protested before now contemplate acts of civil disobedience to protect their land from the dumping of radioactive fluids, resins, tools, machine parts, and clothes that come from reactors, hospitals, and companies throughout the state.

Although state officials assure the local residents that the waste is absolutely harmless and poses no health risk, many citizens have heard about Fernald, Ohio, Rocky Flats, Colorado, and other sites across the nation that have had serious problems with hazardous nuclear waste and whose operators also claimed their procedures were safe and harmless to those living nearby.

"We're not great protesters, but this has really upset

us," said a couple who nailed the "Posted—No Dumping" sign on their front door and to a tree in the yard. The county produces no nuclear waste, and the residents don't want it brought into a community that one resident describes in this way, "Here we are in absolutely the most beautiful part of the earth. It's clean, it's pristine. Why in the world are they talking about bringing nuclear waste here?"[7]

### Baby Jane Doe

"The essence of civil disobedience is to allow yourself to be punished...because you have allegiance to a higher authority," U.S. District Judge Wallace Tashima said. "To deny responsibility, you become nothing more than ordinary law breakers....It is simply hypocritical and nothing more."

In May 1989, a Los Angeles faction of the antiabortion group Operation Rescue and twelve individuals were ordered to pay a $110,000 fine for defying court injunctions by blockading medical clinics in seven California cities. The judge deplored the group's claim to civil disobedience and their attempt to avoid responsibility by asserting they could not be held liable for their actions.[8]

Operation Rescue uses nonviolent, direct action to block and disrupt activities at abortion clinics. With an estimated membership of 35,000 and active groups in at least two hundred cities, it takes the position that it is rescuing lives. Active members receive training in nonviolent action. Carrying an aborted fetus in a jar of formaldehyde, the protesters shout at those running and entering clinics. They stage "rescues" by forming human blockades on the sidewalks outside clinics and try to convince those entering for services to forego an abortion, or as they call it, "baby killing." They exercise passive resistance when confronted by the police, drop to the sidewalk, and are removed to jail.

In 1987, a born-again Christian, Randall Terry, founded Operation Rescue, a militant wing of the right-to-life movement. His followers are largely fundamentalist, white Christians, some of whom have had abortions and feel guilty over the decision.[9] The "rescues" are designed, in Terry's words, "to expose the pro-abortion mind-set that has infiltrated every strata of American society. We are launching a two-pronged offensive; thousands will surround abortion mills to rescue children and mothers, and we will impact state legislatures with equal force."[10]

The most dramatic acts of civil disobedience staged by Terry occurred during the Democratic National Convention in 1988, an event he calls "the Siege of Atlanta," and in May 1989, when more than 1,200 protesters from across the United States returned to Atlanta to demonstrate outside abortion clinics and Planned Parenthood offices. When taken to jail, some gave their names as "Baby Jane Doe" or "Baby John Doe." Before posting bail, some remained locked up for two months.

Demonstrations at abortion clinics and Planned Parenthood offices are noisy, almost always attracting the local media. Increasingly, groups that oppose Operation Rescue arrive at the targeted site to conduct a pro-choice counterdemonstration. The antiabortion movement has a unique aspect to it—active protest against women, physicians, and others attempting to exercise their own civil rights to have or perform a legal abortion or attend a family planning session. The matter of conscience differs —antiabortion or pro-choice—and the two groups are diametrically opposed. In 1986, Operation Rescue took the offensive in this struggle by using street theater, sit-ins, and blockades to gain public awareness of the conflict. Their targets are mostly women who seek abortions or family planning counseling and organizations that support the right to choose abortion. The conflict is intense because a majority of American women resent the personal attacks on their civil rights, and many healthcare workers support the pro-choice position. During 1989 and 1990, at least one act of civil disobedience a week was performed by Operation Rescue groups, usually accompanied by a counterdemonstration. Numerous arrests were the rule.

In 1990, Operation Rescue received two legal setbacks administered by the United States Supreme Court. The high court let stand a ruling banning Operation Rescue protesters from blocking access to New York clinics and fining the organization $70,000 for harassing women seeking abortions. The ruling provides abortion rights lawyers with a new legal weapon against these grass roots protesters by declaring that Operation Rescue has violated the 1987 Ku Klux Klan Act in conspiring to deprive women of their right to get an abortion.

In an earlier decision, the high court let stand an Atlanta judge's strict order forbidding antiabortion demonstrators to block sidewalks in front of clinics and to bother those trying to enter. However, these two legal setbacks have not ended Operation Rescue's efforts to block the entrances to abortion clinics.

### Guerrilla Theater

"We, the species of California's rain forests, demand full representation on the Board of Forestry." This statement was presented to the media at a meeting of the California State Board of Forestry in May 1989. Those responsible for the statement sat in the front row, costumed in masks of bears, eagles, owls, and other wild creatures. They jeered lumber industry spokespersons presenting a petition of the Timber Association of California that proposed changes in the way the state reviews proposals to log private timberlands, a plan opposed by environmental organizations such as the

Sierra Club. The presentation was interrupted frequently with growls, quacks, and coos coming from the costumed members of Earth First!, a newer grass roots group.

Police were summoned and the protesters removed when they occupied the vacated seats of board members during a break. No arrests were made, but by having its colorful theater covered by United International Press (UPI), the group had reached one goal.[11]

Earth First! employs a variety of civil disobedience tactics. Those of a violent nature are discussed in the later section on violent direct action. Frequently, though, they use guerrilla theater, dressed as grizzly bears blocking traffic in Yellowstone National Park or rolling a plastic "crack" down the face of Glen Canyon Dam in Arizona.

In 1981, Earth First! was founded by disenchanted environmentalists who had worked for the Wilderness Society and Friends of the Earth. They were joined by several kindred souls who felt the pace of the environmental movement was too slow. Militancy was necessary, they urged.[12] Earth First! leader David Foreman sums up the group's actions as "a form of worship toward the earth. It's really a very spiritual thing to go out and do."[13] Influenced heavily by Edward Abbey's 1976 novel, *The Monkey Wrench Gang*, Earth First! plays out variations of the book's scenario of a band of environmentalists setting out to halt the desecration of the earth by any means—at any personal cost.

Local chapters are autonomous and free to plan their own acts of ecotage. Within the environmentalists community, Earth First! tactics are controversial, some say counterproductive. David Foreman counters, "The planet is either a collection of resources, or it's alive. That's the real choice. I'm happy there's something bigger than me out there: the natural world. And I'm not gonna throw my life away, but if my death would save the last of the grizzly bears, then fine."[14]

Differences of opinion and choice of preferred tactics have created continuing struggles for Earth First!, particularly during its 1990 Redwood Summer campaign (a campaign to save California's redwoods). The division prompted David Foreman, Earth First! cofounder, to announce that he was leaving his original group to form an organization that is more concerned with "conservation biology and the need for large ecological wilderness preserves."[15] Foreman is reported to believe the original group has gone too far to the left by expanding its activities to include other social activist concerns, such as feminism, Native American rights, and unionism.

Earth First! is a grass roots group that is gaining membership, recognition, and with that visibility, a good deal of internal dissension that is the hallmark of another loosely knit grass roots group—ACT UP.

## Compound Q: Making It Acceptable

Compound Q (GLQ-223) was purchased in China, smuggled into the United States, and became the underground medication for approximately seventy patients who volunteered for a clandestine AIDS study. Compound Q is derived from the root of the Chinese cucumber and is used in China to induce abortions and treat various kinds of tumors. When researchers found in laboratory experiments that the drug had a striking ability to kill cells infected with the AIDS virus, while leaving healthy cells alone, word of this finding spread throughout the AIDS community. The smuggler carried two hundred doses of the compound, which he had purchased at a factory in Shanghai, and, with the help of those in his underground network, he safely avoided customs officials and arrived in San Francisco.

In May 1989, one of the most complex acts of civil disobedience began—an event that has drawn both praise and criticism. The head of Project Inform, Martin Delaney, launched the Compound Q experiment for two major reasons. First, he and others who participated in conducting the experiment had to find out if the promising drug worked before it entered the AIDS self-treatment underground and uncontrolled use became widespread. Second, he and others wanted a reassessment of the federal government's policy on drug testing and approval. Dr. Alan Levin, one of the two founding physicians of the clandestine project, said, "We're not doing this simply because of AIDS. This is the beginning of a reform movement in American medicine. We're empowering the practicing physician to evaluate drugs. We're taking it away from the government and academics."[16] Thus, the Food and Drug Administration and its traditional system of drug evaluation, policy, and ethical concerns were placed in the center of a controversy that will rage for years.

In four cities—San Francisco, New York, Los Angeles, and Fort Lauderdale—patients presented the drug to their doctors and asked that their treatment be monitored and supervised. This procedure was recommended by a lawyer who assisted the underground study's participating physicians. A questionnaire was presented to each potential patient, signed on-camera, and witnessed. This procedure was followed to protect doctors from liability lawsuits and meet the ethical responsibilities of informed consent, according to those conducting the study.

In July 1989, the Food and Drug Administration asked the group to discontinue the unsanctioned clinical trials of Compound Q. They asked for a meeting with Martin Delaney to discuss their letter, which stated that he "should discontinue any further unapproved experimentation and not initiate any new use." Threats of further investigation and sanctions were made. Delaney declined the request, and the patients continued to receive the thrice-weekly treatment. Larry Kramer, the founder of ACT UP, warned, "All hell will break loose if they [FDA and NIH] attempted to crack down on those in the trials. It's heroic what they're doing, and there is an immense amount of support for them."[17]

A major criticism of the clandestine study was that it had no oversight by an impartial committee to examine the clinical process and to protect the patients. Dr. John Fletcher, head of the Center for Biomedical Ethics at the University of Virginia, said, "You begin with a question: Should this study be done at all? Then you submit the study to a disinterested group who could put themselves in the places of those who would be in the study. The premise of secrecy violates the impartial review by others that is the greatest protection for human subjects."[18] In September 1989, when the experiment was completed, the directors of the Compound Q study said they found that the drug may prove to be a significant weapon against the AIDS virus, but that it had dangers attached to its use and it was not the cure they had hoped for. In their preliminary report, they discussed the impact of the drug, both its positive and adverse reactions.

Later, in June 1990, Martin Delaney presented a report on the Compound Q experiment claiming that forty-six patients showed "remarkable improvement in their disease after less than three months" of the unorthodox treatment. Under questioning from several scientists, however, Delaney conceded that a larger and longer study was needed. Further, he said that the drug was highly toxic and that no AIDS patient should use the compound without careful medical supervision.

In 1990, the Food and Drug Administration authorized the firm Genelabs to supply Compound Q to Project Inform in order to continue these once-clandestine human experiments under scientific scrutiny.

This complicated act of civil disobedience will be debated for years, particularly its ethical ramifications. In the meantime, a major shift occurred when the federal AIDS agencies announced the parallel track approach to the use of AIDS drugs. Under this new system, promising drugs would be given to some persons with AIDS at the same time as the drugs are undergoing rigorous university research-based trials. Thus, patients now have access to a promising drug as soon as it's proven to be safe, and the drug can be administered by their own physicians. No placebos will be used in these clinical trials.

While these dramatic policy changes cannot be attributed solely to the clandestine experiment and other acts of civil disobedience by AIDS activists described earlier, profound changes are being made in the way the FDA and NIH conduct clinical trials of promising AIDS drugs. Drugs for other fatal or degenerative illnesses such as pancreatic cancer or Parkinson's disease may also be placed in the parallel track system. However, it is unlikely that the end to clandestine trials of drugs has been seen.

Some act of nonviolent civil disobedience is used almost everyday by the array of grass roots groups, national and local, that occupy the landscape of social activism in America. Many are reported by the media; others go unpublicized.

## Traditional Social Actions

Over the years, social actions have been developed by groups to influence the outcome of policies, legislation, presidential actions, and other decisions that affect either a segment of the population or the entire nation. These actions range from simple letter-writing campaigns to litigation. Some grass roots groups use many of the actions discussed in this section, while others may use only one or two. The decision to use a particular tactic to influence decision-makers depends upon factors inherent in the grass roots group: size, budget, active membership, goals, and staff. Each tactic examined in the following pages has been used successfully and is part of the traditional social action repertory, not necessarily limited to grass roots activism.

### Write a Letter

When a grass roots group has identified the specific public official, company, or legislator whom they wish to persuade, a call is made to its membership to write a letter that expresses the protest or the action desired. Sometimes a suggested form letter is proposed by the group's leaders and hundreds are furnished for easy use by members. Other groups rely on the concerned member to compose an original letter. The White House, congressional offices, mayors, corporate headquarters, and bureaucratic agencies receive thousands of letters every day from members of grass roots groups, and, in most cases, they respond. While letters don't always accomplish the desired goal of the senders, they make the recipients aware of the constituent's position.

*Parents' Campaign in Pendleton, Indiana:* In a small Indiana town with a population of a mere 2,300, upon learning about a drug bust at their local high school, parents organized a parent group to respond to a problem none were aware of or had wanted to recognize: Their children were using dangerous drugs. They organized the South Madison Anti-Drug Organization. With limited funds, but fully aware that reaching others with their message was imperative, in 1978 they launched a letter-writing campaign to inform and persuade.

When they learned about a piece of antismuggling legislation tied up in a House committee and the call for public support from a member of the House Select Committee on Narcotics Abuse, they launched a letter-writing campaign. First, a parent went to the public library and got the names and addresses of every newspaper in Indiana. Then a chain letter was sent to all of them and to all fledgling parent groups in the state. The letter asked concerned citizens to write to their congressional representatives in support of the anti-drug legislation, to send copies of their letters to the local newspapers, and then to recruit at least four other people to write similar letters. The letter exhorted parents with, "Let's form a letter-writing WEB OF COMMUNICATION to let Congress know we are truly concerned about the drug epidemic that has afflicted our youth."[19]

The hundreds of Indiana letters that reached Washington made a big impact on legislators. As Congressman Billy Evans (D., Ga.) noted," We legislators estimate that ten letters from constituents represent the concerns of ten thousand citizens. Anybody who will take the time to write is voicing the fears and desires of thousands more."

This parent group used their WEB letter-writing tactic on many other occasions to reach a shared objective in their antidrug campaign.

---

## TIPS FOR A SUCCESSFUL
## LETTER-WRITING CAMPAIGN

- Determine the focus and intent of the message, (for example, to stop pollution of a local river).
- Recruit others to join you and write letters.
- Select most appropriate recipient(s) (corporate official, elected official, agency director) and address them personally in the letters.
- State concern and suggest specific action (if possible, please stop dumping dioxin in our river).
- State the impact of the dangerous practice (fish are dying).
- Ask for a response to your request.
- Indicate that you will follow up and monitor their action.
- Write original letters. Avoid sending form letters and postcards.
- Encourage genuine letters from children, which have a strong emotional impact.

---

*Save the Rain Forests:*   On August 8, 1989, the Rainforest Action Network (RAN), a grass roots group with its national office located in San Francisco, took out a full-page ad in the national edition of the *New York Times* to urge readers to write on behalf of saving the tropical rain forests in Brazil and Borneo. The ad displayed pictures of eight men who RAN believed would decide the fate of the rain forests and society. The ad said:

Every day we hear something about the vital significance of the rain forest to the future well-being of our planet.
   News stories describe the crucial role it plays supply-

ing the world with water and oxygen.... Scientists explain the unique defense it provides against the "Greenhouse Effect," which may already be raising the earth's temperature to dangerous new levels.

We also hear that this irreplaceable ecosystem is being destroyed at the alarming rate of 75,000 acres a day. And we fear for the future of our planet. And our children.

And yet, all too often, we feel powerless to do anything about it.

The same cannot be said of the eight men pictured above. In the next few months, these men will determine future actions on three separate fronts that, together, significantly affect not only the rain forest, but, ultimately, what kind of world generations will inherit.

The ad urged the reader to "write these men and speak your mind now." It provided the names and addresses of the eight men: names that included the presidents of the United States, Brazil, and the World Bank, as well as the chief executive officers of the Mitsubishi Corporation and Scott Paper Company.

Placing an ad in a large national or urban paper is an expensive undertaking that only a few grass roots groups can afford; however, the national reach is impressive and public awareness is heightened among the readers of these newspapers.

**Send It Back to McDonald's:**   Not every letter-writing campaign is a written statement explaining the position of the sender. In this case, the Citizen's Clearinghouse for Hazardous Wastes (CCHW) planned and continues to execute a mail campaign directed at the McDonald's Corporation.[20] It asks its hundreds of thousands of associates to respond. When the Clearinghouse, headed by Lois Gibbs of Love Canal, launched its McToxic cam-

paign in 1988 to urge the McDonald's Corporation to
discontinue generating 1.6 billion cubic feet of
styrofoam, the company said it would recycle the containers. The CCHW replied,

> Well, the key to make recycling work is volume and the
> way to help McDonald's make its "recycling plan" work,
> we urge you to give McDonald's your styrofoam!
>     You can start now to collect styrofoam and can:
>         a. send it to McDonald's Corporation headquarters,
>            or
>         b. bring it to your local McDonald's restaurant.
> Again, any styrofoam will do, since the key is *volume.*

The CCHW provided a sample address label with the
recipient being the vice president for environmental
affairs at McDonald's headquarters in Illinois. The corporate response to this send-it-back campaign is discussed in chapter 3, "The Opposition: Its Tactics."

### *The Spoken Word*

In order to make their cause known, most grass roots
groups have persons who make public appearances.
Lectures and conferences are standard forums for delivering the spoken word. However, the ability to speak in
public with charisma and wisdom belongs to only a few,
and unless the grass roots group has such orators,
abstaining is the best policy.

The abolitionist movement was blessed with a number
of orators who could hold the crowd and educate. William
Lloyd Garrison, Frederick Douglass, and Wendell Phillips
frequently appeared on the lecture circuit or addressed
antislavery society meetings. Carry Nation held an audience of more than eight thousand spellbound in
Crawfordsville, Indiana. A paid agent arranged her lec-

ture tour in 1901. Both abolitionist and prohibitionist leaders made trips to Europe, especially England, to deliver lectures and to raise funds for their cause. Their popularity with Europeans is legendary. In the nineteenth century, spoken and written words were primary. Today, radio, film, and television augment communication in grass roots campaigns; in fact, many groups find these media tools essential for reaching their membership and spreading their message to the public.

One tactic used by today's grass roots groups that has a long history in this country is the town meeting. Not only does it provide an opportunity to educate and mobilize the public, but it is also used as an organizing and recruiting tool for local grass roots groups.

*The Rocky Flats Raid:* On June 6, 1989, seventy-five FBI agents raided the Department of Energy's nuclear weapons plant at Rocky Flats, Colorado, in search of evidence of surreptitious, illegal burning and dumping of waste contaminated with plutonium. A public outcry was heard throughout the region, and a grass roots group emerged called the Colorado Committee for the Town Meeting on Rocky Flats. The leaders urged citizens to arrange and attend small town meetings in affected communities to confront fear, anger, and confusion over the sudden, unprecedented action by the federal government. The meetings served to organize and educate local groups about the potential dangers of contamination of their air, soil, and water and to plan a course of action to ensure their safety.

The Environmental Protection Agency said in August 1989 that the Department of Energy, which owns the plant, and Rockwell International Corporation, which operates through a government contract, were illegally storing thousands of gallons of mixed radioactive and chemical wastes at the plant and in boxcars adjacent to the plant.[21] The contractor, Rockwell International Corporation, later threatened to close the Rocky Flats weapons plant unless the government guaranteed them immunity from prosecution under laws governing hazardous waste disposal. Town meetings had served to galvanize the region and to bring response from federal agencies and the contractor.

*Garden City's Community Awareness:*  In 1980, the community of Garden City, New York, gradually became aware of drug and alcohol problems among its youth when the results of two local surveys, one for youth and another for adults, demonstrated that most respondents wanted to change the situation in their community. They decided upon "an old-fashioned town meeting to confront modern problems" and gathered more than seven hundred adults and young people to hear a keynote address, attend workshops, and publicly discuss the problem.[22] One parent remarked, "It set the whole community abuzz with excitement. This community has not turned out in such numbers for any event in several years."

The town meeting served as the catalyst to organize a parent network, to forge a social contract between parents and youth, to develop a drug education program at the schools and Neighborhood Watch programs, and to organize "Responsible Sellers Clubs" among local merchants. The superintendent of schools assessed the successful program by saying,"It's a rewarding experience to be part of a process that improves the quality of life for students, families, and neighborhoods." Verbal exchange is superior to didactic presentation in most situations, and ordinary people need to hear the facts, react and question them, and then participate in planning a community response to its shared problem. The town meeting provides that kind of forum.

### The Written Word

Once in a while a book is written that stirs the nation and gives rise to or enriches a grass roots movement. The author may have had no such intention, but, nonetheless, when his message is compelling, his readers are often inspired to take action. Several grass roots movements presented in this book have received impetus from a popular written source.

*Silent Spring* (1962) by Rachael Carson is said by many modern environmentalists to be the book that awakened a nation. When Carson explained the "balance of nature" and man's destruction of that balance by misusing lethal chemicals, readers understood. In the chapter on chemicals and their possible link to cancer, she foresaw the future. She forced a nation to examine the relationship of life to its environment, and millions read and later acted. A grass roots movement did not arise immediately, perhaps because intense controversy surrounded the book's message. The chemical industry, the United States Department of Agriculture, and some university faculty branded it antiscientific and worse. However, over time, the book inspired people to act, particularly against DDT.

The abolitionist movement was aided by the publication, in 1852, of Harriet Beecher Stowe's controversial novel, *Uncle Tom's Cabin*. Without consciously intending to do so, Stowe added members to the ranks of northern abolitionists with her emotional and devastating account of slavery. No other book of its time was more widely read and discussed; it brought the fact of slavery into the floodlight and strengthened the budding movement against it.

In 1975, an Australian philosopher, Peter Singer, released his book, *Animal Liberation, A New Ethic For Our Treatment of Animals.*[23] It questions the world's casual acceptance of animal slaughter, both in research laboratories and on factory farms. In the preface Singer writes, "This book is about the tyranny of human over nonhuman animals. This tyranny has caused and today is still causing an amount of pain and suffering that can only be compared with that which resulted from centuries of tyranny by white humans over black humans. The struggle against this tyranny is a struggle as important as any of the moral and social issues that have been fought over in recent years." Singer's book was widely read. It is used today by animal rights activists, and it was instrumental in inspiring the formation of People for the Ethical Treatment of Animals (PETA).

Grass roots movements concerned over AIDS within the gay community were strengthened by Randy Shilts's book, *And The Band Played On* (1987). This book about politics, people, and the AIDS epidemic traces the inception of the disease, the reaction in the gay community, research efforts or lack of them, government responses, and the numerous obstacles and developments that emerged during the course of the epidemic up to 1987. The documentation gives a detailed account of the people who helped and hindered, as well as of those who died along the way. The author provides the most complete written history of the epidemic to date.

Some books inspire those frustrated with what they perceive as the slow pace of their movements. One such book, *The Monkey Wrench Gang* (1975), by Edward Abbey, inspired the formation of Earth First![24] Some readers continue to be moved toward radical actions against a technology they believe desecrates the environment. The book glorifies guerrillas who plot to blow up Glen Canyon Dam in Arizona. Its celebration of illegal actions to reach a professed end—saving the ecosystem of the desert—has been criticized by many.

A lesser-known book, but relevant to a particular grass roots group, is Marsha Manatt's *Parents, Peers, and Pot*

(1979),[25] a guide to the parent group movement. More than 200,000 copies were printed and distributed by the federal government printing office. The book quickly became the guide for organizing parents against drug use.

Major national organizations that interact with grass roots groups frequently prepare and publish important books and reports. Several have been mentioned earlier. An important book, *Crossroads: Environmental Priorities for the Future* was released in 1988 by the Natural Resources Defense Council.[26] It contains short essays written by leaders of the diverse environmental movement. Contributors examine the past and look into the future. Its editor, Peter Borrelli, writes, "We are at a crossroads that requires more of us than we have ever given. This time the challenge is neither to subdue nature nor to protect it from ourselves but to act as both a part of nature and a member of a global community. As many of our contributors note, if there is not also an emotional and spiritual commitment to these objectives, enlightened policy and politics will be of little avail."[27] This book contains diverse and compelling ideas about the environment and actions required by individuals, this nation, and all others who inhabit the planet.

*Coming Full Circle: Successful Recycling Today* was released by the Environmental Defense Fund (EDF) in 1988.[28] Because recycling is now enjoying renewed public attention and participation, this report is timely and instructive. The report describes some of the ways municipalities around the country choose to make their waste into usable products.

In conjunction with their book on recycling, the EDF launched a national media campaign with the Ad Council. Over the past three years, the doubling of news coverage, legislation, and lobbying for environmental causes has raised public consciousness as well as citizen action. In an August 15, 1990, letter to its members, the EDF called attention to some gains:

- The Environmental Protection Agency reported a 30 percent increase in the amount being recycled.
- The number of convenient curbside recycling programs more than doubled, from 600 to 1,500.
- More than 100,000 Americans called EDF to get information about recycling.

The written word thrives in the grass roots, both among those who produce it and those who read it. It can inspire, document, instruct, criticize, define, implore, and confuse—the written word is an essential aspect of any movement.

## Boycotts

Consumer groups and labor unions have used boycotts for decades, often effectively. Grass roots groups are beginning to use the boycott, and some feel it is the most effective tactic at their disposal. It works if people don't buy a large volume of a particular product or refuse to patronize a service, or if the manufacturer receives the glare of unfavorable publicity. The two central aims are to cause a drop in sales and profits and to educate the public about the cause. Grass roots groups that use this tactic successfully must have a large membership network, committed members who can influence others to join them, a good communication system to inform, and the ability to influence the media to cover the story, and creative ways to introduce and maintain the boycott until objectives are reached. The clearer the objective is made for the public, the more the success of a boycott is assured. Localized, smaller, specific boycotts use procedures similar to those presented here but require less money and a much smaller network to accomplish objectives than national boycotts do.

*The Hamburger Connection:* On April 14, 1984, Rainforest Action Network (RAN), Friends of the Earth, and Earth First! targeted Burger King, starting with a series of guerrilla theater protests across the country. They called for Burger King and other fast-food companies to "stop purchasing beef exported from Central America because of dangerous ranching practices that continue to destroy much of Central American rainforests," said Randy Hayes, director of RAN.[29]

The Rainforest Action Network operates nationally and internationally to protect the world's tropical rain forests. It uses direct actions ranging from letter-writing campaigns to boycotting products made from materials and practices that RAN feels destroy the rain forest. With 150 local RAGs (Rain forest Action Groups) it organizes demonstrations at corporations and government agencies that are believed to contribute to the destruction of rain forests.

In 1986, after more than a year of demonstrations and picketing at local Burger King outlets across the country, RAN placed a full-page ad in the *New York Times* calling for a national boycott of Burger King. They subsequently mailed over a million packets to concerned citizens asking that they join the boycott. Thousands of letters were directed to Burger King's corporate office.

In their ad, RAN stated:

> Millions of acres of Central American rainforests are destroyed so U.S. hamburger chains and pet food companies can get cheap meat.
>
> It's called rainforest beef. Which means it comes from marginal grazing land i what used to be rainforest.
>
> Before the rainforest was bulldozed and burned, it was home to thousands of rare and exotic species. After

the cattle have come and gone, it's an eroded wasteland practically empty of life.

Burger King is one of the biggest fast-food buyers of rainforest beef, a driving force behind this environmental disaster. So we're calling for a national boycott.

Fifty thousand acres of rainforest are being lost worldwide every day. At that rate, the last refuge for half the plants and animal species on earth will vanish in a single human lifespan.

You can do your part by boycotting Burger King. And by telling others the rainforest must be saved.

This well-organized tactic brought a response from Burger King on August 25, 1987. In a letter to RAN, they announced that they would no longer buy beef from tropical rain forest areas. Burger King said it would remove all rain forest beef by September 1, 1987. RAN accepted the pledge and announced an end to the boycott.

According to Randy Hayes, Burger King had a 13 percent drop in sales during the boycott. The food chain was targeted because it was the only major fast-food corporation that was positively identified as using rain forest beef. Other fast-food chains claimed they used only American-produced beef, but these claims were difficult to substantiate.[30]

Later, Burger King was asked to provide independent verification that they had ceased purchasing beef from rain forest regions. However, the company failed to provide further information for a year after the end of the original RAN boycott.

On July 25, 1988, RAN renewed the boycott and asked people to write the company. They requested that Burger King prove they were not using rain forest beef. In the press release, Randy Hayes said, "We applaud any action by Burger King to discontinue the use of rain forest beef, but we must have a system of verification. American corporations have a track record of hiding the complete truth and for disregarding the serious ecological impacts of their actions. People have a right to know for sure if the hamburger they are eating is destroying rain forests, because it is a life and death matter."

In October 1988, RAN reported that Burger King verified that they had not used rain forest beef in their food since September 1987. The second phase of the boycott had thus brought victory for RAN. Taking the issue to the public through a boycott resulted in the reversal of a practice of a major corporation, a reversal that RAN plans to continue monitoring. RAN announced, upon its victory, "For every quarter pound of hamburger that comes from the rain forest, 55 square feet of forest life— millions of individuals and thousands of species—are sacrificed. Because of the wastefulness of Central America's cattle industry, RAN's position is that beef imports from rain forest regions should be banned from the United States altogether. Therefore, we have shifted our focus from boycotting a specific company to the broader issue of halting the import of rain forest beef."[31] Being capable of shifting to other tactics strengthens the grass roots position.

***Cruelty-Free Cosmetics:*** Cosmetics firms are ending animal testing as a result of a three-year boycott organized by People for the Ethical Treatment of Animals (PETA). In its "cruelty free" campaign aimed directly at Avon, Revlon, Benetton, Amway, and several others, PETA gained support from other animal rights activists and consumers. Many film and stage celebrities support their actions, make personal appearances and public service announcements, and attend events sponsored by various groups.

PETA's position is that tests on animals for cosmetics and other products are not required by law but that, every year, an estimated 14 million animals die in painful experiments to determine the safety of cosmetics and household products. PETA's "compassion campaign" against tests for household products is discussed in chapter 3.

The Food and Drug Administration (FDA) only requires that each ingredient in a cosmetic be "adequately substantiated for safety" prior to marketing, or that the product carry a warning on the label that its safety has not been determined. The decision to test and which tests to administer is made by individual firms.

The two most frequently used tests are the Draize test and Lethal Dose 50 (LD50), both painful and sometimes lethal for animals. Once the tests are administered, animals that have not died as a result of the tests are routinely exterminated.

The Draize Eye Irritancy Test was invented in 1944 and has been used to test substances that might accidentally get into the human eye. Albino rabbits are used because their ineffective tear ducts prevent them from blinking and washing away the substance that is tested while the animal is immobilized in stocks from which only its head can be seen. Rarely is anesthesia used, and the rabbit's eyes may react by swelling and bleeding or becoming ulcerated or blind.

The Lethal Dose test was developed in 1927 and is widespread. This acute toxicity test determines the amount of a substance that will kill part of a group of test animals. The substance under study is forced into the animals' stomachs through a tube or injected in the skin, veins, or abdomen. Some experimenters mix it with food. The animals' reactions are observed to detect convulsions, diarrhea, constipation, skin eruptions, and bleeding. The test continues until 50 percent of the animals in the test group die; sometimes the test extends from two to four weeks.

PETA urges that cosmetics companies use alternatives to animal tests: "Non-animal testing methods have proven to be more reliable and less expensive than animal tests. Alternatives include the use of cell cultures, corneal and skin tissue cultures, chicken egg membranes, corneas from eye banks, and sophisticated computer and mathematical models. Companies also have the option of making products using the many ingredients or combination of ingredients already determined safe by the Cosmetics, Toiletry and Fragrance Association."[32]

The conflict between PETA and the cosmetics industry has been intense. In a *New York Times* article, August 1, 1989, the reporter states:

> So far, industry leaders see the world differently. Those that have stopped testing have generally issued press releases but have not advertised the change widely.
>
> The main reason for such reticence, most industry experts say, is that the large companies fear the legal consequences of ending animal testing. These experts say that consumers who suffer adverse reactions to a product may have an easier time proving corporate negligence if the product has not been tested on animals before reaching the market.[33]

*Avon Killing*: In March 1989, PETA launched a boycott called "Stop Avon Killing" when Avon refused to permanently stop using animals for testing cosmetics. In response to the worldwide boycott, animal rights activists placed three million cards on doors across the nation that stated "Avon Killing," a takeoff on the well-known "Avon Calling." In March, Avon's president told the press, "We expect to end all animal testing within the next three months," and, on April 5, Avon declared, "The company no longer uses the Draize test." However, within a short time, Avon was lobbying in California to defeat state legislation to ban the Draize test as well as the LD50 test. PETA gave the president of Avon the Pinocchio award and activists sent false noses to Avon's corporate headquarters. PETA continued the boycott until Avon made a firm commitment to end animal testing, a few months later.[34]

Boycotts were launched against other cosmetics firms such as Revlon, Amway, and Benetton. In December 1988, PETA began its "True Colors of Benetton" campaign to persuade the company to discontinue animal tests for its new line of cosmetics and toiletries. Joined by PETA affiliates in England, Italy, Canada, Bermuda, Mexico, and West Germany, boycotts and demonstrations were held in cities across the world. A poster portraying a rabbit in distress from the LD50 test was displayed with this wording: "This bath and shower gel ate away the skin of the rabbits it was tested on. Yet the company says it's safe for you to use." Many of those picketing wore rabbit costumes and carried signs saying "The True Colors of Benetton," and more than a quarter of a million "Boycott Benetton" flyers were distributed at their stores in Westport, Connecticut. Later, Benetton agreed to the "cruelty free" cosmetics pledge and ended animal testing.[35] When Revlon ended animal testing, the spokesperson declared, "We don't think it brings any substantial risk either to ourselves or to our customers."

The PETA boycott of cosmetics firms is organized with five steps for consumers to follow:

1. *Take the "cruelty free" pledge.* Buy only products that are made without hurting animals. (PETA gives a list of those companies.)
2. *Get others involved.* Ask your local stores to stock only cruelty-free cosmetics. Send the "cruelty free" pledge brochure to a local reporter. Distribute petitions.

3. *Write or call the manufacturer of the product.* Tell them why you dropped out of their market.

4. *Join PETA's National Action Phone Tree to learn about the campaign.* Provide your telephone number and expect to receive requests to act in your community.

5. *Write your congressional representatives and ask them to support relevant legislation on animal rights.*

These steps have been followed by most of PETA's 350,000 members and others who support their programs. More than two hundred cosmetics manufacturers have taken the "cruelty free" pledge, including some large companies targeted by the boycott.

The brochure describing PETA says,

> People for the Ethical Treatment of Animals is a nonprofit charity organization, headquartered in Washington, D.C. PETA was incorporated to educate policy makers and the public to the issues involving the intense, prolonged, and unjustified abuse of animals, and to promote an understanding of the inherent rights of sentient animals to be treated with respect and dignity. Founded in 1980, PETA is the fastest growing animal rights organization in the United States.
>
> PETA is headed by Alex Pacheco and Ingrid Newkirk. "PETA may pose the greatest grass roots challenge to the scientific and medical communities. Its members are young, articulate, and dedicated," says a 1983 Harvard University Study.[36]

**Save the Dolphins:** Citing consumer pressures in letters, postcards, and petitions, the three largest tuna canners pledged in April 1990 that they would not buy or market tuna caught in a way that kills or injures dol-

phin. What they did not mention was a consumer boycott of canned tuna effectively launched and guided by
Earth Island Institute and Greenpeace. Starkist,
Chicken of the Sea, and Bumble Bee brands, which sell
about 75 percent of the tuna eaten in the United States,
took this "voluntary" action. They also favor congressional legislation that would require producers to disclose whether their tuna was caught with technology
that protects dolphins. This corporate reversal signifies
one of the most successful boycotts applied by consumers and demonstrates the power of grass roots
groups to arouse the public to take action.

For years, Greenpeace has been alerting the American
public to the destruction of dolphins and whales:

> For unknown reasons, schools of yellowfin tuna often
> gather just below herds of dolphins. The tuna fleets
> watch for dolphins to locate their catch. And then the
> hideous roundup begins. Tuna boats chase down the
> dolphins with helicopters and speedboats. Exhausted
> and terrified, the dolphins are encircled in purse
> seines, nets up to three-quarters of a mile long, that are
> drawn closed at the bottom. The animals are trapped.
> Because they breathe air just as you and I do, they suf-
> focate or drown. . . . The fishing companies say dolphin
> deaths are incidental to their work. But the dolphins
> are, in fact, *intentional targets* . . . sought to maximize
> tuna company profits.

Greenpeace and Earth Island Institute continue to
pressure tuna companies, especially Bumble Bee Sea-
foods, to ensure that they comply with their pledge to use
only dolphin-safe tuna-catching techniques. The boycott
was successful; however, grass roots groups have
learned to be eternally vigilant to maintain their
accomplishments.

For a boycott to be effective, the leaders must have access to the public, a good communications system, and activists who take the time to continue to pressure the company. Combining the product boycott with petitions, letter writing, demonstrations, and picketing was used in the three boycotts discussed in this chapter. Each was successful.

### The Plebiscite

A vote by which the people of an entire state or district express an opinion for or against a proposal is called a plebiscite. As a direct form of democratic decision making, the initiative process began in 1911 when California Governor Hiram Johnson called for sweeping political reforms in the state. One reform made it possible to place an issue on the ballot for vote in a general election by gathering a specified number of valid signatures. During the almost eighty years of voter initiative in California, the electorate has placed approximately 212 state propositions on the ballot, with 67 winning approval.

Of the twenty-six states that have the initiative provision in their constitutions, seventeen are west of the Mississippi River. Californians overwhelmingly approve of the ability to vote directly on an issue (73 percent favor the process), and one-third of the 212 propositions initiated by citizens since 1911 have been placed on the ballot since 1982. It is believed that voters are dissatisfied with their legislators, feeling that the latter are increasingly unable to function in the public's interests, partially because of their ties to political action committees and lobbyists. While the initiative process can be used—and is at times—by grass roots groups, it is time-consuming and expensive to get an initiative on the ballot. Also, the intent of the measure may be changed by the courts or legislature, or implemented without fulfilling what the electorate had in mind.

Some initiative campaigns have cost as much as $130 million, and much of that money is used for media campaigns, to pay for mailings, and, recently, to hire high-priced consulting firms. In fact, the initiative process has given birth to a new industry in California—firms that work to get the initiative on the ballot and try to win the vote. This emerging business approach is not consistent with the grass roots process of citizens identifying a grievance or need and organizing to accomplish it; in fact, this commercialization denigrates the grass roots appeal of the initiative. The process is also being used by candidates and incumbent legislators to promote political issues to win favor with the electorate or to circumvent the legislative process.

"Instead of serving as a safety valve, the initiative has become an uncontrolled political force of its own," says Professor Eugene Lee at the University of California at Berkeley. Others feel that the process, established to give ordinary citizens the possibility for grass roots action, has been harmed by financial interests who have taken over the initiative process. In spite of these criticisms, the initiative process is still supported by many. Former Governor Jerry Brown writes," The initiative process allows for political choices that are stymied in the normal legislative process. In fact, the problem is not the initiative but the lack of political leadership."[37] Whatever may be said against the process, though, it still gives citizens a way to confront an unresponsive government.

*Proposition 65:* In 1986, the California electorate overwhelmingly passed Proposition 65, a tough provision supported by grass roots environmentalists and the Environmental Defense Fund as well as a number of other public interest groups. The law says that no business may produce and sell a product that exposes people to chemicals that cause cancer or birth defects without giving "a clear and reasonable warning." This law calls for stronger warnings about products than those imposed by the federal government and places the onus on business, not government, to prove when exposure to a product is safe.

The food industry in California lobbied to win federal exemption from the law but failed. Led by the Grocery Manufacturers of America, a toll-free number was set up to provide the warning. Formed by a consortium of industry groups, the Ingredient Communications Council operates the toll-free line and answers specific questions about specific products. However, the caller cannot ask for a list of products containing toxic chemicals.

Public concern arose when, after 28,000 calls to the Council during the first fourteen months, only 488 warning messages were provided. The system became known as "800 BALONEY" because consumers felt it did not provide adequate warnings. They wanted producers to place warning symbols on the products themselves or on the grocery shelf to alert potential buyers to ingredients possibly causing cancer or birth defects.[38]

When, in 1989, the California attorney general planned to file a lawsuit to have the system ruled invalid, the Ingredient Communications Council sued the attorney general, hoping to obtain court approval for the toll-free system. At the trial, evidence was presented that more than 8,300 products were represented by the telephone service, although only about five-hundred products were deemed by their manufacturers to require warnings. Shoe polish, spices, and tobacco products were registered after an advisory panel established by the law set exposure levels for toxic chemicals specified in the law.

In August 1989, a California judge ruled that the toll-free number set up by manufacturers so consumers could find out about toxic substances in products did not meet the requirements of state law. "Clearly this does not constitute an effective warning system," Judge Eugene Gualco noted. "Customers are not likely to take the time necessary to call and inquire about relatively inexpensive, routinely-purchased products. Although consumers may make inquiries about an automobile or major appliances, little time or thought is usually extended prior to the purchase of routine grocery or household products." The judge added that a toll-free number might work if it were coupled with signs or symbols in stores pointing out which products require warnings.[39]

A statement from the Ingredients Communication Council called the decision disappointing and likely to be appealed, in court, but no legal action was taken by the Council.

Under the provisions of Proposition 65, any citizen can bring a suit against a producer for failure to warn about toxic content in the product; it requires notification to the California attorney general's office of a suspected violation and gives the state sixty days for enforcement. Consumer groups and the attorney general's office want manufacturers to abandon the toll-free system and use labels, signs, or other product-specific warnings to alert the consumer.

Critics of the law say risk assignment is vague, and they question how "significant risk" is applied. They believe existing federal standards are adequate. The issue for the voters is that the "warnings" be available to them. The court ruled that they were not being adequately warned by the toll-free system.

Grass roots environmental groups have been successful in getting initiative measures on the ballot and in winning voter approval in California as well as in other states having this process.[40] In fact, when one state is successful in winning voter approval on a specific proposition, other states often follow suit, spurred by their own grass roots activists.

## Lobbying

To lobby is to conduct activities aimed at influencing public officials, especially members of a legislative body, on legislation. Grass roots groups lobby for causes that range from legislation on pesticides limits to medical care for the elderly. In 1838, William Lloyd Garrison launched a petition campaign against slavery in which the United States Congress was deluged with 320,000 petitions—at the time, the largest petition drive in the nation's history. John L. Thomas, in *The Liberator*, wrote,

> Garrison had pioneered in the organized use of the antislavery petition in Vermont back in 1828 and was well aware of its advantages. In the first place, the right of petition was guaranteed in the Constitution; Congress was obliged to receive petitions and to take some kind of action, however unfavorable, which meant invaluable publicity for the abolitionists. Then, too, petitions were cheap, easy to circulate, and effective in bringing the slavery question before the country.[41]

The Southern forces in Congress, led by Senator John C. Calhoun of South Carolina, retaliated by trying to deny the petitions. He called them "a foul slander on nearly one-half of the states of the Union" and was able to gain the support of the Congress to counter the abolitionists. After much debate and behind-the-scenes maneuvering, the Pinckney gag rule was enforced. It provided that "all petitions, memorials, resolutions, propositions, or papers relating in any way to any extent to the subject of slavery, shall, without being printed or referred, be laid upon the table and that no further action whatever be taken thereon." The gag rule remained in force from 1836 to 1845. Garrison lost interest in the petition drive and abandoned that tactic.

Lobbying was ineffective in the abolitionists' cause. However, subsequently it has been successfully used by grass roots groups as well as corporations that oppose the efforts of those groups. Full-time, paid lobbyists are used by some grass roots groups, but mostly their efforts are confined to members' letter writing, telephone calls, and direct confrontations with legislators when they return to their home districts during congressional recesses. To be effective, the lobbying must be concentrated, specific, direct, and widespread.

***Grass Roots Rebellion Against Medicare Law:*** When Congress took its summer recess in August 1989, legislators returning to their home districts met angry, elderly constituents aroused over the Medicare Catastrophic Coverage Act of 1988. Congress mandated that the measure be funded by the aged themselves, mostly through a surtax on the high-income elderly. It was the first provision in history in which the cost of medical care insurance was based on a person's income. Of the elderly constituents, about 40 percent were asked to pay for the bulk of the program under the plan. The program was financed by a flat premium of $4 a month deducted from the Social Security checks of the 33 million Medicare beneficiaries and a surtax of $22.50 on every $150 of income taxes paid by the elderly. Five percent of the beneficiaries paid the maximum surtax of $800 annually or $1,600 per couple. The latter amount was slated to be increased to $2,200 in 1993. The ensuing grass roots rebellion by the elderly who were paying for most of the program surprised everyone in Congress. The bill did not cover the catastrophic costs of long-term nursing care, a much desired provision most elderly thought was included. Many did not understand the bill; some were shocked to discover they had to pay; and all felt betrayed by Congress and the President.[42]

The grass roots rebellion began during the 1988 presidential election in retirement communities in Florida, California, and the Southwest. It reached its fever pitch when an organization, the National Committee to Preserve Social Security and Medicare, sent flyers to its 5 million members to urge them to work for the act's repeal, calling it "Repeal the Seniors–Only Income Tax Increase Costing Up To $1,600." Letters, petitions, and telephone calls flooded congressional offices.[43] At first, Congress tried to ignore the revolt. Some media framed the issue as a battle between the elderly rich and the poor. "The Elderly Duke It Out—Who Should Pay for Catastrophic Health Insurance? The Debate Pits Rich Against Poor," said a *Newsweek* headline on September 11, 1989. A *New York Times* article, reprinted in the *San Francisco Chronicle* on August 31, 1989, read "Congress Getting Fed Up With 'Greedy' Elderly."

This massive lobbying campaign resulted in the repeal of the act. The House of Representatives voted 360 to 66 for repeal. Only sixteen months earlier, it had voted passage by 328 to 72, calling it a piece of landmark legislation for the elderly. Shortly after the House repeal vote, the Senate voted 99 to 0 to repeal the surtax and to retain only the long-term hospital benefits. The 1988 Senate passage vote had been 86 to 11. The repeal vote was sent to a joint committee for compromise. However, on November 16, 1989, the Senate voted to repeal the entire catastrophic care law after months of fruitless negotiations on revisions with the House of Representatives. Some said repeal was necessary to clear the air and allow Congress the opportunity to pass legislation acceptable to the elderly. The turnaround was remarkable.

This effort demonstrates the power of grass roots lobbying. While the controversy over who should pay for catastrophic health care and how to finance it will rage on for years, the history of the failed 1988 law is important because it clearly demonstrates that lobbying as a grass roots tactic can influence legislation.

*Drunk Driving Crackdown:*  Mothers Against Drunk Driving (MADD) and Remove Intoxicated Drivers (RID) lobbied in Sacramento in 1989 to encourage state lawmakers to pass several bills to "close up loopholes in drunk driving laws." California followed the example of Oregon, Utah, and Maine by passing legislation on the level at which alcohol impairs a driver. The percent was lowered from .10 to .08, the equivalent to about one drink an hour.

In MADD's and RID's prediction, the lower level will serve as a deterrent to drivers and reduce the number of drunken driver arrests.[44] A 30 percent reduction in the number of alcohol-related accidents was recorded after the state of Maine had cut the legal limit to .08 percent. MADD's and RID's lobbying for stricter laws and more diligent enforcement has been credited with making the nation's highways safer. The first effort to gain legislative support of drunken driver reform was launched as early as 1978 by RID's founding chapter in New York.

MADD's and RID's tactics have evolved over more than ten years of operation and include an array of goals and programs:

*Legislative reform*: Strengthen the laws against alcohol and other drug-impaired driving and gain support for enforcement and prevention programs.

*Education and public awareness*: Develop youth education programs and sponsor poster/essay contests, as well as annual candlelight vigils, Project Red Ribbon, and K.I.S.S. (Keep It a Safe Summer).

*Victim support program*: Support victims with information about the judicial process, individual and family support groups, and a victim hotline.

*Case watch and court monitor*: Obtain copy of the traffic crash report, obtain the driver's driving record, attend the court hearings, contact the probation officer to discuss the case, and speak out if the procedure does not appear appropriate.

*Seller awareness*: The Community Prevention Intervention Program works to change consumer and seller awareness in order to keep the drunk driver off the road and encourage responsible sales of alcoholic beverages.

MADD members write to, meet with, and telephone state and federal congressional lawmakers in well-financed, carefully organized campaigns to influence legislation. With four-hundred chapters in forty-nine states (Montana being without a chapter) and about 1.1 million members, MADD is a visible organization that also works on educational programs for children and community groups and on monitoring the justice system to see how it handles drunken drivers. RID, a rapidly growing grass roots organization, has chapters in forty-one states and a national budget of approximately $100,000.

**Stockholders' Meeting:** Stockholders who have owned over a thousand dollars worth of a company's shares for over one year can bring a resolution asking other concerned stockholders to join them in voting on it. Further, they can make statements at shareholder meetings to try to gain support for their position on an issue. This tactic has been used repeatedly by People for the Ethical Treatment of Animals (PETA).[45] In 1983, PETA brought its first animal rights campaign to a stockholders' meeting. By 1987, it had presentations and resolutions at three stockholders' meetings and, by 1988, it had added six more, reaching a total of nine annual meetings. In 1987, the resolutions asked the targeted companies to halt animal testing not required by law. In 1988, all proposals asked targeted corporations to disclose information to shareholders about their testing and to continue to work toward eliminating the use of animal tests.

***Animal Testing at Procter & Gamble:*** The PETA struggle with a multinational giant, Procter & Gamble, has been important because the tactics of both sides show the intensity of PETA's grass roots effort to obtain change away from animal to alternative tests for product safety. The corporate battle to block the proposed change and to continue using animal tests has been equally intense.

At the 1988 Procter & Gamble annual stockholders' meeting, PETA presented a resolution asking the corporation to report to shareholders on the scope and cost of its animal testing for nonmedical consumer products.

The following are excerpts from the Shareholder Proposal No. 3 and the Procter & Gamble Board of Directors' recommendations for a vote against the resolution:

### Shareholder Proposal No. 3

*Ms. Susan D. Knapp, 12 Boulder Road, Norwalk, Connecticut 06854, owning 330 shares of Common Stock of the Company, and the People for the Ethical Treatment of Animals, Inc., P.O. Box 42516, Washington, D.C. 20015, owning 20 shares of Common Stock of the Company, have given notice that they intend to present for action at the annual meeting the following resolution:*

*RESOLVED: That the Board of Directors is requested to review P&G's use of live animals in research and testing of non-medical consumer products, whether conducted directly by P&G or on P&G's behalf by independent laboratories, and report to shareholders its findings on the scope and cost of live-animal testing, including:*

*—Species and numbers of animals used annually, including dogs, cats, guinea pigs, hamsters, rabbits, mice, rats, ferrets, gerbils, "mini-pigs," and others;*

*—Identificaiton of independent laboratories with which P&G contracts for live-animal research and testing;*

*—Costs to P&G of animal testing, including purchasing, housing, and maintaining animals; training and employing animal care staff, veterinarians, and technicians; and performing experiments on animals, including the aggregate amount paid annually for animal testing at outside laboratories;*

*—A list of experimental procedures performed, including eye irritancy, oral toxicity, and lethal dosage tests, and the means by which euthanasia is performed on animals;*

*—Expenditures made by P&G in its efforts to reduce animal usage, showing support for in-house and independent development of nonanimal alternatives, refinement of in-house test procedures, and proposals made to government agencies or industry associations.*

*Such report shall omit trade-secret information.*

*The proponents have submitted the following statement in support of their resolution:*

*P&G uses thousands of animals every year in research and testing of non-medical consumer products including soaps, laundry detergents, and deodorants manufactured under its Laundry and Cleaning and Personal Care lines. In 1986, P&G ranked in the top*

ten among American companies in number of live dogs
(1,264) reported used in all types of in-house research,
according to an independent analysis of government
data.

Development and testing of some of these products
causes pain and suffering to the animals involved.

In recent years, P&G has been exploring alternatives
to live animal tests, and we encourage it to move
ahead with such efforts.

Nevertheless, shareholders presently have little data
by which they can know the full scope and the costs
of P&G's animal testing program. Without such information, shareholders cannot intelligently evaluate the
company's present use of animals or its progress
toward reform.

P&G reports filed with the government under the
Federal Animal Welfare Act, for example, routinely exclude rats and mice. Moreover, P&G has acknowledge
that, besides its own in-house research, it "uses at
least 10 outside laboratories" for animal tests. ("News
for Investors," Investor Responsibility Research Center,
VOl. XIV, No. 10, November, 1987, p. 219.) As outside
laboratories do not report the allocation of animal
usage among their corporate clients, there is no way—
short of disclosure by a corporation—that shareholders
can ascertain the true scope of their company's use of
animal tests.

In short, shareholders do not know how many animals P&G uses, in which facilities, in what kinds of
experiments, or at what cost.

In a 1986 report to Congress, the U.S. Office of Technology Assessment concluded: "Whole-animal tests
can be far more costly than in vitro and nonanimal alternatives, largely because they are labor-intensive."

How much does P&G's animal testing program cost
shareholders every year? Shareholders have a right to
know.

This resolution seeks the information by which
shareholders can evaluate P&G's animal testing pro-

*gram and make informed judgments as to whether such tests and expenditures are consistent with a continued financial investment in P&G.*

### P&G Board of Directors Recommendation

*The Board of Directors recommends a vote AGAINST this resolution for the following reasons:*

*Procter & Gamble has a moral and legal responsibility to insure that all of its products are safe. Animal testing, in conjunction with appropriate in vitro testing, remains the only scientifically reliable approach to providing this assurance of safety.*

*At last year's annual meeting of shareholders, this same submitting organization, People for the Ethical Treatment of Animals, Inc., presented a resolution which, in the Company's opinion, was directed against Procter & Gamble's continued use of animals as part of its efforts to assure the safety of its products. Over 97 percent of shares participating were voted against this proposal. In the Company's opinion, the current proposal deals with substantially the same subject matter, although presented as a request for information.*

*Within the limitations necessary to assure safety of its products, Procter & Gamble is fully committed to the principle of humane and responsible use of animals. It is the Company's policy and practice to use animals in testing only when necessary and when no acceptable alternative exists. This policy is carried out across all Divisions of the Company and applied to testing by outside laboratories as well as within the Company itself. The policy is overseen by a Corporate Animal Care and Use Committee made up of top scientists in the Company and responsible directly to an executive officer of the Company.*

*The Company's efforts over many years have greatly reduced its dependence on animals in safety testing. Since 1984, the use of animals in consumer product safety studies (both within the Company and at out-*

*side laboratories under contract) has been reduced
more than sixty percent. Alternative methods developed by Procter & Gamble to replace the Draize Test
and the classical oral lethal dose (LD50) test are not
being used by the Company but are also being used
by other companies and have been internationally
recognized. Procter & Gamble continues to invest
heavily in inside and outside research efforts to develop predictive nonanimal alternatives to a variety of
tests. These alternative methods include the use of
tissue culture, organ culture and other in vitro test
systems. The Company's policy is to publish the results of its alternative test method research so that the
learning can be available to everyone. The Company
continues to advocate formal acceptance of these alternative methods by governmental agencies, both
domestic and international.*

*Procter & Gamble is recognized worldwide as a
leader in the search for alternatives to animal testing.
Earlier this year, The Council on Economic Priorities,
one of America's leading consumer interest organizations, awarded Procter & Gamble its first annual
Corporate Conscience Award in the Animal Rights category. This award recognizes the Company's longtime
leadership in seeking alternative testing for animals
and honors what the Council considers exemplary corporate social responsibility.*

*Similarly, government, industry and academic orga-
nizations such as the Congressional Office of
Technology Assessment, the European Chemical Industry Ecology and Toxicology Center, and the New
York Academy of Sciences have recognized the Company's leadership in alternative safety testing by
inviting Procter & Gamble scientists to play key roles
in their panels and task forces. Company scientists
have been sought out by the National Institute of
Health, The Society of Toxicology, the National Academy of Science, and the International Congress of
Pharmaceutical Sciences to make presentations on
this subject to their memberships. Government agen-*

*cies, including the Environmental Protection Agency, the Food and Drug Administration, and the Organization for Economic Cooperation and Development, as well as members of Congressional staffs, have approached Procter & Gamble to participate in discussions on alternative safety research.*

*The Board of Directors believes that the detailed information requested by the proposal would serve no practical purpose in advancing the goal of reducing animal use in safety testing of consumer products and therefore would impose an unwarranted burden of record keeping and reporting.*

*In view of the above facts, the Board of Directors recommends a vote AGAINST this proposal.*

PETA staff members believe their efforts with corporations are gaining attention because of public exposure to the issues of animal testing, especially on cosmetics and household products, and that corporations are on the defensive.[46] For a grass roots group to be able to confront the second largest American producer of consumer products (Philip Morris Companies is larger) gives credibility to the organization. At the 1988 Procter & Gamble annual meeting, mothers, scientists, Procter & Gamble employees, and a seventh-grade student spoke in favor of the PETA proposal. The PETA resolution received 2 percent of shares voted.[47] PETA plans to reintroduce the resolution if they are able to obtain sufficient support from Procter & Gamble stockholders.

The shareholders' resolution strategy provides grass roots groups an opportunity to present their case to a segment of the population not normally reached: boards of directors, shareholders, and their families. Proxy statements of the resolution and the vote are sent to all shareholders, thus extending the reach of the communication. While none of the resolutions has won a majority vote, support ranged from 2 to 16 percent.

With pressure placed on them from PETA at their

shareholders' meetings, corporations that use animal tests are, according to industry spokespersons, seeking to find ways to eliminate those tests. In chapter 3, the opposition tactic of Procter & Gamble to PETA's proposal is discussed.

Greenpeace and other grass roots groups have used the resolution tactic at shareholders' meetings to accomplish their goals as well. Being able to obtain the necessary number of shares to qualify may be a problem for some of the smaller movements, but the use of this tactic is spreading. In a recent Council on Economic Priorities research report, Myra Alperson wrote, "After decades of being considered part of the social fringe, animal rights advocacy in the United States has entered the mainstream as a legitimate grass roots movement."[48] Some believe the shareholders' proposal tactic has been partially responsible for that shift in public opinion.

***Exxon Valdez Oil Spill:*** In (what was at the time) the worst oil spill in history, the *Exxon Valdez* oil tanker spilled 240,000 barrels, or 10 million tons, of oil into the Alaskan waterways in March 1989, mostly in Prince William Sound. A forty-one-year-old fisherman quickly bought ten shares of Exxon stock and went to the Exxon stockholders' meeting on May 18, 1989, to air his grievance. With two thousand shareholders at the meeting, he said, "Exxon is going to have to earn the restoration of its public image." For more than four hours, the annual meeting was turned into a spirited debate. Outside, protesters rallied and conducted guerrilla theater to draw attention to the meeting.[49] Unlike the PETA formal resolution, the group at Exxon issued its challenge from the floor. They demanded that Exxon's chairman resign, that Exxon set aside $1 billion a year to repair the damage from the spill, and that the company assure the public that it is equipped to deal with future emergencies.

At the meeting, Chairman Lawrence Rawls said, "We've accepted the responsibility. In time, when the job is done, I'm confident that it will be evident to every fair-minded person that our employees met this major challenge with a high level of determination and professionalism."[50]

Exxon management did agree to place an environmentalist on its board, but critics said the concession was not enough and they doubted that Exxon could clean the Alaskan area by its September 15, 1989, deadline. It did not, in fact, meet the deadline and pulled out from the damaged area for the winter of 1989, promising to return in the spring of 1990, if needed. With oil remaining in Prince William Sound, Exxon-paid crews returned in spring 1990 to renew the cleaning process. The work force was less than ten percent of the summer 1989 crew. Alaska officials said the plan did not meet the cleanup needs.

Public support for greater environmental efforts, regardless of cost, has dramatically increased since the *Exxon Valdez* oil spill. In a *New York Times* poll conducted from June 20, 1989, through July 15, 1989, 80 percent of the 1,497 people interviewed by telephone said they agreed with the statement: "Protecting the environment is so important that requirements and standards cannot be too high, and continuing environmental improvements must be made regardless of cost." Only 14 percent disagreed. The *New York Times*/CBS News polls have been tracking this issue (unqualified environmental support) since 1981, when only 45 percent agreed and 42 percent disagreed with the statement.[51]

When a grass roots issue enjoys broad public support, those using the shareholders' meeting as a forum usually gain substantial public exposure and awareness and find some sympathetic shareholders willing to back their position.

## Litigation

Getting an issue in court is frequently sought by grass roots groups, often with success. The tactic is costly, time-consuming, and strongly countered by the defendant in many cases. Because of these factors, some grass roots groups are reluctant to use litigation as a weapon in their arsenal. The defendants in most lawsuits brought by grass roots groups are government entities, corporations, universities, or small businesses. At times, the grass roots group itself is sued; that counter-tactic is examined in chapter 3. Two large, respected environmental organizations, the Environmental Defense Fund and the Natural Resources Defense Council, have their roots in litigation and, although they are no longer considered grass roots groups, they continue to file suits on behalf of environmental causes, frequently joining other public interest groups in the courtroom.

*Vietnam Veterans and Agent Orange:* Agent Orange, a chemical defoliant, was used by United States forces during the Vietnam war in the 1960s to clear dense jungles and, according to the Defense Department, "to enhance the military's operation against Vietnamese resistance." The defoliant contains dioxin, a potent carcinogen that many veterans and others believe to be the source of cancer, skin ailments, birth defects, and other serious health problems they are encountering. In 1984 the manufacturer, Dow Chemical Company, settled a class-action suit filed by the Vietnam Veterans of America, a grass roots group that sprang up in the 1970s, out of court for $180 million. The suit brought charges that Dow Chemical knew dioxin was carcinogenic and did not warn those using it of its dangers. Also in 1984, Congress passed the Dioxin Act to provide compensation to herbicide-exposed veterans and their survivors.[52]

Following the enactment of that legislation, Vietnam veterans filed Agent Orange-related claims with the U.S. Veterans Administration (now the Department of Veterans Affairs), but of the 33,272 cases claimed, the Veterans Administration gave disability compensation to only five. Despite the intent of the law, the agency demanded that claimants prove a causal link between their illness and Agent Orange. In 1985, the Vietnam Veterans of America filed a suit in federal court on behalf of its 35,000-member organization and thirteen individual veterans. They charged that the Veterans Administration had violated the 1984 congressional Dioxin Act.[53]

In his May 1989 ruling, U.S. District Judge Thelton Henderson declared that the Veterans Administration had imposed an "impermissibly demanding test" on veterans to substantiate their claims and that "in refusing to give veterans the benefit of the doubt, the Veterans Administration tipped the scales against veterans claimants."[54] In the beginning, the Veterans Administration classified only one ailment, a skin condition known as chloracne, as a basis for granting benefits, and dismissed all others.

The judge also said that the 1984 law did not demand a cause and effect relationship in determining Agent Orange claims: "It is unlikely that Congress would legislate a system in which veterans would actually be made worse through the rule-making process."[55]

Following the decision, Veterans Affairs Secretary Edward Derwinski announced that his agency would reconsider the question of whether Agent Orange had injured tens of thousands of soldiers during the Vietnam war. He further said that the court decision would not be appealed to a higher court. Barry Kasinitz, the attorney for the Vietnam Veterans of America, said, "The ruling is a tremendous victory. We always felt that the principal battle was to force the federal government to live up to its responsibilities."[56] In effect, the ruling requires the Department of Veterans Affairs to set new eligibility standards and reconsider the claims of the 33,272 veterans exposed to the herbicide.

In early 1990, the Department of Veterans Affairs acknowledged for the first time that exposure to Agent Orange may have caused cancers among the 3.1 million U.S. military personnel who served in Southeast Asia. The decision was a breakthrough in the long struggle over whether dioxin in Agent Orange was a carcinogen. The Department of Veterans Affairs now acknowledges a link to soft-tissue sarcomas (malignant tumors found on muscles and connective tissues and in body fat.)

Frustrated once again by their inability to win benefits for Vietnam veterans exposed to Agent Orange, however, veteran groups took to the courts anew in August 1990. The American Legion, joined by Vietnam Veterans of America, filed a suit in the U.S. district court, calling for a federal judge to direct the government to complete a study mandated by Congress in 1979 to determine the herbicide's effect on those who served in Vietnam. The veterans' groups charge that the study was discontinued in 1987 due to White House pressure on the Department of Health and Human Services, a charge denied by government officials.

***On Behalf of Alaskan Wildlife:*** In an unprecedented suit, the Wildlife Federation of Alaska, the National Wildlife Federation, and the Natural Resources Defense Council filed suit in September 1989 in the Alaska Superior Court in Anchorage accusing Exxon of gross negligence, creating a public nuisance, and of misleading the public concerning its efforts to clean up the *Exxon Valdez* oil spill. The suit asserts that bears, otters, birds, salmon, and other animals should have standing in a court action, and it asks Exxon to pay for restoration of the Alaskan environment and wildlife damaged by the *Exxon Valdez* oil spill.[56]

The lawsuit asks the question, "Who has a property interest in the over 3,000 otters and seals killed and the thousands of birds? The suit contends that those animals are owned by the public.

"As a consequence of the defendants' gross negligence and willful acts and the resultant ravaging of the coastline, Exxon's spilled tons of oil are responsible for the death of animals at every level of the food chain," according to the suit. Further, the suit calls on Exxon to restore the Alaskan environment by establishing a fund overseen by an independent group to conduct studies on the short- and long-term effects of the spill and to restore and replace the wildlife and the ecosystem's diversity. The suit is stalled, awaiting the disposition of other suits filed against Exxon.

In early February 1990, officials of the Exxon Corporation and the U.S. Justice Department met to work out a plea bargain that would free the corporation from liability in exchange for an agreed-upon, undisclosed sum of money, some of which would be earmarked for environmental restoration. This plea bargain ploy was roundly denounced by Alaska state officials and environmental groups. On February 27, 1990, a federal grand jury in Anchorage indicted Exxon and its shipping subsidiary on five criminal charges that carry more than $700 million in penalties. The five charges are

- Willfully and knowingly violating a regulation prohibiting any person from being engaged on a crew if such person is known to be physically or mentally incapable of performing his or her duties.
- Violating the Port and Waterways Safety Act.
- Violating the Clean Water Act by illegally discharging pollutants into Prince William Sound.
- Unlawfully discharging refuse, the oil.

• Violating the Migratory Bird Treaty Act, a count
which stems from the deaths of more than 36,000
birds as a result of oil pollution.

The Exxon Corporation challenged the U.S. Department of Justice, saying it could not be held criminally
responsible for actions of its subsidiary, and it further
challenged the government to name any corporate official who committed crimes. All parties expect judicial
delays, and a court decision is unlikely within the next
two years.

*Environmental Defense Fund: From DDT to Recyc-
ling:* The Environmental Defense Fund (EDF) began at
the grass roots level, with scientists and an attorney
presenting six days of testimony in a New York courtroom in 1967. They were in court to stop Suffolk County
from massive spraying of DDT to kill mosquitoes. The
ordinary citizens argued that the pesticide was killing
the osprey, the peregrine falcon, and the bald eagle
population. They won the suit, and that case was the
first of many, ending with a ban of DDT in 1972 by the
Environmental Protection Agency (EPA).

In 1988, in one of hundreds of cases over the years, the
EDF returned to court, the U.S. District Court of Appeals
for the District of Columbia, and won a consent decree
that compelled the EPA to issue regulations requiring
federal agencies to purchase paper, tires, insulation, and
lubricating oils, all made from recovered materials. Recycling was given a new life.

"This settlement is a turning point for an important
program that has been too long delayed," said EDF
attorney Michael Herz. "For twelve years, EPA has ignored its statutory duty to issue these regulations, and
its attitude toward the procurement program has varied
between disinterest and outright hostility."[57]

The 1976 Resource Conservation and Recovery Act (RCRA) requires federal agencies to buy recycled products when they are both available at a reasonable price and adequate for the intended purpose. The EPA is required to implement the act by designating specific products for purchase. It had given only one guideline by 1987. The Environmental Defense Fund, along with several other national consumer and public interest groups, sued to force the EPA to carry out the law. The 1988 consent decree settled the lawsuit.

The decision to select a particular traditional social action tactic remains with the grass roots group. Some, notably PETA and environmental groups, utilize a range of these actions. Having adequate resources, informed staff, experience, and commitment to follow through is important. Those opposing these actions—government, corporations, and universities—usually have all of the above and more.

## Violent, Direct Action

The use of violence by grass roots groups is rare in recent history, and most of the direct physical action used by the groups analyzed in this book is against material objects rather than people. In contrast to the violent methods used in the abolition and prohibition movements, passive, nonviolent resistance is the preferred choice today.

***John Brown's Body:*** John Brown, consumed with religious fervor, frequently said, "The price of liberty was less than the cost of repression." And his target, American slavery, was described by him as "the foulest and filthiest blot on nineteenth-century civilization." He decided to make war on slavery and dedicated his life to bringing this institution down. The leading abolitionist, William Lloyd Garrison, spoke for nonviolent resistance and perfectionism and developed a large following during the thirty-five years of his writing, speaking, and peaceful organizing. Brown, on the other hand, spoke for the radical wing of the abolitionist movement and decided that "God's use of him was first and foremost to free the slave."[58]

Support for slavery was strong. The federal government, Southern white plantation owners and merchants, and the United States Congress, led by Senator John Calhoun, resisted all attempts to abolish the institution. In 1850, the U.S. Congress passed the Fugitive Slave Act, and the matter of slavery moved directly north when bounty hunters searched for runaway slaves as far north as Boston. Thoreau, Garrison, and Brown were enraged by this piece of plantation legislation. Overnight, the abolitionist movement grew in numbers and fervor. The battle in the 1850s centered on Kansas and Nebraska: would they be admitted to the Union as free states or slave states?[59]

The first acts of direct, violent action used by an abolitionist were John Brown's raids in Kansas, where he took a small group of men, mostly his sons and friends, to Pottawatomie to massacre the Border Ruffians, a group of proslavery diehards determined to make Kansas a slave state at any cost. Brown came to Kansas to wage war against slavery and, at Pottawatomie's Ruffian encampment, in the dark of night, his group entered and killed five leaders in cold blood. The news of the massacre shocked the nation, and revenge was quick. Pro-free-soil partisans were attacked. Brown went into hiding but later conducted his second Kansas raid at Black Jack, where he attacked and killed another band of Ruffians. With these victories, his fame spread, and the governor of Kansas proclaimed, "He was the only man who comprehended the situation and saw the absolute necessity of some such blow and had the nerve to strike it."[60] His last Kansas raid at Osawatomie, in 1856, ended in a withdrawal, but not without a spirited fight against a force six times as large as his. When he left Kansas, he said, "I have only a short time to live and only one death to die, and I will die fighting for this cause. There will be no peace in this land until slavery is done for. I will give them something else to do than to extend slavery. I will carry the war to Africa."

In this sentence, Africa meant the Southern plantations, and John Brown spent the next three years planning his "African invasion," which would begin with the raid on the federal arsenal at Harper's Ferry to obtain guns for his new army. He believed Southern slaves would rebel and join his armed forces when he marched south from Harper's Ferry into the "Great Black Way," as he called the South.[61]

In October 1859, John Brown led his secret, carefully planned attack on the United States arsenal with twenty-one men who had trained for four months for this mission. He took the town of Harper's Ferry and the arsenal and held it for almost two days before he surrendered to a detachment of the United States Army commanded by Colonel Robert E. Lee.

At his trial, Brown said, "I am ready for my fate. I do not ask for a trial. I beg no mockery of a trial—no insult— nothing but that which conscience gives or cowardice would drive you to practice." The trial was speedy, and the sentence, hanging. At its pronouncement he commented:

> "Now, if it is deemed necessary that I should forfeit
> my life for the furtherance of the ends of justice, and
> mingle blood further with the blood of my children and

with the blood of millions in slave country whose rights are disregarded by wicked, cruel, and unjust enactments, I say, let it be done."[62]

John Brown's actions, both his violent attacks on slavery and his resolute belief in the cause of abolition, became an inspiration to many in the North, and Ralph Waldo Emerson called him "the new saint who will make the gallows glorious like the cross." He succeeded in dramatizing the deep moral chasm between the industrialized North and slavery in the South, and slavery was abolished in 1865 after a bitter civil war.

## *"Hatchetation"*

Before she died on June 2, 1911, Carry Nation told a group of supporters, "I have done what I could." She had. Although she is best known for her direct, violent action, mostly against property, she utilized an array of grass roots tactics: lectures, guerrilla theater, two newsletters, a sit-in, litigation, letter writing—to name only a few. She is best remembered for smashing saloons with her famous hatchet.

Like John Brown's, Carry Nation's exploits began in Kansas, in a small town named Kiowa. She arrived in 1900 in a horse-drawn buggy with her armaments: rocks, brickbats, and several large bottles. (The hatchet was introduced in a later raid.) She was on a "mission of God" to wipe out American saloons, which she knew harbored drunken men and women who neglected their families and drank away the profits of their labor. In her autobiography, she describes this moment: "I stacked up these smashers on my left arm, all I could hold." She stood in front of Dobson's, a popular saloon, and yelled to those inside, "Men, I have come to save you from a drunkard's grave!" Ignoring pleas from the owner, she launched the missiles that soon left the saloon in a shambles. Upon physical victory, with the establishment shattered, she began the second phase of her moral crusade by singing the hymn "Who Hath Sorrow? Who Hath Woe?"[63]

After wrecking two other bars, Carry stood in the streets of Kiowa and shouted, "Men of Kiowa, I have destroyed three of your places of business! If I have broken a statute of Kansas, put me in jail. If I am not a lawbreaker, your mayor and councilmen are. You must arrest one of us."[64] She was taken by the marshall and then released when she pointed out that, by Kansas law, saloons were illegal. Finally, after a public squabble with hundreds of Kiowanians looking on in disbelief, Carry Nation was told to "go home" by the marshall. Within a short time, the Kiowa saloon smashing was national news, and her career as a home defender who resorted to violence had begun. Eleven years later, at the age of sixty-four, Carry Nation died, leaving a profound mark on the country she loved and wanted to save. Her followers in this violence-prone wing of the Temperance movement were largely Bible students, women, and ministers. Hers was a moral issue; she never mentioned the deleterious effects of alcohol on the body. She was troubled by "the devil's grip on the soul" that came from drunkenness and neglect of the family.

The hatchet was used for the first time in 1901 at the smashing of Shillings Lounge in Enterprise, Kansas. Later, she sold small pewter hatchets as souvenirs to finance her saloon forays across the nation. These violent encounters landed Carry Nation in jail many times, and she made the most of jail time because, as an early member of the Woman's Christian Temperance Union (WCTU), she had served as jail evangelist and knew her way around. Her jail time was spent trying to convert fellow prisoners and answering correspondence that poured in from admirers and antagonists. While in the cell, she also planned her next assaults.

These two historic grass roots movements changed the course of America. That violence was a central part of them may reflect a young frontier nation that saw violence as almost ordinary. Slavery was violent; westward expansion was violent (particularly against Native Americans); the Civil War was violent. Accomplishing social change today is far less violent than in the earlier days of this Republic. Nonviolent civil disobedience has become almost synonymous with grass roots activism. However, some acts of violence have been used recently to force change by factions within several movements. The violence perpetrated is, however, almost always against property—not other people.

*Animal Liberation Front:*  In Eugene, Oregon, in October 1986, members of a local chapter of the Animal Liberation Front (ALF) broke into the University of Oregon laboratories and removed a large number of animals used for various experiments. In the raid, ALF members destroyed more than $150,000 in laboratory equipment and left a warning, "This is just the beginning. We cannot allow the slaughter to continue without resistance." This violent action against property was defended in a statement released by the ALF: "Action goes beyond acts of protest. Animals will always be rescued where possible, but the main purpose of the action is often economic sabotage. Property and "things" hold no sacred value—the opposite, in fact, if they are used to cause pain and death. To stop the very real violence of torture and killing, inanimate objects must be rendered unusable. When equipment is broken, insurance rates go up and so do security costs, making the enterprise less profitable." They further stated, "Animal experiments may be legal but morality will eventually change these oppressive laws as it has changed all such laws before."[65]

## Monkey Wrenching

Sabotage, ecotage: whatever it's called, the principle is to conduct violence against technology. Earth First! calls it "defense" in the book *Ecodefense: A Field Guide to Monkey Wrenching.* Author David Foreman, one of the founders of Earth First!, was arrested in May 1989 by agents of the Federal Bureau of Investigation and charged with conspiracy to sabotage federal energy plants. His arrest came shortly after FBI agents arrested three other persons said to be trying to disable a tower that carried high voltage lines to the central Arizona project. The power was to be used for a large irrigation system in the Arizona desert. Earth First! and others opposed its operation.[66]

In addition to this direct, violent action, Earth First! members have been accused of other acts of vandalism, such as spiking trees with metal rods, pouring sugar and sand in bulldozers at timber company operations in old growth forests, and burying salt in the dirt airstrip in an Idaho wilderness to encourage deer to dig up the runway. These and other acts of ecotage are described in Earth First! literature. Some members have been apprehended and charged with crimes.

In its most visible effort to date, Earth First! launched Redwood Summer during 1990 in the timber country of Northern California. The aim of acts of civil disobedience by some two hundred volunteers was to slow down the logging of all redwoods and to end logging of old-growth redwoods, which are 150 to 1,000 years old. This radical environmental action was designed to alert California voters to the plunder of the redwood forests, which are a unique ecosystem, and to the 1990 ballot initiative, "Forests Forever," sponsored by environmentalists. This proposition called for severe restrictions on the harvest of old-growth redwoods as well as for other forest conservation measures. It was defeated in the November 1990 election.

Redwood Summer began inadvertently in Oakland, California, with a violent action on May 24, 1990: the explosion of a pipe bomb in the car of two Earth First! organizers. Both environmentalists were injured and subsequently arrested. Federal and local law enforcement officials initially stated that they suspected the two of possessing and transporting an explosive device. The police questioned many persons and released information linking the bomb to the environmentalists. The latter denied any knowledge and countercharged that the bomb had been placed in their car by foes of Earth First! After two months of criminal investigation, no formal charges were filed by the Alameda County district attorney.

A coalition of environmental groups, including mainstream organizations such as the Sierra Club and the National Audubon Society, called for a congressional probe into the pipe bomb explosion. The coalition accused the Oakland police and the FBI of selectively leaking information to the press about the ongoing criminal investigation, of conducting warrantless searches, and of refusing to let one of the injured activists see his attorney while being questioned for four hours by the FBI. Shortly after the coalition's request, the decision was made not to file charges.

Whether, over time, violent, direct action will increase in the United States is unclear. Certainly, terrorism has escalated in other nations—terrorism against people as well as physical objects. At this point, the vast majority of American grass roots movements eschew violent direct action. The violent tactics of the two nineteenth-century movements have been relegated to history books, but they serve as reminders that, in that stage of America's growth, violence was a fact of life.

During the civil rights struggle of the 1960s and the Vietnam war protests, persons and groups used violent direct action. In the ghetto riots and burnings, violence was generally against property, but many died, both rioters and police officers. Some antiabortionist activists continue to bomb and set fire to abortion medical clinics in violent protest. Most are apprehended and tried in court for crimes against property.

Grass roots groups have many tactics to choose from. Leaders report that boycotts, media exposés, and acts of nonviolent civil disobedience are especially effective. They place less value on tactics such as rallies, telephone calls to officials, and speeches. Consensus at the time of choosing tactics promotes greater group participation. As soon as tactics show results, opposition mounts. Scott Tucker of ACT UP suggests: "Make the right friends and enemies. The best defense is a good offense."

# 3

# The Opposition: Its Tactics

The tactics of corporations, government agencies, and private associations are employed to apply counterpressure on grass roots groups. Often well-financed, the opposition seeks to disrupt, discredit, and disarm the groups, as well as to gain public approval for their own position. Their tactics are both defensive and offensive in nature, not entirely unlike grass roots tactics themselves.

## Big Three Against Animal Rights

No other grass roots movement in the past decade has been the target of a better financed, more concerted, and more persistent opposition campaign than the animal rights movement. It has found itself engaged in a complex and visible struggle with a government agency (Department of Health and Human Services), the American Medical Association (AMA), and corporate giants, particularly Procter & Gamble. Although each of these counteractions was developed independently, each plan of attack alludes to the need for a coalition of public and private groups in opposition to the activities of the various animal rights groups.

An American Medical Association memo dated June 1989 gives a detailed plan of action to oppose animals rights activists, primarily the Animal Liberation Front, the Animal Rights Militia, and the leadership of People for the Ethical Treatment of Animals (PETA).[1] The memo states four specific aims of its opposition to these grass roots groups:

### The AMA Action Plan

To defeat the animal rights movement, one has to peel away the outermost layers of support and isolate the hardcore activists from the general public and shrink the size of the sympathizers. This can be done by exploiting the differences that already exist over goals and tactics—especially the use of violence. The extreme goals and tactics of the hardcore activists must be exposed fully for the public to see. This is a prime goal of the American Medical Association (AMA) Action Plan.[1]

To reduce public support and sympathy, i.e., isolate the hardcore activists, the violent elements must be prosecuted vigorously. The theme should be "no person is above the law, whatever the cause." The hardcore types and the activists will not alter their views. They are dedicated. The sympathizers however are soft and the general public is up for grabs. These people can be scared away if they come to see the violent tactics of the movement as dangerous and counterproductive. This is an important part of AMA's strategy.

The animal activist movement must be shown to be not only anti-science but also: a) responsible for violent and illegal acts that endanger life and property and b) a threat to the public's freedom of choice. This is particularly important given the importance of "life-style" issues to the public. The public must be made to understand that animal rights radicals and "moderates" are opposed not only to the use of animals in medical research but also their freedom to eat as they choose (meat), dress as they choose (leather and fur) and enjoy various forms of entertainment (hunting, zoo's [sic], circuses, rodeos etc.). This may have more immediate and personal impact on many audiences than arguments about the importance of using animals in research—an issue which may not be perceived by most as affecting them personally.

Finally, inherent in the AMA Action Plan are approaches designed to take the humane treatment issue away from the animal activists by showing that the research community supports humane treatment of animals used in biomedical research, and that it is taking action to insure that humane standards are observed. This should ease the concerns of the largest part of the general public and allow the AMA to say that the legitimate concerns of the animal welfare proponents are being addressed (as opposed to the extreme and unreasonable demand that no animals be used in such research) and help isolate the hardcore activists from the broader public. [Additional excerpts from the AMA June 1989 memo can be found in Appendix A.]

The AMA defines its opposition in political terms and sets forth to discredit animal rights groups as extremists with a hard-core leadership and several layers of decreasingly active supporters who can be reached. The memo states, "If the animal rights movement is to continue to be successful in the political arena, it must mobilize activists and sympathizers." The AMA is concerned over several successes of animal rights groups: congressional support for bills that impede the use of animals in research, the rising cost of this research, prescribed minimal cage sizes, requirements to maintain the psychological well being of primates, and the passage of "pound laws" in some localities. Grass roots groups have learned that, as their success mounts, so does the reaction of those they seek to change. The AMA memorandum acknowledges the influence of animal rights activists and proposes ways to seize the initiative from their opponents:

> Until now we have allowed the activists to define the issues, choose the arena, and set the agenda—reacting from time to time only when pressed. But this strategy is not working and must be changed. The frontal attack on biomedical research can be won only through a strong concerted effort by many individuals, groups, and organizations dedicated to preserving biomedical research and resulting in advances for clinical medicine. . . .

The AMA further acknowledges that, to implement their plan, they must expend money and other resources:

> Many organizations have been working diligently to assure proper understanding of the role of animals in biomedical research. These organizations include the National Association for Biomedical Research, the Foundation for Biomedical Research, the Incurably Ill for Animal Research, and a number of other important groups. Each of these groups has contributed in an important way to the preservation of biomedical research. However, the proactive participation of the medical community is an essential—and to date, underrepresented—element in this effort. These efforts must be expanded and continued.
>
> The American Medical Association is making a major commitment of time, resources, and personnel to implement the tactics and strategies in this Action Plan. Implementation of the plan will require a major financial commitment from many sources. The AMA will sustain its commitment for whatever length of time it

takes to turn the tide of this public issue. The preservation of biomedical research and continued advancement in clinical medicine are dependent upon this effort succeeding. Together we can succeed.

For the most part, the AMA Action Plan focuses on education and reeducation of the medical profession, its affiliates, and the general public. It also calls for coalition with others in government and the business community, and the labeling of animal rights activists as "antiscience" and "against medical progress." It plans to "position the biomedical community as moderate—centrist—in the controversy, not as polar opposite."

The AMA plans to employ a public relations firm to "enhance a public education campaign to counteract animal rights propaganda." A major focus will be "activities specifically designed to educate children and teachers."

The AMA's coalition-building will concentrate on "education and mobilization of physicians, scientists, and the general health-care community." This effort seeks to build a broad, informed base of support for the use of animals in biomedical research, convincing others that this practice is essential to medical progress. While most of its actions are designed to educate and convince, it does state three objectives that appear to acknowledge problems to which animal rights advocates call attention:

- Promote and aid the training of scientists, technicians, and caretakers in biomedical research laboratories in the areas of law, regulations, standards, techniques, husbandry, etc.
- Develop procedures to address potential misconduct toward animal subjects in laboratories so that the public can have confidence that the biomedical re-

search community is conducting research in the most humane manner possible.

- Educate the profession about systematic development and validation of nonanimal testing techniques and significant efforts to reduce the use of animals in biomedical research.

In its objectives pertaining to legal sanctions and strategies directed at preventing restrictive legislation and protecting freedom of scientific inquiry, the AMA proposes the following actions against animal rights groups:

- Development of legal means for contesting the tax exempt status of animal rights groups.
- Development of legal defense strategies for, and funds to be made available to, scientists targeted by animal rights groups.
- Promote formation of special investigative units within government to examine animal rights activities.
- Consultation with state, local, federal, and international policing authorities about illegal activities relating to animal rights groups; stress importance of animal rights violence being placed high on priority list; lobby for creation of Justice Department database to monitor and prosecute illegal activities of animal rights groups.
- Building private database on animal rights activities and reported abuses of animals by researchers; report significant incidents to proper authorities.
- Development of coalition groups at the state and local level, built around county medical societies (including local physicians, scientists, other health-care professionals, patients, business and community

leaders) to monitor animal rights activities and educate the public about the necessity for animal use in
biomedical research.
- Develoment of Foundation for Animal Health to attract funding away from animal rights groups; funding to support critical research on companion
animals and laboratory animals.

The American Medical Association has a large and
well-financed membership, as well as a powerful lobby in
Washington, D.C., and state capitals. Their opposition to
grass roots activism within the animal rights movement
indicates a determination to shift public opinion. Cen-
tering the campaign on violent activities of a minority of
animal rights activists to paint all members with the
same brush is a tactic that has been used before, especially during the McCarthy era in American politics.

### The Federal Response

A primary target of many animal rights groups is the
federal government. Its many departments, agencies,
and institutes fund and conduct research using animals. Animal rights groups have organized extensive
nonviolent civil disobedience against offices in departments such as Health and Human Services, Agriculture,
Defense, and Transportation, to name only a few. They
have focused a campaign against the National Institute
of Mental Health for its use of animals in psychological
experiments as well as drug addiction investigations.
Their actions have created a response, especially in the
National Institute on Mental Health.[2] Excerpts from a
memorandum that was circulated to key personnel in
NIMH describe the beginning of an action plan to
counter and oppose the animal rights movement (the
complete memo is in Appendix B):

DEPARTMENT OF HEALTH & HUMAN SERVICES

Memorandum

Date: September 29, 1987

From: Director of Intramural Research, NIMH

Subject: Reflections Following the 9/28/87 Meeting on the Animal Rights' Movement

1. The stakes are enormous. The animal rights' movement threatens the very core of what the Public Health Service is all about.

2. The "bunker" strategy is no longer tenable.

3. The health research community must participate with patient groups, voluntary health organizations, the American Medical Association, and other groups of health professionals. Wherever feasible, the research institutions should leave the "out front" activists to the other groups. The PHS [Public Health Service] and its agencies should find some acceptable way to provide funding for some of these efforts and technical support for others.

4. Although it is important that we continue to work toward "having our house in order," we must realize that by making this our major focus, we tacitly accept the premise of the animal rights' movement and play into their hands.

5. The pro-active posture should focus in two directions:

    a) Contemporary examples of health advances directly dependent upon animal research. Here we should draw liberally from those areas that already enjoy wide public and congressional support, i.e. AIDS, dementia schizophrenia, various childhood disorders, etc. We should draw up a list of such illnesses and the research upon which treatment is dependent keeping in mind the existence of various specialized groups such as Danny Thomas and so forth. The example of the Juvenile Diabetes Association should be instructive.

b) A pro-active stance should include a vigorous focus on the fundamental philosophical underpinnings of the animal rights movement, namely the moral equivalence between human beings and animals. This could be highlighted by some of the more outrageous quotes from Elizabeth Newkirk and Alex Pacheco, that dramatize how the movement's philosophy is based on a degradation of the concept of human nature.

6. The research institutions need to have effective spokespeople available, but they should not generally be the researchers themselves. A scientist whose laboratory has been raided is the least likely person to be effective as a spokesperson. The NIMH Intramural Program has developed four clinical investigators who have been trained in the arguments of the animal rights' people and who have had media training.

7. The PHS and the DHHS [Department of Health and Human Services] need a more concerted legislative strategy. All budget presentations should include a discussion of overly stringent animal regulations and their impact on the cost of research. Answers to questions from Congress concerning what we are doing (or why we are not doing more) in a given area should include reference to the difficulties imposed by restrictive regulations and by the activities of animal activists.

9. The PHS and/or its agencies should pull together groups to think of more creative ways to counter the long-term threat posed by the animal rights'

movement. For example, it might be possible to fund special fellowships in research advocacy for investigators who may wish to include a year or two of such activity in their career. Although most investigators are not interested in such advocacy and are not skillful at it, there are a few who would be interested if there were financial incentives. A corollary would be the creation of research advocacy awards that could convey some of the prestige available for traditional research awards.

10. The Department of Education should be contacted concerning infiltration of high schools by the animal rights' people. PHS should sponsor countereducational efforts, in collaboration with the voluntary health organizations and the grass roots health provider organizations such as the AMA.

11. The Department should fund a contract to provide assistance to the agencies in conducting and coordinating the myriad tasks associated with these efforts. This would include the collection and preparation of materials, the analysis of data on the cost of animal rights' destruction, and the cost of regulations. Brief packets of material could be prepared for direct use and for integration into budget testimony and into speeches, talks and articles prepared by our political and scientific leaders, as well as individual scientists.

12. In marshalling these various near term and long-range efforts, we should not lose sight of the fact that the NIH-NIMH Intramural Programs are facing a demonstration on November 9, probably to be preceded by a break-in. It is critical that contingency plans be worked out in advance, and that all levels of the Department approve them promptly.

13. In summary, I am suggesting a strategy at the
    other end of the spectrum from the "bunker strat-
    egy": we must consistently, aggressively, and
    unashamedly portray the importance of animals
    in research in every way that we possibly can. Al-
    though initially this may heighten opposition, it
    is far better in the long run because it is intellec-
    tually honest and, therefore, more credible. Our
    caution will signal lack of conviction and resolve.
    Without these, we cannot expect others to help
    us.[2]

Frederick K. Goodwin, M.D.

cc: James Wyngaarden, M.D.
Ms. Frankie Trull (FBMR)
Salvatore Cianci, Ph.D.

Opposition tactics planned by the National Institute of
Mental Health are largely similar to those presented in
the Plan of Action by the American Medical Association.
While the NIMH memo was written almost two years
earlier than the AMA plan, this federal agency proposes
collaboration with the American Medical Association in
points 3 and 10, calling the AMA a "grass roots health
provider." Both groups plan internal and public education, coalition-building, advocacy by researchers, lobbying, and putting aside their "bunker mentality."

The director of NIMH proposes using taxpayers' dollars
to "fund special research advocacy for investigators" and
to "answer questions from Congress concerning what we
are doing (or why we are not doing more) in a given area"
by including "reference to the difficulties imposed by
restrictive regulations and by the activities of animal
activists." Apparently NIMH would excuse its failures to
Congress by casting itself as the victim of animal
activists.

This original NIMH memorandum was distributed in

September 1987, and, from that date, NIMH staff have participated in the National Institutes of Health (NIH) Animal Welfare Initiative. A group within NIH was assembled to prepare the 1989–1990 Goals and Action Plan to address animal welfare issues within NIH and in December 1988, this group met in a retreat setting to begin to plan the Initiative. On April 5, 1989, a draft of the Goals and Action plan of NIH's Animal Welfare Initiative was released intramurally.

Shortly after the draft of the Goals and Action document was distributed, a copy of an article written by Kenneth P. Stoler, M.D., entitled "The Secret of NIH," appeared in volume 2, number 3, of the magazine *Animals' Voice*. The article calls into question the expenditure of "billions of public dollars a year—most of which involve animal research" spent by thirty-one public agencies, including the National Institutes of Health. The author asserts, "In order to obtain basic research grants, the biomedical scientist often is compromised into publishing less than meaningful papers. The 'grant' is the bottom line in academia, and being well-published is the best way to obtain grants. One's whole career in academia depends on obtaining this funding to pay salaries, build up points for tenure, etc. Once the grants start coming in, you have to make sure they keep coming in year after year.... Here is where animal research comes to the rescue."

The author proceeds to describe numerous experiments funded by NIH and other federal agencies. They include drug addiction, electric shock, burn, and microwave experiments in which animals are used. Stoller lists the grants by name, the funding agency, the grant amount, the recipient university, and the number of times the grant was renewed.

When this article was given for review to the NIH

associate director for science policy and legislation, his written reply on June 12, 1989, was, "The attached article, 'The Secret of NIH,' recently appeared in *Animals' Voice*. Our initial reaction was not to dignify such non-sense with a response; however, we probably should be prepared to be attacked further on some of the research identified in the article.... We will probably use the information you provide for internal purposes only, but I believe we need your input to help make the decision as to how best to deal with the exaggerations and half-truths being promulgated by animal rights groups in articles such as this one." Signed: Jay Moskowitz, Ph.D.[3]

## A Corporate Response

Joining the American Medical Association and the National Institutes of Health in their carefully planned and expensive opposition to the animal rights movement is the Procter & Gamble company. In chapter 2, one conflict between this company and the movement was discussed pertaining to the resolution about Procter & Gamble's use of animal experiments at their shareholder meetings. On June 9, 1989, the director of issues management in Procter & Gamble's Public Affairs Division sent a letter to the chief executive officers of a number of large corporations (Bristol-Myers, Eastman Kodak, IBM, Johnson and Johnson, Merck, Monsanto, Syntex, 3-M, Colgate Palmolive, Lever Brothers, and Gillette) proposing that they "form an industry coalition to support responsible use of animal testing to assure product safety and efficacy"; the letter also carried an invitation to attend an initial organizing meeting in July 1989. Excerpts from the letter describe a proposed coalition. (The complete letter is in Appendix C.)

*June 9, 1989*
*Retention Limit: 7/90*

Mr. G.S. Gandall
    Subject: <u>INDUSTRY COALITION ON ANIMAL</u>
    <u>TESTING</u>

*This proposes that we proceed with establishing an industry coalition to augment current trade association efforts to address the growing issue of animal testing. Specifically, with Mr. Smale's agreement, we propose that he send out invitations for an initial organizational meeting which would include the CEO's of key companies concerned about this issue. We would like to hold this meeting by mid-July.*

*A statement describing the proposed mission, role and membership, developed by Ms. Linda Ulreay, is provided in Exhibit I. Briefly, we see the mission as follows:*

*To sustain a public and legislative environment which supports the judicious use of animal testing as a necessary part of a corporation's responsibility to manufacture and market safe and effective products.*

*The key role of the coalition would be to direct public relations and legislative activities to support this mission. In addition, it would provide a forum for sharing learnings about activist activities. We see this coalition as a supplement to current trade association and Company efforts. It is not intended to replace or usurp current responsibilities.*

*Our proposed organization approach is to form an independent coalition, but primarily work through the Foundation for Biomedical Research (FBR), a nonprofit public education group which has been support-*

ing the use of animals for medical research and product safety testing for many years. They are highly experienced with this issue and well-regarded for their effectiveness, as is their Federal legislative lobbying sister organization, the National Association for Biomedical Research (NABR). A fact-sheet on these organizations is provided in Exhibit II, and we have additional materials available. We would coordinate public education and legislative efforts closely with CTFA, SDA and other trade associations....

The Coalition would be directed by an Executive Committee. This group would also serve as the Product Safety Advisory Committee for FBR to provide direction for programs. In addition, the Coalition would be represented on the Board of Directors and Executive Board of FBR. Prior to the initial meeting, we plan to establish a small organizing committee to work logistics. Further details of governance would be addressed by the organizing committee following the initial meeting...

We have developed a prototype three-year educational and legislative plan (see Exhibit III). Key elements include a broad-based public relations and advertising program, legislative education and lobbying efforts focused on key states and development of a school education program. Our initial cost estimate is roughly $5MM per year, with an additional $2.5MM start-up expenses in Year I to develop materials, etc....

We have drafted a sample invitation letter, which is also attached. In addition to the CEO, we suggest a senior Public Affairs and technical representative from each Company be invited. Further, we suggest Mr. Smale consider issuing the invitation jointly with at least one other CEO.

We would welcome Mr. Smale's input on the mission statement, proposed membership and any expectations he may have on how this organization will *operate. In addition, we would appreciate Mr. Smale's selection of a meeting date (no later than mid-July) and location (we recommend New York), so we can proceed with arrangements. We look forward to moving ahead quickly with this vital organization.*

*C.R. Otto*

Procter & Gamble proposes the coalition mission: "sustain a public and legislative environment which supports the judicious use of animal testing as a necessary part of a corporation's responsibility to manufacture and market safe and effective products." In the plan, they propose a national public relations program, directions for influencing legislation (including coordination of activities with other industrial parties; e.g., trade associations, lobbyists), and a forum for sharing learning about activists' activities. The proposed membership includes eleven additional corporations.

The coalition education and legislative plan lists a third objective: "Block attempts to legislate prohibitions on product safety testing using animals." A budget for the first year is estimated at $7.5 million, with $5 million for each of the following two years.

This coalition of corporations proposes to work with two existing nonprofit, tax-exempt public foundations: the Foundation for Biomedical Research (FBR) and the National Association for Biomedical Research (NABR). The FBR has concentrated on "responsible animal research in the development of treatments and cures of diseases." Procter & Gamble proposed that the group expand its mission to include product safety testing and profit from its reputation as lobbyist: "They are highly experienced with this issue and well regarded for their effectiveness." Procter & Gamble uses animals to test household products, not in cancer or diabetes research.

They plan to buy the reputation of the Foundation for Biomedical Research as a cover for their more mundane use of animal testing and they propose the FBR change its mission.

The mission of the other foundation (NABR) is "to activate and represent member institutions in national policy-making which affects the use of animals in research, education, and product safety testing." Both foundation have been longtime opponents of animal rights groups. The circle is now complete: The animal rights groups have aroused powerful opposition from several federal government agencies, multinational corporations, and the American Medical Association, and each has developed its plan of action to contend with this grass roots movement. Strategies and goals for plans among the three opponents are strikingly similar, and

---

Dear Mr. Artzt:

I am appalled that Procter & Gamble continues to use animals for needless product tests while other companies have abandoned such cruel and inhumane practices. Perpetuating the animals suffering is more than bad science, it's bad business. Until you join the growing ranks of "cruelty-free" companies and support, rather than fight legislation that would end the horrors of the LD50 and Draize tests, I shall boycott your products.

Sincerely,

Name _____

Address _____

City, State, Zip _____

*Please Place 15¢ Stamp Here*

TO:
**Edwin Artzt, CEO**
**Procter & Gamble, Inc.**
**P.O. Box 599**
**Cincinnati, OH**
**45201**

each plans to reach out to the other. Also, each is well financed and has powerful members, staff, and resources.

**The Corporate Plan Is Tested**  During 1990, Procter & Gamble was confronted by In Defense of Animals, a group that launched a boycott against P&G when it learned of the coalition's $17.5 million plan. Members of In Defense of Animals (IDA) sent the postcard opposite to Edwin Artzt, Procter & Gamble's chief executive officer.

Postcard senders received a reply from P&G to counter "their blatant lies and misrepresentations." Excerpts from the P&G letter explain the company's position on animal testing and question the legitimacy of In Defense of Animals. (The complete letter is contained in Appendix D.)

*THE*
*PROCTER & GAMBLE*
*COMPANY*

*GEOFFREY PLACE*  *P.O. BOX 599*
*VICE PRESIDENT–RESEARCH*  *CINCINNATI. OHIO 45201-0599*
*AND DEVELOPMENT*

*May 1990*

*Mrs. Jack Earle*
*P.O. Box 18114*
*S. Lake Tahoe, CA 95706*

*Dear Mrs. Earle:*

*Our Chairman and Chief Executive, Ed Artzt, received your postcard, sent at the request of In Defense of Ani-*

*mals, and he has asked me to response to you. We are gravely concerned about their blatant lies and misrepresentations of Procter & Gamble.*

*Our Company remains committed—as it has been for years—to reducing animal use. We have made significant progress in this area. Over the past five years, P&G's use of animals for personal care and household product safety testing is down over 80% worldwide.*

*Further, we are committed to eliminating animal research wherever science allows, through the development of alternate test methodologies. For the three year period 1986–89, we spent over $10 million developing alternatives. In March, we announced the first recipients of grants from the University Animal Alternatives Research Program we sponsor. When the program reaches full operation in two years, this will represent $450,000 in new additional funds annually for in vitro research.*

*Beyond this, let me share some other facts that In Defense of Animals' letter neglected to mention:*

> *—Promising developments are continuing to unfold in the relatively new field of alternative test methodologies. But, new methods aren't all that's needed—the methods must be validated as predictive and useful, and then they must be accepted by the scientific, government and regulatory community alike.*
>
> *P&G has been a leader in all of these arenas. Since 1987, P&G has published or presented over 70 papers on alternatives, helping to advance scientific and regulatory acceptance of alternative methods. Also, we have met with regulatory agencies to discuss acceptance of these new methods. P&G no longer uses the Draize or LD50 tests. Instead, we use alternatives developed by P&G which use fewer animals and are less distressful....*

*We're glad to know you care about animal welfare. To be certain that your funds are directed toward truly helping animals, check with the Council of Better Business Bureaus' Philanthropic Advisory Service. This clearinghouse exists only to help prospective donors learn more about philanthropic programs, fundraising and finances. To date, In Defense of Animals has refused to provide information to this service. Perhaps In Defense of Animals is embarrassed to reveal how your funds are being used. To the best of our knowledge, none of it has gone for direct aid to animals.*

*We hope this helps you to better understand the real situation. P&G is very committed to further progress and results. If you want more information on this important issue, please contact us.*

Sincerely,

Geoffrey Place
Vice President
Research and Development

*11u2368/5–6*

The founder of In Defense of Animals, Elliot Katz, a veterinarian, responded to the letter by urging others to join his grass roots group's campaign: "This past year, with the help of thousands of people like yourself, IDA has been protesting P&G's cruelty with demonstrations and direct actions in hundreds of cities across the country.... And we have initiated a boycott of P&G products. Deciding to boycott a multibillion dollar corporation like P&G was not an easy decision. We knew of their power to discredit and hurt us, but earlier attempts for change, like pleas of physicians and shareholder resolutions, had proven useless.... And so I ask you to act today." The complete text of his letter is in Appendix E.

The action Katz requested was to send a second

postcard to P&G. Thousands responded. The card counters:

---

Dear Mr. Artzt:

Your rhetoric and poison-pen letters directed at In Defense of Animals will simply not work.

**I WANT HONEST ANSWERS!**

Why did your company oppose a shareholders' resolution that would have made available the kinds and numbers of animals used per year in your product testing? I want to know how many animals are blinded, burned, poisoned and killed each year in your laboratories, including those harmed and killed in outside contract labs.

Why did your company wage a campaign to defeat California Bill AB 2461, a bill that would have banned the use of the outdated Draize test (a test P&G supposedly no longer uses)? Will your company oppose the bill when it is reintroduced again this year?

Until you answer these questions and join the ranks of other major corporations that have stopped harming and killing animals in their product testing, I will continue to urge my friends and associates to join me in boycotting your company.

In the past, I thought of P&G as standing for purity and progressiveness. Now I equate the letters P&G with pain and greed.

I look forward to hearing from you.

Name

Address

City/State/Zip

---

In Defense of Animals led a demonstration at the October 1990 shareholders' meeting of P&G in Cincinnati and organized hundreds of other demonstrations at P&G sites nationwide. Their purpose was to call attention to animal testing of household and personal care products. Prior to the demonstration, P&G developed an elaborate plan to counter the demonstrations, but their confidential, for internal-use-only plans were leaked to members of animal rights groups, a frequent action by sympathizers within the organization. (Grass roots leaders have been extremely successful in learning about the opposition's tactics from personnel within the organizations. These leaks create distrust and cause costly reactions.) Procter & Gamble's plan to cope with the animal rights protests in October 1990 included the development of a P&G public statement, a list of questions and answers for P&G personnel to use with the media, a plan for how to deal with the media, and a company brochure, "Human Health and Safety Assurance."

In dealing with the media, personnel were advised to "stick to the scripted statement,": "You are not obligated to respond to a question just because someone asks it....Avoid specific mention of demonstrators....Avoid bashing demonstrators...Do not refer to their campaigns or efforts in any way that could be construed as derogatory...Bashing reduces our [P&G's] credibility and has potential to create a backlash." The complete documents are in Appendix F.

In Defense of Animals selected Procter & Gamble to receive the IDA 1st Annual Corporate Hypocrisy Award in November 1990 "for their contradictory attitude toward animal testing, for their lobbying efforts to kill the California bill that would have banned the Draize test, their refusal to back up rhetoric that they have reduced animal use, and their attempts to initiate a $17.5 million program to scare the public into accepting animal testing and to block animal protection legislation."[4]

Over the coming years, the conflicts between these groups on opposing sides of the use of animals in research will be fought not only in he media, but also in

Congress, boardrooms, and the community. Animal rights groups will continue to boycott products that have been tested on animals or that are made from animals. They will write letters, be present at shareholder meetings, use nonviolent civil disobedience, lobby, and use a host of other grass roots tactics. If they continue to grow in membership and effectively counter the broad opposition planned and presented in this account of their three opponents, the struggle promises to be lively. If their tactics include direct violence, their opponents will make a strong public case against them. Both sides will vie for public approval and condemnation of the other.

### Hazardous Waste Disposal: Curing Garbage Headaches and Creating New Ones for Grass Roots Groups

Dealing with hazardous waste has sparked controversy in thousands of communities across America. No other issue has mobilized more local grass roots groups and consumed more time, money, and other resources of businesses than waste disposal. In classic struggles, public and private waste disposal groups take on opponents who battle to keep their communities, families, and homes safe from toxic waste. "It's got to go somewhere" comes up against "Not in My Backyard!" The local grass roots groups call for waste reduction, recycling, and eliminating the use of toxins. They believe that industrial pollution should be handled at the production site. The Citizen's Clearinghouse for Hazardous Wastes (CCHW) leads a national grass roots environmental justice campaign that calls on industry and government to:

• Reduce the amount of waste that is created.

- Change production methods to eliminate waste that cannot be handled safely.
- Recycle or reuse remaining waste.
- Destroy, in safe ways, wastes that cannot be eliminated or recycled.
- Permanently clean up existing sites—using safe technologies.
- Employ pollution prevention practices within industry and government.

The Citizen's Clearinghouse for Hazardous Wastes was formed in 1981 by Lois Marie Gibbs, the Love Canal activist-mother, to assist grass roots groups in their efforts to end land disposal and unsafe incineration of hazardous wastes. The Clearinghouse recommends to local groups a host of tactics ranging from traditional social action to nonviolent civil disobedience. Barry Commoner says these local grass roots groups take the "hard path":

> The frontline of the battle against chemical pollution is not in Washington but in their own communities. For them, the issues are clear cut. In these battles, there is little room for compromise; the corporations are on one side and the people of the community are on the other, challenging the corporations' exclusive power to make decisions that threaten the community's health.[5]

The conflict between these opposing factions is often highly visible and spirited. Opposition tactics of corporations and government agencies against environmentally focused grass roots groups include adverse labeling, public relations, litigation and infiltration, and the creation of counter groups.

In a CCHW handbook entitled "The Polluters' Secret Plan," the CCHW staff writer, Will Collette, says, "I'm not trying to make you feel paranoid by reciting this litany of measures industry and government undertake to advance their goals and win. The point is: don't be näive. In these struggles, there's a Golden Rule. Whatever you do, they can do too. Even though they have more money to do it with, they probably won't be able to do it as well as you do. Why? First of all, because you are right and they're not. Second, they're hired guns, doing what they've been paid to do. In contrast, your main motivation is the passionate defense of your family and home.[6]

## Opposition Tactics

### Adverse Labeling and Waste Site Selection

In the mid-1980s, the media began to report on a term coined by industry to describe community grass roots groups that opposed hazardous waste disposal in their communities. NIMBY ("not in my backyard") was coined to frame the image of these groups. By resisting the waste disposal plan, these grass roots groups are said to display selfish, unrealistic attitudes. Members are labeled emotional, hysterical, antiscience, and antijob. The aim is to make the members appear unpatriotic and concerned only with property values—putting their own personal interests above the greater good of society. Members of some other grass roots movements also recieve similar negative labels, especially animal rights and radical environmentalists.

Since opposition is growing in communities across the nation against building hazardous waste facilities, industry and government planners target those areas least likely or able to resist. These vulnerable communities are usually rural, open to promises of economic benefit, low in income, high in minority population, and located in the South, Southwest, and Midwest. Finding a location for hazardous waste that requires transporting the toxic materials across state lines is becoming more difficult each year. Several Southern states have passed legislation prohibiting the acceptance of other states' hazardous waste. Alabama, the site of the nation's largest hazardous waste facility (Emmelle) and a target state for additional sites, passed legislation in 1989 to block further acceptance of such waste from other states.

### Public Relations

The author of "Polluters' Secret Plan" describes a public relations plan developed by Fanfare Communications, a group advising the city of Boston on how to sell its sludge disposal plan: "(a) support mainstream environmental groups who are raising public awareness of the problems with Boston Harbor, since this would soften up the public to the plan; (b) sell the concept that it's everybody's problem and everybody's fault; (c) it's in the public interest to go for a quick solution, even if it's a hard sacrifice for somebody; and (d) use sports stars from the Red Sox, Celtics, and Bruins to sell the plan to blue-collar Boston, because if you win them over, they can help the city literally steam roller the opposition."[7] The sludge disposal plan is being implemented in Boston.

The use of carefully selected euphemisms is a popular public relations tactic: "resource recovery" instead of "incineration," "sanitary landfill" instead of "dump," and "solid waste integrated management" to describe a plan to build an incinerator and expand local landfills to accept the ash and unburned waste.

Risk assessment and acceptable risk are two terms frequently used by firms and government agencies to gain support for their plan. A risk assessment expert may say that the presence of part of a toxic substance will only cause one additional cancer death per million. These terms mean little to most citizens, but the goal is to reassure citizens that exposure to toxins is minimal.

Nelson V. Mossholder, vice president of GSX Chemical Services sums it up: "There is a profound lack of understanding in our society of the level of risk associated with our everyday lives. So the community demands a zero risk standard for chemical waste management and all other activities they fear. This standard is reflected in NIMBY situations by the community's refusal to accept sites, technologies, as well as companies because they are less than perfect... There are no easy solutions to the NIMBY problem. It is clear, however, that there are no perfect sites, no perfect technologies, and no perfect companies. Since the public's expectations cannot be met, we must do our best to change their expectations so that they become more realistic. This will require a substantial, grass roots educational effort."[8]

Waste management companies expend large sums of money to convince political leaders and their constituents that their fears are unfounded. Most public relations efforts are made at specific community sites to soften local public resistance rather than through national campaigns.

## Marketing Ecology

Preceding and following Earth Day 1990, big manufacturers began courting environmental groups with offers of money to link their products with ecology. This marketing strategy attempts to convince the public that buying specific products is tantamount to being environmentally conscious. In 1990, the Coca-Cola Company launched an aggressive campaign with one of its products, Minute Maid juices, in conjunction with the National Parks and Conservation Association. For each carton purchased, the campaign provided a match of 75 cents to help pay for planting trees in Redwood National Park in California.

Caution is advised by such groups as Friends of the Earth and the Sierra Club. In an article appearing in the *New York Times*, Rosemary Carroll, director of development for the Sierra Club in San Francisco, said: "There is a lot of schlock out there right now. We've been approached by manufacturers of tampons, toilet paper, and automotive parts, and we are not in the position to evaluate whether they are environmentally sensitive or not." Others feel credibility with the consumer will be lost if everything in the marketplace has the imprimatur of an environmental group.

### Promises

As organized local resistance grows, enticements are used in campaigns to win over those protesting the disposal plan or to neutralize opponents. The best available technology, recycling as part of the plan, limits on landfill use or air pollution, and, especially, more jobs are promised. In 1989, most state officials opposed a site within their borders for storage of nuclear waste produced at U.S. Department of Energy-operated nuclear energy sites. In order to convince governors to agree to having disposal sites in their states, economic enticements were used as a last resort. Few governors wish to counter public opinion solidly against the location of nuclear waste, and only a few were swayed by economic baits.[9]

Public relations firms are discovering the difficulty of finding ways to counter local opposition, partly because the failure of the Superfund to clean up contaminated sites has added to the woes of hazardous waste management companies. Each scandal or failure at a hazardous waste or nuclear facility exacerbates the problem.

### SLAPP and SLAPP Back

In order to muzzle public protest and disarm citizen participation, some public and private operators are filing lawsuits against grass roots individuals or groups. These lawsuits are called Strategic Lawsuits Against Public Participation (SLAPP) a term coined by University of Colorado law professor George Pring. These suits are brought to name a private individual or group as the defendant, accuse that individual or group of libel and slander, insure that the suit is known to the public, and intimidate the defendants with threats of financial retaliation.

The Citizen's Clearinghouse for Hazardous Wastes keeps a record of these suits.[10] They report the following, among numerous others:

- In Pearland, Texas, the operator of several toxic sites sued a grass roots leader for libel. The charge: the grass roots leader had called his "sanitary landfill" a "dump."
- In Culver, Indiana, leaders of a grass roots group named STOP were sued for slander and causing the business to lose revenue. The business is a hazardous waste site.
- In Warren County, New York, county supervisors individually sued 328 grass roots leaders for $1.5 million each for actions to stop the sale of municipal bonds for the construction of a garbage incinerator.

Intimidation tactics such as SLAPP focus on citizens' fears of financial loss and public humiliation. Ordinary people in grass roots movements fear these lawsuits because their own resources, jobs, public standing, and personal welfare are placed in jeopardy. The Citizen's Clearinghouse reports that few of these libel and slander suits against individuals or groups have been won—most are dismissed. The Clearinghouse recommends "SLAPP-back," a countersuit to protect the right to free speech and to participate in the democratic process. The Clearinghouse staff has developed a workshop entitled "How to Deal with Trouble" to assist local grass roots leaders in coping with these threats. They provide advice on systematic responses to the lawsuit.

## Infiltration

Earth First!, People for the Ethical Treatment of Animals, Operation Rescue, In Defense of Animals, ACT UP, Rainforest Action Network, and some grass roots groups that oppose hazardous waste sites and dangerous toxic polluters fear infiltration. These groups believe that opponents intentionally join their organizations or tempt members to their viewpoint in order to create problems within the organization. The actions they report or suspect range from simple intelligence gathering to plants who encourage provocative acts that discredit the group.

For those groups that employ surprise civil disobedience tactics such as disabling a logging operation, shutting down an abortion clinic, guerrilla theater to embarrass a corporation, a raid on an animal research laboratory, the possibility of infiltration is not unlikely. The need for surprise requires secrecy. Dirty tricks campaigns to discredit are used extensively in political campaigns and, to employ them effectively, opponents seek to learn about the group they target. The more direct-action, violent tactics a grass roots group considers or uses, the more likely their ranks will be infiltrated. However, little specific evidence has been found to substantiate widespread covert infiltration with the intent to harm individuals in a particular group.

Two militant grass roots groups, Earth First! and the Animal Liberation Front, are being investigated by the FBI for the increase in sabotage and vandalism on remote western ranches. "Richard Whitaker of the FBI office in Las Vegas warned the annual Nevada Cattleman's Association ... that recent attacks on remote ranches are believed to be the work of the same people suspected of torching meat plants and bombing offices in California and Nevada," according to a front page article in the *Los Angeles Times* dated November 19, 1989. Admissions to these violent acts are also printed with statements from members of the ALF and Earth First!

"We are trying to eliminate the livestock industry. We do not believe in eating animals," said the person from ALF. In a telephone statement from Earth First!, the caller said, "We believe the grazing of livestock has a devastating effect on the flora and fauna. Our position concerns the health of the wild."

The FBI and other law enforcement agencies have increased surveillance of the remote ranches and the activities of these two groups in "an effort to end the attacks on beef and wool growing ranchers."[11]

However, keeping tabs on grass roots groups is a common practice by corporations and government agencies. In the account that opened this chapter, each of the three groups opposed to the animal rights movement proposed plans to gather intelligence on these groups, as shown in the following excerpts:

The American Medical Association plans to promote formation of special investigative units within government to examine animal rights activities"; and aims at "building private database on animal rights activities."

The National Institute of Mental Health states: "a proactive stance should include a vigorous focus on the fundamental philosophical underpinning of the animal rights movement... This could be highlighted by some of the more outrageous quotes of Elizabeth Newkirk and Alex Pacheco [PETA leaders] that dramatize how the movement's philosophy is based on degradation of the concept of human nature."

Procter & Gamble plans to "provide a forum for sharing learnings about activist activities."

Private firms are employed as clients of large corporations to observe, monitor, and assess activities of some grass roots groups. In a few firms, undercover staff infiltrate the movement, but most study newsletters and publications to learn trends and practices of a group. Their specific objective is to help the targeted corporation neutralize the group. "What's amazing about private surveillance is that there's no legal protection against it," according to David Kairys, a student of this subject.

"International Barometer," a newsletter published in Washington, D.C., since 1985, "report on activist movements, personalities, and issues, with a particular emphasis on how they affect business. It covers campaigns by consumers, environmental, church, and other organizations that directly pressure business, and those that seek changes in public policy of importance to business... in order to facilitate dialogue between business and activists." This publication examines worldwide issues and has featured articles on the Rainforest Action Network, animal rights organizations, Nuclear Free America, and opponents of toxic waste disposal in landfills and by incineration. The publishers are currently compiling a series of "Profiles in Activism"—about those individuals who are the influential leaders of the activist community supporting issues designed to promote social, economic, and/or political change."

Pagan International, a Washington-based public relations firm, publishes the "International Barometer" in addition to developing dossiers for corporations on activist groups such as Greenpeace. The Citizen's Clearinghouse for Hazardous Wastes alerts its members to Pagan International in "Action Bulletin No. 24": "Another firm, Pagan International, noted for its soldier of fortune approach to union-busting, does active espionage on groups opposing corporate practices, like a recent spy mission for Shell Oil Company on church groups leading an international antiapartheid boycott."

Pagan International prepared a secret plan, the Neptune Strategy, to assist the Shell Oil Company to undercut the antiapartheid boycott of its products led by a religious group, the Interfaith Center on Corporate Responsibility. These documents and others pertaining to Pagan International are available at the San Francisco-based Center for Investigative Reporting.

Any grass roots group can expect to have its activities monitored by those it opposes. Likewise, many grass roots have been successful in obtaining confidential documents and plans from groups they confront. Infiltration and intelligence gathering can and does work both ways.

## Creating a Counter Group

In the early 1980s, when the parent group movement was visible and effective in calling attention to the problems of drug use and abuse among young people, a parents' counter group called MAMA, Mothers Against Marijuana Abuse, was formed in Oregon. One of their goals was diametrically opposed to most parent groups: They pushed for "responsible use" of marijuana, a position that was anathema to the National Federation of Parents for Drug Free Youth. Some members of MAMA were marijuana growers in Oregon, a state which at that time had liberal laws regarding personal marijuana use. Their goal was to weaken the message of traditional parent groups and to confuse the public. With tongue in cheek, MAMA tried to trivialize the issue and ridicule the strong stand taken by some parent groups against any marijuana use.

Those communities in which struggles rage over siting of a hazardous waste program often face opposing citizen groups. The Citizen's Clearinghouse for Hazardous Wastes identifies some of these local groups in "The Polluters' Secret Plan." They suggest that some of these groups are industry-sponsored. Whenever a hazardous waste issue appears on a ballot for vote by the citizens, opposing groups attempt to gain vote approval.

### Tokens, Pilots, and Other Diversions

When industry and government are under attack from grass roots groups, one reaction is to set up a pilot program to test an approach that may lead to an acceptable solution. Two examples of this strategy follow.

*Archie McPuff:*   When the Citizen's Clearinghouse for Hazardous Wastes (CCHW) launched its McToxics campaign to "send-it-back" to McDonald's, the environmental vice president for the McDonald's Corporation, Shelby Yastrow, developed a plan in May 1989. According to an article in the CCHW "Action Bulletin No. 22," Yastrow says, "It [Styrofoam] is one of the most recyclable products there is. . . . It's the most harmless thing in the world to incinerate at the right temperature. I'd like to buy an incinerator for every McDonald's restaurant in the country." CCHW charges that, starting in the Chicago area, McDonald's received a permit from the Illinois Environmental Protection Agency to install "Archie McPuff" incinerators for use in Yorkville and Woodridge. They are designed to burn the Styrofoam directly at the restaurant. With the passage of ordinances in more and more localities that ban plastic and Styrofoam packaging, businesses using those products are seeking ways to cope with grass roots opposition, and the practice of burning Styrofoam in a community is being challenged by the CCHW and their affiliated groups. McDonald's claims the incinerators are "no more toxic than the average backyard barbecue," according to the CCHW "Action Bulletin No. 22."[13]

In an article in the August 1990 issue of CCHW's new publication, *Everyone's Backyard*, CCHW staffers report on the latest round in the Archie McPuff fight. McDonald's abandoned its plan to dispose of styrofoam by burning the toxic waste in incinerators behind their fast-food outlets. The new campaign, dubbed the McRecycle Program, commits McDonald's to buying $100 million in construction materials made from recycled materials. At local restaurants, customers are urged to place their foam food boxes and cups into the restaurant's recycling bins. The polystyrene will be rendered into small plastic pellets for recycling.

"There's no taking away from the achievements of the McToxics campaign. It's forced McDonald's to spend a fortune to clean up its image, if not its act. Its concrete concessions are a certain victory for the grass roots movement, but also McDs efforts to blunt criticism. The other advances, such as institutional bans and local plastic bans, are added bonuses."[14]

When the McRecycle program was launched in northern California in the spring of 1990, advocates from the California Public Interest Group rallied at a McDonald's site to protest the program. They urged using paper packaging rather than recycling polystyrene. They also pointed out that, nationally, about half of all the food in foam containers sold at McDonald's that have drive-through window service will probably not be returned by customers for recycling.

The CCHW article made another important point: "McDonald's, in alliance with the plastic industry, had undertaken a multimillion-dollar defense plan. In a nutshell, that strategy was to redefine the debate by focusing on end of the production line solutions rather than the key community demand of waste reduction."[15]

The campaign against McDonald's use of styrofoam was joined by the Environmental Defense Fund (EDF). In a rare alliance, EDF and the McDonald's Corporation formed a joint task force to identify new ways to reduce the trash generated by the more than 11,000 McDonald's restaurants worldwide. The decision to cooperate was initiated in 1989 when McDonald's approached EDF for help with its solid waste problems.

At a press conference held on November 2, 1990, a major grass roots victory was declared. Even though McDonald's declared to the end that its foam packaging was safe and environmentally sound, its U.S. president, Ed Rensi, said, "Our customers just don't feel good about it, so we're changing."

The alliance of EDF and McDonald's was an uneasy one. Up until the last week before the final announcement, McDonald's had planned to continue its recycling plan. Upon learning of McDonald's continued resistance to switching from Styrofoam to paper packaging, EDF warned the corporation that it was prepared to oppose the recycling program publicly. McDonald's then acquiesced. A November 2, 1990, *New York Times* article described the victory for grass roots groups in the following accounts: "McDonald's has gone far beyond being a mere seller of hamburgers—it is a national institution. So the last thing it needs is to have schoolchildren be told it is an evil force, damaging society. If it appeared to be

putting profit over the environment by stubbornly stay-
ing with a material widely regarded as detrimental to the
environment, the company risked alienating many of the
same young customers who avoided buying tuna caught
by methods that kill dolphins."[16]

The EDF's decision to work with McDonald's concerned grass roots groups such as CCHW. In an October
1990 editorial, CCHW said, "EDF consulted with no
group, national or local, on the frontline of the war
against fast-food waste." But two important lessons for
grass roots groups are worth noting. First, boycotts and
other tactics that focus on the public image of the
corporation appear to work, and, second, coalitions,
even unintentional ones, can combine the power of local
grass roots opposition and a nationally recognized organization to work for a common end.

### Cloth vs. Disposable Diapers

"We want to convince parents to give up the use of
disposable diapers, except when they're absolutely necessary—like when camping or traveling," said Lisa Waugh,
the chairperson of a grass roots group called Concerned
Citizens for Cloth Diapers. This group was founded in
May 1988 in Boulder, Colorado, in response to a growing
concern over what to do about the 16 to 18 million plastic
disposable diapers used per year, which the group dubs
as "really not disposable at all. They hang around for
hundreds of years, long after the child has lived to old
age and died."[17]

In 1988, in the United States, the billions of throwaway
diapers created 3.7 million tons of garbage, or 2 percent
of solid waste that cities must dispose of. The problem is
not only placing nonbiodegradable plastic in landfills;
health risks also cause concern. Although instructions
on disposable diaper boxes encourage the user to empty

the contents of the dirty diaper into the toilet before throwing it away, most parents do not. Most cities ban disposal of raw sewage in landfills but routinely ignore the laws when soiled diapers are dumped. The diapers carry a host of disease-causing microbes. Carl Lehrburger of Energy Answers Corporation in Albany, New York, reports that fecal matter from babies is especially dangerous since babies are effective carriers of viruses and are usually immunized with live vaccines such as the polio virus.[18]

According to the Environmental Protection Agency, 80 percent of all garbage is put in landfills and nearly one-third of the country's landfills will reach capacity by 1994. Cities are facing a crisis in solid waste disposal and health concerns for those who work with this contaminated waste.

Disposable diaper manufacturers have taken this industry from $90 million in 1969 to $3.3 billion in 1988. About 80 percent of all disposable diapers are sold by Kimberly-Clark and Procter & Gamble. These two companies will lose financially if grass roots groups succeed in reversing consumer preference for the plastic product because convenience—to parents, day-care centers, and hospitals—is a big factor in promoting large sales of disposable diapers on the market. Within three months the Boulder, Colorado, grass roots group succeeded in getting a large local community hospital to switch from disposable to cloth diapers in its nurseries, and several local child care facilities are making the shift as well.

Concerned Citizens for Cloth Diapers' next action is to push for several pieces of legislation at the state and local levels in Colorado: a product disposal charge on each package, landfill bans on disposable diapers, and positive incentives for recycling and using cloth diapers. Some states and communities have already passed or are considering similar legislation. Nebraska legislatures have banned the sale of nonbiodegradable diapers by 1993, and their counterparts in Iowa, Washington, and Oregon have considered similar laws. Not all proposed legislation has passed. In 1989, Washington state legislators defeated a bill that would have required diaper packages to carry this label: "Soiled diapers contain viruses and microbes which may transmit diseases to the general population when disposed of improperly. Fibrous material must not be disposed with garbage or trash."

Diaper laundry services cost an average of $10.50 a week, compared to $13 to $14 a week to purchase disposable diapers. The Lehrburger study, "Diapers in the Waste Stream," estimates that cotton diapers cost about 15 cents each from a delivery service compared to 22 cents for each disposable diaper. Babies require 6,000 to 10,000 diaper changes over a three-year period. The National Association of Cloth Diapers reports that delivery service increased from 15 to 20 percent during 1989.[19]

## The Corporate Response

In June 1989, *NBC Nightly News* aired a segment that discussed the three issues pertaining to disposable diapers—the landfill crisis, possible health risks, and other dangers to the environment. In this national news broadcast that reaches millions of viewers, questions were raised by environmentalists, legislators, and concerned citizens about long-term problems caused by the product. The possibility of legislative action has stirred the manufacturers. Within a week, a spokesperson for Procter & Gamble (makers of Luvs and Pampers, with $1.6 billion in sales) said, "We believe as a company it is our responsibility to insure that our products are good not only for the baby but that they are good for the environment and can be easily recycled, decomposed, and incinerated."[20] Procter & Gamble announced a pilot recycling program in Seattle, Washington, that would recycle used disposable diapers into garbage bags, building insulation, park benches, flower pots, computer paper, and cardboard products. In Seattle, the Solid Waste Utility and Rabanco Company will collect used disposable diapers from one thousand volunteer households. The company will sanitize the reusable plastic lining as well as the paper pulp from the padding and transform it into recycled products. In St. Cloud, Minnesota, Procter & Gamble will provide money and soiled diapers to Recomp Inc. to transform the waste into humus, a form of soil that can be used as fertilizer.[21]

"In defense of their industry, Procter & Gamble and other manufacturers cite studies indicating that the use of cloth diapers requires three times the energy and may cause nine times the air pollution because cloth must be laundered and oftentimes delivered."[22] Environmentalists counter by citing studies that demonstrate the extent of the problem of disposable diapers on landfill, as well as potential public health hazards.

Naming disposable diapers the biggest consumer waste item after newspapers and drink containers, the Environmental Defense Fund calls for long-term solutions rather than this stopgap measure. Others doubt the economic feasibility of these recycling efforts. Carl Lehrburger is quoted as saying, "I applaud their efforts in seeking alternatives to the environmentally harmful disposal of their products. He added that Procter & Gamble seems determined to maintain its product rather than change its disposable diaper. Barry Commoner and other environmentalists point out that "the primary issues are excessive and wasteful practices and the best approach is waste reduction."[23]

In March 1990, a bill was introduced in the California

legislature that would require manufacturers of disposable diapers to warn consumers that the diapers are contributing to the nation's garbage crisis. Under this measure, all packages of disposable diapers would have to carry environmental warning labels stating: "Single-use disposable diapers pose significant environmental problems and costs when disposed. The State of California recommends that you consider reusable diapers for your daily diaper needs." Strong opposition greeted this bill. Bills that would ban, restrict, or tax sales of disposable diapers are before lawmakers in at least eight other states. The only state to enact legislation has been Nebraska, which requires the use of biodegradable disposable diapers by 1993.

For those in grass roots groups advocating a return to the cloth diaper as the only environmentally sound option, the recycling plan misses the point. The groups want the use of the disposable diaper discontinued. The industry, on the other hand, believes that disposable diaper sales can be maintained because customers feel the product offers benefits, primarily convenience. Once again, grass roots groups are bucking corporations with ample resources that greet the controversy with token pilot projects.

### The Bureaucratic Response or Lack of It

Some grass roots action is taken because government agencies entrusted with the responsibility to regulate and monitor fail to do so or because they withhold critical information.

When attacked by groups for perceived wrongs or shortcomings, bureaucracies respond in different ways. Their leaders may deny the charge, blame the failure on a lack of clear legislative or administrative mandate, say it's another agency's task, claim they have inadequate budget and staff, or seek support for opposition tactics from groups and companies in the private sector. More than anything else, bureaucracies want to remain invisible, hoping those accusing them will go away or self-destruct, and they can silently slip away from the glare of negative publicity.

Mothers and Others for Pesticide Limits began because parents believed that two federal agencies had failed. The Environmental Protection Agency, charged by law with establishing safe limits for pesticides in food, and the Food and Drug Administration, charged with monitoring food to detect pesticide residues and enforcing the limits established by the EPA, were specifically accused of failing to protect children from pesticides in the food they consume. Mothers and Others for Pesticide Limits say:

- The EPA did not take children's eating patterns into account when it set virtually all the current limits for pesticides in food.
- Because the EPA underestimates children's consumption of most foods, pesticide exposure levels in children's food that our government claims are legal can greatly exceed safe levels.
- Adequate testing hasn't been done on the health effects of many pesticides.
- Even pesticides that are known to be hazardous are allowed to stay on the market while under special EPA review.
- The EPA allows significant levels of cancer-causing pesticides in food.
- The EPA's methods for setting legal limits for pesticide residues for food don't adequately protect children.

- In enforcing legal restrictions on pesticide residues, the EPA food sampling program is extremely limited.
- The tests used by the FDA for analyzing pesticide residue levels are too limited.
- The FDA monitoring program is plagued with delays and doesn't serve as an effective deterrent.

These charges are brought in a book, *For Our Kids Sake*, published by Mothers and Others for Pesticide Limits in 1989.[24] One of the book's primary messages and an overriding concern of parents is that these two large bureaucratic agencies have failed. Also concerned about the produce parents buy, the authors point out: "As a consumer, you can exercise your power in the marketplace and work to get your supermarket to stock pesticide-free produce."

When five small U.S. and Canadian supermarket chains pledged to stop selling fresh fruit and vegetables treated with cancer-causing pesticides by 1995, reaction was swift from the EPA, large supermarket chains, and the Food Marketing Institute. The September 12, 1989, issue of the *Washington Post* reported responses from these groups. An assistant administrator from the EPA said," We are concerned that the campaign could cause confusion for consumers and unnecessary economic hardship for both consumers and American farmers." Representatives of the nation's largest supermarkets denounced the campaign as an unwarranted and irresponsible attack launched by "misguided zealots" in consumer groups. A spokesperson from the Food Marketing Institute accused campaign organizers of using "scare tactics" and "blackmailing" supermarkets to join their movement or face consumer boycotts.[25]

Opposition tactics include adverse labeling, bureaucratic delay, discrediting the movement, shifting the blame, and collusion between federal agencies and private groups.

## Withholding Crucial Information

"Federal records show that the government knew as early as 1948 that radiation releases from its Hanford nuclear weapons plant posed a serious risk to human health, yet it rejected secret advice to tell workers they were in danger."[26] Information about exposure to radiation was obtained by the Hanford Education Action League when it filed a request under the Freedom of Information Act. The release of the report marked the first time the government has publicly acknowledged that radioactive releases from its nuclear arms factories could have harmed human health. Yet, the government was made aware shortly after the Hanford plant began operating in 1944 that airborne contaminants pose a serious health problem.[27]

Records shows that experts warned the Atomic Energy Commission (AEC) of this condition as early as 1948, but their recommendation to inform workers of the radiation danger was rejected by the AEC. This inaction may have endangered the health and lives of thousands of workers and residents of areas surrounding the Hanford nuclear reservation. Currently, the U.S. Department of Energy is conducting a five-year study on the amount of radiation absorbed by the exposed population and the concomitant dangers. Without the dogged determination of the Hanford Education Action League and the Hanford Downwinder Coalition, this dark secret would have remained locked in the bureaucracy's voluminous files. Tom Bailie, a farmer and member of a grass roots group, describes the anguish: "There is a fine line of morality that none of us can cross and still claim membership in the human race. The government's nuclear gang deliberately crossed it. The price we had to pay, you say? We think we were worth much more!"[28]

## The Right to Know

Until Congress acted in 1966, individuals and public interest groups found it difficult to obtain sensitive information that their government possessed but that directly affected them. With the passage of the Freedom of Information Act (FOIA) in 1966 and the Privacy Act in 1974, the right to know and the premise that government information, within limits, belongs to the public, were assured.[29]

Under the Freedom of Information Act, some grass roots groups have obtained investigative reports, information on corporate product development and marketing practices, scientific information on nuclear hazards, background reports on consumer products, data on the efficiency of specified drugs, nutritional content of food products and processed foods, and safety records of transportation vehicles.

The FOIA guarantees a citizen's right to inspect government documents. If refused access, the specific government agency must explain the reason(s) for denial of the request. If denied, an appeal process is available, and, if the appeal is rejected, the requesting party can seek legal action in a federal district court.

The Privacy Act of 1974 was passed to allow individuals to review almost all federal files pertaining to them, and the files must be accurate and up to date. If found inaccurate, the requestor can challenge the information contained. The act gives individuals significant control over how the information concerning them is used. Grass roots leaders are often the subject of government agency investigations, and they may wish to learn if their rights to privacy are being violated.

Both acts are simple to implement, and grass roots groups can consider this simple process:

- Conclude what information you desire and describe it in as precise a manner as possible (i.e., a study on hazards associated with plutonium release in water at the Rocky Flats, Colorado, plant).
- Indicate in a letter to the respective agency (i.e., Department of Health and Human Services) that you are making an FOIA request.
- Place a telephone call to the agency and follow up with a short letter explaining your specific request.
- Make no effort to explain the purpose of your request. (The agency cannot question your intent.)
- Be sure also to ask for all documents related to your request.

The government agency has ten days to reply. If costs result for the search and copying the document, you will be asked to pay for them. Find out how much the costs will be prior to obtaining the information.

Not all government information can be released under the Freedom of Information Act. There are nine exceptions, such as national defense, information concerning financial institutions, trade secrets, and personnel and medical data. You may challenge the use of these exceptions by the government agency.

Some state governments have similar freedom of information legislation, and the request process is similar to the federal one.

### Inaction: A Form of Opposition

During the 1980s, a number of environmental law organizations spent large sums of money and a great deal of legal talent to counter inaction, failure to comply with

congressional mandates, lack of regulation and enforcement, and policies they deemed damaging to the environment that were initiated by federal and state agencies
responsible for the use and protection of this nation's
natural resources. In court, federal and state agencies
defended their practices and frequently sought delays in
meeting court-ordered decisions against them. The Natural Resources Defense Council (NRDC) was active during the 1980s in seeking to force federal agencies to
comply with legislation. The following examples demonstrate the range of actions taken by the NRDC to protect
the environment and the resistance of many federal
agencies entrusted with a responsibility to the citizens.

- When the EPA was sued for its failure to adopt
  regulations that limit pollution increases in areas
  that are relatively clean, based on standards required
  by the Clean Air Act, the EPA conceded its duty to set
  these regulations but asked the court for a five-year
  delay. When given further evidence by the NRDC, the
  court ordered that the regulations be completed in
  two years.
- Proposition 65, the Safe Drinking Water and Toxics
  Enforcement Act, a law requiring the governor of
  California to issue a list of chemicals known to cause
  cancer or reproductive hazards so that discharges of
  those chemicals into drinking water can be prohibited, was passed by California voters. The governor initially listed only 29 chemicals known to cause
  cancer. The law requires the governor to list *all*
  known chemicals, and a suit was won in court by
  NRDC, with massive grass roots support, to force the
  governor to extend the list to approximately 250
  known carcinogens.
- In 1986, the Bureau of Land Management and the
  U.S. Forest Service set a grazing fee formula that

charged livestock owners far less than market value. This action resulted in increased grazing on public lands and environmental damage. The NRDC filed suit in federal district court, challenging the fee structure. In a favorable ruling, the court noted that the two federal agencies had failed to follow public participation requirements in setting the fee.[30]

These and many additional examples of litigation to force resistive or passive federal agencies are available from public interest law groups.

### AIDS—Turning Their Back on It

In 1987, Randy Shilts, a San Francisco journalist, wrote, "The United States, the one nation with the knowledge, the resources, and the institutions to respond to the [AIDS] epidemic, had failed. And it failed because of ignorance and fear, prejudice and rejection." In his book, *And the Band Played On*, Shilts documents the incompetence, bureaucratic infighting, and lack of leadership and disdain shown by the Reagan administration in dealing with the AIDS (acquired immunodeficiency syndrome) crisis.[31] While as early as 1983 AIDS was dubbed the "number one health priority" by the Department of Health and Human Services, funding had to be virtually forced upon it by Congress.

The administration took a wait-and-see attitude during the first few years of an epidemic that was first identified in Los Angeles in 1981, when a physician noted that five young men had contracted an uncharacteristic disease, *Pneumocystis carinii* pneumonia. From those five cases, the epidemic grew to include more than 170,000 persons by mid-1991. The number one health priority of the Reagan administration was largely ignored because those who developed AIDS were not seen as "part of the general population" by the secretary of Health and Human Services and a large segment of the population.

Grass roots activism to force a nation to face the facts was essentially the only meaningful response to the crisis. The Department of Health and Human Services had failed to adequately fund federal efforts to fight the AIDS epidemic, according to a report prepared by the Intergovernmental Relations and Human Resources Subcommittee. The subcommittee investigation revealed that despite administration claims that sufficient funds were being spent on AIDS, important surveillance, epidemiological studies, and laboratory research at the Centers for Disease Control (CDC) and the National Institutes of Health (NIH) had been undermined because of inadequate funding.

Most education, care, and treatment for the disease was done by the gay community, a community that struggled with its own internal problems, aside from the disease's ravages. Until 1985, the gay community based its policy toward AIDS in its own political terms, and an internecine struggle between different factions only exacerbated the general neglect. When health authorities failed to respond to either research needs or provide treatment, an underground developed in the gay community that delivered unauthorized, often useless, medication to those suffering from the fatal disease.

As early as late 1983, the first official recognition of negligence was reported in a press release issued by Representative Ted Weiss (D.–N.Y.) announcing a House of Representatives report dated December 6, 1983:

*House Report Documents Inadequate Response to*
*AIDS:* "Tragically, funding levels for AIDS investigations
have been dictated by political considerations rather
than by professional judgments of scientists and public

health officials who are waging the battle against the epidemic," said Weiss. "The inadequacy of funding, coupled with inexcusable delays in research activity, leads me to question the Federal Government's preparedness for national health emergencies, as well as their Administration's commitment to an urgent resolution to the AIDS crisis."

Government inaction was compounded by an international controversy that developed in 1984 over who should get credit for discovering the virus that caused AIDS—the Pasteur Institute in Paris or the National Cancer Institute in Washington, D.C. This political maelstrom interfered with scientific research and added fuel to conflicts raging between the National Cancer Institute and the Centers for Disease Control.[32]

Lack of official interest, turf wars inside the Department of Health and Human Services, repressive measures against high risk populations proposed by some, and the public's lack of knowledge about or appearance of concern for those afflicted or those at risk accounted for the frustration that eventually helped to mobilize the gay community. Gays knew who opposed them, and why, and they could envisage the mounting death toll unless constructive steps were accelerated.

It was not until 1989 that the groups reached some measure of mutual communication and action, when government officials and those dying and in danger of acquiring the disease agreed on parallel tracks for clinical trials of promising drugs such as ddI, compassionate use of experimental use of aerosolized pentamidine and pressuring pharmaceutical companies to lower price for Zidovudine. The truce is an uneasy one.

In no other case of opposition to a grass roots movement has the record of the bureaucracy been more carefully documented and shown to be as negligent and destructive as that reported by Randy Shilts.[33]

## Revolving Doors

During Senate hearings on Alar by the Subcommittee on Toxic Substances, Joseph Lieberman (D.–Conn.) and Harry Reid (D.–Nev.), expressed concern over a possible violation of government ethics laws. They charged that seven of eight members of the EPA's Scientific Advisory Panel were receiving income from the chemical industry while serving on the panel. Extreme concern was focused on two panel members who left the panel to work on behalf of Uniroyal, the manufacturer of Alar, the chemical under discussion at the subcommittee meetings.

The controversy arose over the EPA's position that removing Alar from the market would take eighteen months due to a federal law requiring extensive reviews and procedures. "A spokesman for the EPA told the committee that the data do not support a finding of an imminent health hazard, a prerequisite for an immediate ban."[34] Alar was removed from the market several days later when the apple industry said that growers would voluntarily stop using the chemical by the fall of 1989.

The ethical question is, Did the EPA Scientific Advisory Panel members, who were paid by the chemical industry, influence EPA's original position—refusal to consider the chemical a health risk?

Critics have charged over the years that Washington, D.C., is the hub of the revolving door—that powerful people move back and forth between government appointments and corporate boardrooms. Recent scandals at Housing and Urban Development, the Pentagon, and in the savings and loan industry have uncovered the same pattern of former administration officials, members of Congress, and corporate officials playing musical chairs or peddling influence to gain government contracts, policy changes that favor the industry, and consultant fees.

Grass roots groups concerned with toxic waste disposal regulations enforcement are uneasy that the president of Browning-Ferris Industries (BFI), William Ruckelshaus, was twice director of the Environmental Protection Agency. BFI is the second largest corporation among those in waste management, and is often the target of local groups opposed to putting sites in their communities or to the technology used, such as incineration.

With constant reminders by the media about corruption and ethical lapses among key officials in government and in private life, grass roots leaders should remain vigilant.

**Positive Directions—Cooperation instead of Conflict**

Not all tactics used by corporations and governmental agencies are negative or counterproductive to grass roots groups. During 1989, a number of breakthroughs brought cautious praise from some activists. Motivated largely by economic and political factors, companies have introduced new technology, policies, and products, partly in response to pressure from grass roots groups and also to capture a favorable position in new market trends.

*An Alternative Test—Animal Free*

Molecular Devices Corporation in Menlo Park, California, has announced a sensitive new instrument that could limit toxic tests currently performed on animals. In October 1989, the silicon incrophysiometer was reported on in *Science*, and important journal. Tests such as Draize and Lethal Dose-50 could be largely eliminated by the new instrument, which uses human cells—such as those of the human cornea—to grow on the surface of an electric sensor. As chemicals pass over the cells, the extraordinarily sensitive device can detect changes in the health of the cells. The device is available for commercial distribution. A version of the instrument is undergoing tests by Procter & Gamble, a target of animal rights protesters.

Meanwhile, the U.S. Department of Agriculture is working on a new set of regulations to improve the welfare of animals in research laboratories. Under an order from Congress, the Animal and Plant Health Inspection Services (APHIS) has produced a report, including 133 pages of regulations, which took four years to write. Some of the proposed rules would require laboratory researchers to ensure

- That dogs be housed, preferably in groups in cages four times as large as the current requirements or be released for exercise and socialization for 30 minutes a day.
- That nonhuman primates be housed in groups that do not fight or that they be released for at least four hours of exercise and social interaction a week.
- That standard cages for guinea pigs and hamsters be one-half inch taller.
- That isolated apes or monkeys be able to see and hear fellow creatures or have "positive physical contact or other interaction with their keeper or other familiar and knowledgeable person" for at least an hour a day."[35]

Animal rights groups describe the regulations as "ranging from beneath bare minimum to simple and moderate." A spokesperson for the National Association for Biomedical Research, a nonprofit corporation that represents the scientific and corporate community, is critical of the regulations, saying, "Some of these emotional and sentimental ideas have no scientific foundation. In many cases, there is no evidence that spending all this money will benefit the animals."

The APHIS report, while controversial, is an attempt to improve the welfare of animals used in research. It does not recommend elimination of or alternative tests that use animals, positions taken by animals rights activists.

### Corporate Code on the Environment: The Valdez Principle

The Coalition for Environmentally Responsible Economics, a group of environmental, religious, and investment organizations, introduced a code of conduct in 1989 to use in judging which corporations are environmentally responsible. It is called the Valdez Principle, named after the Exxon oil spill in Alaska and it contains ten points on which judgments are made. The thrust of the code is for corporations to assess the effects of products and production processes on the environment, employees, and communities. It includes a requirement that companies appoint environmental experts to their boards. The code also calls for an annual environmental audit to determine compliance with the code.

Corporations are being invited by the coalition to endorse the Valdez code. The code also proposes to help socially aware investors choose companies for investment, to urge college students to consider which companies are in compliance with the code when weighing job offers, and to urge companies to develop internal environmental efforts.

The most significant feature of the development of this code is that it brought investors, grass roots organizations, and environmental groups together to support environmentally sound economic growth.

## The Green Consumer

In April 1990, the Opinion Research Corporation, a polling firm based in Princeton, New Jersey, released a report of a survey that indicated environmental concerns have a powerful effect on American consumers. "Consumer interest in environmentally safe products is very high. That should send a strong message to companies to do more to show their concern for the environment," the report concluded. Respondents to the survey questions volunteered that more than one-fourth of them boycotted products because of a manufacturer's prior environmental record, and more than 70 percent said they had switched brands because of environmental concerns.

If companies produce "green" products, grass roots consumers are ready to purchase them. The voice of the public is being heard, and, as consumers talk and buy based on environmental or ethical concerns, corporate officials are beginning to listen and respond. A sound environmental image equals money.

Ben and Jerry's Homemade Inc., an ice-cream company in Waterbury, Vermont, introduced an ice cream called Rain Forest Crunch, made with Brazil and cashew nuts imported from virgin rain forests. Their point is that rain forests need not be cut down in order to be economically productive.

Habitat Designs, a British furniture manufacturer, uses the save-the-rainforest theme by eliminating tropical hardwoods in their furniture making.

Aveda cosmetics introduced a refillable metal makeup bottle, which eliminates throwaway plastic containers.

In 1989, 5,700 packaged goods were expected to be

introduced according to Marketing Intelligence Service. Retail outlets are designating "green products" with shelf signs or labels placed on products and expect to tap the new consumer preference. Some environmentalists are cautious about the explosion in "green" products and urge that they be carefully tested for accurate labeling and truth about their claims before being designated "green."

In April 1990, four retail and grocery chains in the western United States announced a program letting shoppers know which products meet tough environmental standards, including advertising claims. "The environmental seal would be awarded if a product is made from at least 50 percent recycled materials, if it has no detected residue of highly toxic emissions, if it will not deplete the ozone, if advertising claims for the product and packaging can be verified, and if the manufacturer adopts an aggressive policy for reducing solid waste."[36] If the product qualifies, it may carry a seal of approval as well as a seal on store shelves.

In responding to grass roots pressure from Greenpeace and other environmental activists, the Federal Trade Commission (FTC) announced in September 1990 that it will investigate environmental claims of products ranging from trash bags to hairsprays. The FTC will pursue charges of deceptive advertising and misleading packaging.

Atlantic Richfield introduced a new gasoline called EC-1 for emission control as a replacement for its leaded gasoline used by older vehicles without pollution control equipment. The new gas cuts emission pollutants such as benzene, sulfur dioxide, and carbon monoxide. Consumer response in 1989 was called good by ARCO officials. The move was made in anticipation of tighter pollution controls contained in the revised Clean Air Act of 1990.

Alexander Fruit and Trading Company in Geyserville, California, is substituting popcorn for plastic foam to pack its produce for shipping. Popcorn is biodegradable and can also be used to feed birds or as mulch for gardens. Also, its cost is one-third below that of plastic foam kernels.

\*     \*     \*

Grass roots groups are learning from and sharing information with each other about the tactics their opponents use. Exchange between opposing sides in the array of issues presented in this book demonstrates the volatility and drama of the conflict.

# 4
# Media: The Trade-Offs

I will be as harsh as truth, and as uncompromising as justice. On this subject I do not wish to think, or speak, or write with moderation...I am in earnest—I will not equivocate—I will not excuse—I will not retract a single inch—AND I WILL BE HEARD.

William Lloyd Garrison wrote these fiery words in his editorial on January 1, 1831, when he brought out the first issue of *The Liberator,* a modest, four-page periodical. Though a young man of only twenty-five, Garrison launched in print his antislavery creed and continued to publish bellicose indictments of slavery until 1866, when, on its thirty-fifth anniversary, his *Liberator's* final editorial announced:

"The object for which *The Liberator* was commenced—the extermination of chattel slavery—having been gloriously consummated, it seems to me especially appropriate to let its existence cover the historic period of the great struggle; leaving what remains to be done to complete the work of emancipation to other instrumentalities."

With his life work completed, Garrison put down his pen and rejoiced; the millions of slaves in the United States were free—the people had abolished slavery. The words of his paper's masthead were realized: "Proclaim Liberty throughout all the land, to all the inhabitants thereof." Although *The Liberator* counted only three thousand subscribers at the peak of its circulation, most historians agree that this periodical had extraordinary influence during the abolitionists' struggle to the death with those favoring slavery. Garrison heaped scorn and denunciation upon his opponents in editorials, never succumbing to the fear of retaliation, although he experienced much abuse himself. In 1835, a mob gathered in front of *The Liberator's* makeshift office and seized Garrison, tied a rope around his waist, and dragged him through the streets of Boston to the city hall. The mayor placed him in jail for his own protection from the unruly mob that planned to tar and feather him.

From its first edition, *The Liberator* provoked outrage among Southerners, who passed laws to exclude the periodical from their stores and to levy fines and prison terms to prohibit free Negroes from buying or reading it. The state of Georgia placed a price of five thousand dollars on Garrison's head.

In the abolitionist cause, John Brown used the gun; William Lloyd Garrison, the pen. During the nineteenth century, words, both written and spoken, were the media, and those who used them well and with conviction had influence. Whenever Garrison could raise the funds, he printed the periodical, setting the type, writing the articles, and running the small press. By financing and publishing *The Liberator* solely by himself, he controlled its editorial position, contents, and style. He spoke for the nonviolent abolitionists and stirred the grass roots. In 1832, he established the American Anti-Slavery Society and later helped the Underground Railroad take slaves form the South to Canada. Both tactics received dedicated grass roots support and contributed to the success of the movement. However, it was his antislavery trumpet, *The Liberator,* that most aroused the nation.

## Times Have Changed

The Media today are vastly different from their simple beginnings, and understanding these differences is crucial for leaders and participants in modern grass roots movements. Dominated by television, media today are big business, and their first obligation is to turn a profit for their owners. Broadcasting in the public interest is of minor concern. Mass media are owned and controlled by a corporate elite that join with the elite in government to induce conformity or a mainstream view of society. Allowing little public access to this power, media giants often succeed in making citizens passive observers. In their search for corporate profits, largely gained from advertising revenue, the corporate elite determine program content and news events coverage in concert with the media elite.

A new grass roots group called Fairness & Accuracy in Reporting (FAIR) advises active citizens to ask an important question about the ownership of the media: "Our society demands that politicians and government officials disclose their financial involvements; why shouldn't the media disclose theirs?"[1]

Because the media's reach is vast, grass roots leaders need to understand the following twelve points about the mass media (television, radio, and daily newspapers) in order to plan how to use them effectively or defend against them. Some media operations are controlled by the same elite: newspaper corporations own 30 percent of the television network (ABC, NBC, CBS) affiliates and independent stations.[2] For example, the Tribune Company in Chicago owns the *Chicago Tribune,* a newspaper; WGN, a passive superstation with a potential television audience of 30,756,000 million (34 percent of American households); an AM radio station, WGN; and it also owns the Chicago Cubs baseball team. In some cities, a corporation may hold a virtual monopoly on daily newscasts and columns, providing the public with a single editorial slant to the news events.

The media can be and often are powerful allies to grass roots groups; to learn about them is crucial. Grass roots organizers should understand these twelve points:

1. *Decision-making power rests with media personnel.* Whether the group's story or event is covered or reported depends on the judgment of the news editors. *Example:* Almost every grass roots group has experienced a lack of response to a press release or press announcement sent to local media. Either no one arrives to cover the story or the covered story is not presented. In 1989, when Rainforest Action Network held its third annual World Rainforest Action Network Week, it received scant local coverage and no national attention. Jeff Cohen, the founder of FAIR asserts, "Media managers are counting on people to be intimidated by their assertion of authority. It's clear that those who own the media would rather have us be a nation of mindless consumers than a nation of active citizens."[3]

2. *The media try to balance issues in a story and depend on their regular sources to present the other side if the event or story is reported at all. The code of balance and objectivity often neutralizes the story's impact. Example:* In a *New York Times* article, dated August 1, 1989, the headline

reads: "Cosmetics Companies Quietly End Animal Tests." The article states, "Several leading cosmetics companies have quietly stopped testing products on animals. The moves are in response to years of pressure by animal rights groups and reflects growing confidence in the reliability of alternative testing methods." Further into the article, the president of the Cosmetics, Toiletry, and Fragrance Association is quoted as saying, "we are not dealing with rational opponents. We are dealing with zealots who cannot comprehend that a child's life is more important than a dog's, who see nothing wrong with making a child the ultimate guinea pig instead of an animal."[4] The reporter did not include a rebuttal statement from PETA or any other animal rights group spokesperson.

3. *The media frame the issue; they determine the meaning and parameters of the issue, and they allow little opportunity for those making the news to influence the framing.* If the decision is made that the event has little public significance, it can be blanked out. If the event is flamboyant, the way it is reported rests with those reporting. Setting the agenda for what gets reported and how it will be reported rests largely with media decision makers; thus, the opportunity for communication of the veracity of their issues and concerns in the popular media is basically lost to grass roots groups. *Example:* The issue of timber cutting in old forests—redwood and Douglas fir forests over two hundred years old—has been framed by some media as a contest between owls and loggers. In a June 1989 issue of the *San Francisco Chronicle,* the headline reads, "Loggers Say They're Endangered, Owl Isn't." The story is reported as follows: "In a show of solidarity, thousands of northern

California timber workers joined forces here yesterday to tell the federal government that their
livelihoods are in much greater danger than the
northern spotted owl." The executive director of
the Sierra Club legal defense fund sees it in another light. He writes in defense of the owl and old
forests,

> The loss of timber industry jobs is, in fact,
> automation and log exports....According to
> the Oregon State Employment Division: "The
> reasons for these [mill] closures are complex,
> more complex than the industry of the media
> have usually reported. The problem is not
> merely a decision to...save some old-growth
> forests. What is really happening is the con-
> tinuing long-term modernization and restruc-
> turing of the lumber and wood products
> industry, a process which began in the late
> 1970s and has accelerated during the reces-
> sion of the 1980s....This process will proba-
> bly not be complete until virtually all of the
> remaining mills are of the new automated
> variety.
>
> "The result of modernization? Today, the
> wood products industry in the Pacific North-
> west employs one-third fewer workers than it
> did ten years ago while it produces more
> lumber than ever before"[6]

4. *A grass roots leader can be made a celebrity if the
   media choose to place that person in the spotlight.* Some grass roots movements find that the
   media determine the spokesperson for the group
   and direct questions and attention only to the new
   celebrity. The "cult figure" syndrome can be detrimental if it robs the movement of access to the

media by persons other than the media's anointed celebrity. Reporting on the personality of the leader reduces the concentration of the media on the issues the grass roots group may wish to communicate. Celebrity status within a grass roots group can become an internal problem. Decentralized leadership is important to those in a movement who want their voices heard. *Example:* Randall Terry, the leader of Operation Rescue, has emerged as a media celebrity for the antiabortion force. Members of this grass roots group block abortion clinics and Planned Parenthood offices to disrupt their services to would-be clients. The media have created celebrity status for Terry. In an article in the May 1, 1989, issue of *Newsweek,* Terry is said to have "turned a small band of antiabortion activists in Binghamton, New York, into the fastest-growing wing of the right-to-life movement. The group now has 35,000 followers in 100 cities. How did he do it? Terry, a fiery speaker, traveled around the country addressing conservative church groups."

When the U.S. Supreme Court announced its decision in *Webster* v. *Reproductive Health Services* on July 3, 1989, the media, both television and print, focused on Randall Terry as the major spokesperson for antiabortion forces. They recorded his prediction: "This Supreme Court decision will create an avalanche of new legislation on abortion." In the July 5, 1989, issue of the *New York Times,* an article said, "Randall Terry, national director of Operation Rescue, said his organization would continue its strategy with increased vigor. 'We're calling on thousands of pro-life Americans to peacefully blockade these killing centers with their bodies to prevent children from dying, and we will launch an equal force against state legislatures to chip away at Roe.'"

5. *Radio and Television newscasts usually break at three and seven minute intervals for commercial advertisements, prohibiting an in-depth discussion of an issue.* Commercial media provide only a sketch or outline of significant news stories, framed with tantalizing sound bites. Newspapers and magazine stories provide the opportunities for a more thorough discussion of a particular grass roots issue. Public radio and television are likely to provide even greater expanded coverage and exploration. *Example:* On October 26, 1989, "NBC Nightly News" reported in a 10-second news bite that the McDonald's Corporation had announced plans to recycle its plastic hamburger containers and other packages. The news report did not mention the boycott, public pressure, additional environmental hazards, and the criticism of McDonald's by grass roots group such as the Citizen's Clearinghouse for Hazardous Wastes. The report appeared to give McDonald's credit for initiating a sound environmental solution to polystyrene waste. On the following day the *New York Times* carried an article in its business section that discussed the plan and mentioned the pressure: "McDonald's has been widely criticized for using plastic containers because they often end up as litter and add to waste disposal problems." It went on to quote Jeanne Urika of the Environmental Action Foundation in Washington, D.C., who said, Recycling does not address the issue of pollutants generated in the making of polystyrene. There is pollution at every step of the production process."[6]

The *Times* article does not include a statement from the Citizen's Clearinghouse for Hazardous Wastes, the group that engineered the "McToxins—Send It Back" campaign discussed in chapter 2. Reporters depend on reliable, consistent sources when they balance an article; they often eschew quotes from grass roots leaders considered marginal or fringe. Many reporters are unaware of them and their organizations.

6. *The media can trivialize an issue, reducing its importance to the public. By presenting the grass roots issue in a way that minimizes the serious nature of a movement, they misrepresent the issue and make it seem marginal.* Being trivialized is deadly. *Example:* Newspaper and television accounts of the activities of Earth First! frequently trivialize or label the group as deviant. A San Francisco Chronicle account stated, "Radical environmentalists began tree sitting in seven states, vowing to remain perched aloft on platforms to protect logging operations they say are destroying the USA's forests." On October 1989, the same newspaper included a negative comment about Earth First! in its article featuring the conflict with loggers who said they were endangered, not owls: "although there was no sign of anyone from Earth First!, an environmental group staging anti-logging protests this week, the boisterous crowd was urged to treat them courteously if they did show up.

'We don't want any of them to be stopped on the way to the welfare department to pick up their checks,' joked one of the speakers."[7]

Media managers' tendency toward balancing viewpoints and trivializing the story also distorts the message. Martin Lee and Norman Solomon say, "Active media watchers have...complained about the 'no culprits, no solutions' style of journalism found in many reports on the environment or on poverty. In this type of journalism, reporters thoroughly lay out a problem, then throw up their hands in desperation at the possibility of a solution—carefully avoiding the issues of who caused the mess and what solutions are being proposed by independent public interest experts."[8]

7. *The media's attention span is extremely short, and to keep the story before the public requires creative thinking. Example:* When Lois Gibbs led the grass roots movement at Love Canal, she said, "we had to keep the media's interest. That was the only way we got anything done. The residents forced New York State to answer questions. They kept Love Canal in the public consciousness. They educated the people about public wastes." Love Canal residents planned a picket line to block construction work at the canal because they felt that the city's putting up a chain link fence could not stop chemicals from leaking out and affecting the citizens. The image of a fence in their neighborhood angered the residents. Gibbs said, "During the first week, people continued to get arrested. After six weeks, the picketing lagged. People got tired of coming out every morning, and we weren't getting anywhere. We hadn't stopped the construction. All we had accomplished was to aggravate the truck drivers. But it did keep our story in front of the public—and that was important."[9]

8. *If a grass roots movement targets a corporation, as is often the case, the media are likely to protect the powerful group under attack.* The reporter may trivialize, negatively frame, or ignore the ac-

tion. More than one grass roots group has found its message falling on deaf ears in the media when its target is a large corporation. *Example:* The "Send It Back" campaign, in which the Citizen's Clearinghouse for Hazardous Wastes targeted the McDonald's Corporation. The CCHW urged people to return styrofoam containers to the fast-food chain to recycle when McDonald's proposed that method to deal with the vast amount of those containers produced in the United States. The CCHW campaign did not receive media attention.

Advertisers pressured the networks (broadcasters) to keep them from airing an *Audubon Society* documentary on the cutting of forests. The documentary made the point that cutting the trees would destroy the habitat of the spotted owl, already a threatened species. Stroh's Brewing Company withdrew $600,000 it had planned to spend underwriting a series of films produced by the National Audubon Society. The remaining sponsors, including Exxon, New York Life and Dean Witter Reynolds also pulled advertising under pressure from the timber industry.[10] The documentary was later aired on Ted Turner's cable network.

FAIR's Jeff Cohen reminds grass roots leaders, "Be conscious of who the advertisers and sponsors are. Remember, when you're watching NBC, you are watching the network owned by GE. Remember that the other broadcast networks and mass media are owned by big business."

9. *Those issues or approaches of grass roots groups that are compatible with the views of those in control of the media enjoy greater success in obtaining positive media coverage than those whose cause rests outside the mainstream of social acceptance. Example:* The campaign to

remove intoxicated drivers from the nation's roads has been successful, not only in reducing lives lost in alcohol-related accidents, but in changing social norms about drinking. Mothers Against Drunk Driving (MADD) has enjoyed widespread, positive media coverage in print, radio, and television. The MADD campaign deals with a concern that is endorsed by the majority of Americans. The beverage industry has supported it because they do not view it as prohibitionist—rather, the campaign has focused on responsible drinking and the designated driving program.

10. *An unforgettable visual is worth a thousand words.* In this regard, television has a jump on print or the spoken word. An image, reinforced and repeated, conveys the message a grass roots group uses to arouse its members as well as the public at large. *Examples:* The following are some of the memorable visual images that television has communicated:

- Medical waste, especially syringes, washing up on the pristine shores of the East Coast.
- The AIDS quilt with the panels depicting names and mementos of those who died from AIDS.
- The corroded Civil War stone statues and discolored metal plaques at Gettysburg, victims of acid rain.
- The wall in Washington that stands as a memorial to Vietnam veterans.
- The loaded garbage barge from East Islip, New York, floating around the world in search of a site for dumping and finally returning to New York with its original load of waste.
- Thick smog hanging above an urban area with long, billowing plumes of smoke rising from smokestacks, blocking out the sun.

- The *Exxon Valdez* oil spill at Prince William Sound, Alaska.
- An albino rabbit with its pink eyes infected and raw with pain caused by substances administered in a Draize experiment for a cosmetics firm.
- An automobile crash with mangled bodies of teenagers spread across the highway and empty beer cans rolling from the wreckage.
- Dead waterfowl floating in a wildlife refuge.
- Children using alcohol and other illegal drugs.

11. *Never go unprepared when engaging the media. Ignorance of a subject or surreptitious manipulation of an event can backfire, and the negative impact of a poorly staged media event seen by the public on television can be difficult to overcome.* Reporters ask probing questions and can spot a setup. Incoherent or false messages given by a grass roots leader, recorded for public consumption, can cost a group its credibility. *Example:* During the summer of 1989, WWOR-TV, a television station in New York, covered a protest rally by citizens in a nearby New Jersey town. In their protest against a waste disposal site, the pickets gave the appearance of setting up the reporters for their own advantage. When the reporters arrived and began to question the demonstrators, a confrontation occurred. The reporters dismissed the demonstration as a publicity stunt and gave a negative appraisal of the group. The group's spokespersons were unable to convince the reporters of their case or sincerity.

12. *Social change rarely comes overnight, and even with ubiquitous national news media, grass roots groups need to engage reporters for a sustained period of time with the best available information*

*in order to gain credibility and ultimate accep-
tance.* Grass roots groups must be prepared to
engage representatives of the media as frequently
as possible in order to encourage accurate reporting of their causes and activities. Without credible
information, reporters may trivialize or scant the
groups' actions.

*Example:* From the early days of the AIDS epidemic, gay activists expressed concern and anger
that the press and television ignored the threat of
the fatal disease and labeled it the gay plague.
When it got any media mention, the slant was
toward blaming the "victim," a term gay activists
began to deplore. Even into the fifth year of the
epidemic, little was said about AIDS or its prevention, treatment, and research. Partly because of
the persistence of such writers as Larry Kramer
and Randy Shilts, coverage improved and expanded. Larry Kramer's exchange of letters with
the editor of the *New York Times* is instructive,
and the dialogue, among other things, has increased the coverage of the AIDS story by the
*Times.* Kramer says, "A writer—this writer, any-
way—can only write well about what he's interested in....

"I don't consider myself an artist. I consider
myself a very opinionated man who uses words as
fighting tools. I perceive certain wrongs that make
me very angry, and somehow I hope that if I string
my words together with enough skill, people will
hear them and respond."[11]

In addition to Kramer's persistent efforts to get fair
and accurate reporting of the epidemic, Randy Shilts's
regular articles in the *San Francisco Chronicle* have
given that newspaper a national reputation for its cogent
and timely news coverage on AIDS.

Grass roots groups often seek to dissolve the concentration of power held by the corporate and media elite. They have confronted the hegemony of the television establishment and made inroads. PETA's compassion campaign; ACT UP's support for the parallel track and compassionate use of AIDS drugs; MOPL's push for organically grown farm produce; and CCHW's campaign against concentration of hazardous waste sites in Southern states are examples of successes. Each campaign focused on deleterious corporate or governmental policies or practices. The media have recently begun to support some grass roots protagonists. However, in each case, the reporter seeks institutional authorities to remedy the ills exposed by ordinary people. Reporters go to university researchers, legislators, federal agencies' staffs, corporate officials, and established national organizations. As values and concerns of reporters and their sources coincide, shared solutions are generated by the experts and reported to the public. Grass roots groups rarely receive credit from the media for coming up with solutions. For the most part, they remain on the sidelines.

## The Fight for Fairness

FAIR was formed in mid-1986 to counteract the exclusion of viewpoints of citizens and groups whose voices were silenced by the corporate-owned media. Jeff Cohen describes FAIR in this way, "We don't just educate; we also agitate. FAIR and its members fight so that public interest voices—peace spokespersons, consumer advocates, environmentalists, social justice activitists—get access to the media."

Leaders of FAIR have seen their group change from a research to a membership organization. They credit the growth of their group to the sense of being on the sidelines that most grass roots leaders experience. Cohen says of this feeling, "I believe the frustration level is at a breaking point. Something has to give. Nothing's more frustrating than being locked out. Look at recent history: being locked out of society's mainstream is what produced the powerful civil rights and feminist movements. FAIR is part of a new movement protesting another lockout: the virtual exclusion of public interest leaders from mainstream TV."[12]

## The Media as Ally

When a message is repeated by the media, interested citizens are encouraged to take action. As the following example illustrates, media reinforcement of a grass roots cause can accelerate the group's mobilization and impact.

### *The Designated Driver*

Americans are thinking differently about drinking in the 1990s than in past eras, but they have a long way to go to remedy a situation in which 25,000 Americans— nearly half of them young—die each year in drinking-related traffic accidents. In addition, 500,000 Americans sustain serious injuries in crashes, and the yearly cost to society of this accident-specific problem is estimated to exceed $12 billion. Remove Intoxicated Drivers (RID) and Mothers Against Drunk Driving (MADD) launched their grass roots movements in 1978 and 1980, respectively. They were joined by others, as pointed out earlier in this book. The role of the media in this struggle is hotly debated: advertisements to promote alcohol consumption generate billions in revenue for the media from the beverage industry, and many people—such as RID members—believe young people are targeted by these ads, while others believe television is effective in delivering anti-drinking and driving messages. But both RID and MADD subscribe to the belief that a change in this dangerous public health problem can be enhanced by media's capacity to educate.

The Harvard University Alcohol Project, conducted by the Center for Health Communications, seeks to convince television viewers that the use of a designated driver in a group drinking occasion is socially responsible and socially correct. The message is aimed at those of legal drinking age, not at minors. During the 1987–88 major network television season, 45 episodes of different network series carried a warning against drinking and driving. The emphasis in the Harvard project is to include the message during prime time episodes as a natural part of the script and in keeping with the character who delivers it. Popular sitcoms such as *Cheers, Family Ties, Hunter,* and *The Cosby Show* have participated.

In the beginning, the Harvard project director proposed trying to persuade television executives to provide free time for short public service announcements to deliver the anti-drinking and driving message. Instead, they were advised that the delivery of a subtle message in the story line of a popular sitcom by a credible character would prove more effective than a thirty-second spot. The decision was wise because public service announcements, even when made by a celebrity, have never been proven to change behavior. The Harvard project director deliberately refuses money from the alcohol beverage industry, although it has been offered and although that industry, along with others, has plugged the designated driver program. Notably, the National Basketball Association and Miller Beer have a public service campaign urging drinkers to "team up" to avoid the drinking and driving danger through the selection of a designated driver. Anheuser-Busch promotes the slogan Know When to Say When, a responsible-use message specifically intended for adults, although children, too, see it on television, and many RID members and other prevention specialists do not forget the highly successful "Spuds McKenzie" commercials which they believe targeted young people.

These media campaigns may have gained some success; the Harvard project director points to a June 1989 Gallup poll reporting that 72 percent of respondents used a designated driver on social occasions all or most of the time. That percentage was up 10 points from 62 percent in 1987 (prior to the Harvard project), when only public service announcements carried the same message. Some may question the veracity of the poll, but the project directors believe the findings support evidence that a social norm is changing—that using a designated driver is now socially acceptable and that the new norm is encouraging others to adopt the practice.

Grass roots groups often receive support from unexpected quarters, and the strategy embraced by the new ally may vary from the grass roots group's original intent or use of tactics. For instance, MADD originally focused on changes in the criminal justice system, and they were encouraged by evidence that the fear of stiff legal penalties may have brought down the alcohol-related accident and death rates. States such as New Jersey, with mandatory penalties and a high conviction rate, report progress. In 1981, according to New Jersey officials, 376 people were killed on the road and 32,000 were arrested for driving under the influence. For 1989, the fatality figure is believed to have dropped to 180, while the figure for arrests is expected to have risen to 41,000.

Recently, the Centers for Disease Control (CDC) reported that 39.2 percent of all traffic deaths in 1989 involved at least one person who was legally drunk, down from 46.3 percent in 1982. Between 1982 and 1989, the number of alcohol-related fatalities dropped by 12 percent, from 20,356 to 17,849. For this significant trend, researchers at the CDC credit new state laws that penalize drunk drivers, better enforcement, higher drinking ages, and increased public intolerance and awareness.

The point this analysis makes is that an array of tactics must be used in order to obtain a desired change or right a perceived wrong. The media serve a role in education and behavior change, often complex and compromised, such as noted in the anti-drinking-and-driving movements. A revision of the criminal justice system's response to the problem has paid off—much more, many believe, than the media campaign. The origin of this grass roots movement can be traced back to a California mother who lost a daughter to an intoxicated motorist and refused to suffer in silence.

## Periodicals and Public Broadcast

Up to this point, most of the discussion has touched on the role of commercial television and newspapers in reporting on issues and actions of grass roots groups. While the market is significantly smaller for weekly or monthly periodicals and public television, these publications and broadcasts do provide an opportunity for a deeper look into a social problem than do commercial television, radio, or newspapers. While some commercially produced documentaries and newscasts probe a complex movement, they are rare. When the Audubon Society produced a special on old forests and the spotted owl, some of their original backers withdrew funds. Stroh's Brewing Company pulled its support for both the production of the Audubon documentary and its planned commercial advertisements during the airing. Ford Motor Company, Sears, and ITT also canceled their commercials. Without this financial backing, the major networks (ABC, NBC, and CBS) were not interested. Turner Network Television (TNT) and PBS did show the documentary without paid advertisements, thus allowing those interested an opportunity to learn about the plight of the ancient forests and the spotted owl. PBS's televised presentation of "Who's Killing Calvert City?" in 1989 gave a serious examination of airborne pollution caused by the incineration of toxic wastes in a small Kentucky community. Ordinary people were interviewed, and the spokespersons of the local grass roots group opposed to the use of incineration for the disposal of hazardous wastes had an opportunity to describe their concerns. Owners of the incinerator, the waste disposal plant, and public officials offered their rebuttal, and the viewer was allowed to decide the merits of the two sides.

The 1989 C-SPAN telecast of the U.S. House of Representatives hearings on Vietnam veterans and Agent Orange provided live coverage of the testimony and charges against the Centers for Disease Control for the termination of a study into causal links between exposure to Agent Orange (dioxin) and health problems for Vietnam veterans and their offspring. The testimony implied that the study was discontinued at the direction of White House officials. Complex issues were placed before the public, and the viewers decided.

A July 9, 1989, *New York Times Magazine* article described the growth of ACT UP and the new militancy of young gay New Yorkers and their friends who, as author David Leavitt put it, "have emerged from the apolitical consumerism of the 1980s and mobilized itself [sic] around the issue of AIDS into a political force to be reckoned with."

*Newsweek* and *Time* magazines frequently report on

social and health crises that have stirred the grass roots. Animal rights as a movement was explored by *Newsweek* in 1989, and *Time* named Endangered Earth the "Plant of the Year" and devoted much of its January 2, 1989, issue to the examination of four major threats to the environment and the inhabitants of the globe: extinction of plants and animals, global warming, overpopulation, and waste.

*National Geographic's* December 1988 issue was devoted entirely to global problems and global solutions, and it asked, "Can we save our fragile planet?" One sentence in this issue of *National Geographic* poses the challenge to every grass roots group: "True equilibrium, true improvement in the quality of all our lives, will happen only when an informed and dedicated population wants it to happen."

## A Movement That Failed in Spite of Radio

Each Sunday afternoon, as many as 30 million Americans crowded around their radio sets to hear his magnificent oratory bursting from large horn-shaped speakers. The priest of the Shrine of the Little Flower, Charles Coughlin, broadcast from WJR in Detroit and became radio's first superstar. Radio was in its infancy when the "radio priest" mesmerized his audience from 1928 through the fall of 1939. His was the largest continuous radio audience in history, unmatched today, and his popularity and following eclipsed those of Jack Benny, George Burns and Gracie Allen, Arthur Godfrey, and Fred Allen, the other giants of early radio.

During the first five years of his regular broadcast, originally on contract with CBS and later through a network of independent stations that he helped arrange (CBS dropped his contract because they considered his addresses controversial), Father Coughlin switched from religious topics, such as birth control and Christian charity, to economic, social, and political issues. In 1929, when the stock market crashed, he leveled a scathing attack on President Herbert Hoover that drew 1,200,000 letters from listeners.

"Among the middle and lower classes, he succeeded in galvanizing a feeling of class discrimination which evolved into class and religious hatred. His followers had become fed up with big business and its tool—the federal government. He gave slashing attacks against the concentration of power in the hands of big business and the government's passivity in the face of crisis," his biographer, Sheldon Marcus, wrote.[13]

From the beginning, he played to the fears of those devastated by the Great Depression. They wanted reassurance, and he spoke their language—a colorful, populist vernacular for the common man; he said damn, swell, hot, lousy. He named names and railed against "economic royalists," "international bankers," and "capitalistic money-hoarding dynasties." He praised the newly elected president and told his audience, "It's Roosevelt or ruin."

David Bennett, a historian of that era, says, "But while his mastery of radio techniques was perhaps a necessary condition for his achievement, the real key to Coughlin's success lay in his ingenious exploitation of not only economic problems his audience confronted, but also the old social and psychological wounds that the Depression opened."[14]

After stirring up enormous grass roots support, Father Coughlin formalized his movement in November 1934. He named it the National Union for Social Justice (NJSJ). By the end of 1935, Coughlin boasted that he had more than 8.5 million members in grass roots local chapters of the National Union for Social Justice, that he received more than 150,000 letters a week, and that each year he was raising $5 million for the Radio League of the Little

Flower, also his organization. The National Union became a giant lobby of grass roots supporters to influence legislation. *Fortune* magazines noted, "So far as the response of his audience is concerned, Coughlin is just about the biggest thing that ever happened to radio." When Roosevelt pushed for the United States to join the World Bank, Coughlin produced 200,000 telegrams with 1 million signatures in opposition. In the early 1930s, Father Coughlin had easy access to Roosevelt, the Pope, Henry Ford, and Joseph G. Kennedy.

Why did the movement finally fail, a movement led by one of the most charismatic personalities in his day. It failed in part because Father Coughlin failed to establish a consistent mission and stable organization. He could not decide where to take his social justice drive, which he based on the writings of Pope Leo XIII and Pope Pius XI. At one point, he wanted to reform the nation's monetary policy; at another, he wanted to follow Mussolini's concept of the corporate state. At first, he spoke of Roosevelt *or* ruin, but when he broke with the President and the New Deal in 1936, he attacked it as Roosevelt *and* ruin. Notwithstanding these constant shifts in thought and loyalties, his populist followers listened to his Sunday broadcasts and read his periodical, *Social Justice*, which he began publishing in 1936. He had a vast, captive audience but failed to deliver on a coherent, credible grass roots issue.

In 1936 the radio priest decided to form a political party, the Union Party, in order to oppose the reelection of Franklin Roosevelt as well as the candidacy of Republican Alfred Landon. But he overestimated his ability to change his grass roots national union into a successful third political party. In this bold (but, as it turned out, unwise) step, he thought he could succeed in channeling the discontent and frustration of millions of ordinary Americans to his political advantage. The Union Party was forged from an alliance of Dr. Francis E. Townsend's

Old Age Revolving Pension Plan, Huey Long's Share the Wealth Party, then headed by Gerald L. K. Smith, and William Lemkie's Farmers' Relief Group. The Union Party received only 882,000 votes in the 1936 election, and the psychological effects of this smashing defeat pushed Coughlin in a sinister direction that cost him his massive following over the next five years.

His grass roots support peeled away as he embraced anti-Semitism, the Ku Klux Klan, the German American Bund, isolationism, and the Christian Front. In *Social Justice* he called for the United States to accept fascism as a bulwark against communism. His increasingly hostile and personal attacks on Roosevelt and the British finally broke the straw, and most of his followers deserted. After the United States entered World War II, many regarded him as a traitor.

This nascent grass roots movement was the first one to appear in the age of electronic media, and its leader was the premier radio personality. The nation was in great need of social and economic justice, and the grass roots were never more fertile. Father Coughlin had the opportunity. He failed, but he taught a nation about the power of the media—for good or for evil. No one since the radio priest has been able to mobilize a radio or television audience of that dimension.

### Children Are Watching, Also

"It's my living room. It's 8:30 Sunday Evening. Why is this coming into my living room?"

Terry Rakolta, incensed at the inappropriate content of prime-time television programs made for adult audiences, but, in fact, also viewed by many children, decided to take action. After viewing an episode of *Married...With Children* on Fox Broadcasting, she wrote a score of letters to the show's advertisers, accusing them of "pandering to and supporting...soft pornography." In her letters, she mentioned the possibility of a boycott of the sponsors' products. In early 1989, network television became the target of a grass roots movement begun by the Michigan mother of three young children.

Terry Rakolta did not accept media's usual position (use critical viewing!), knowing only too well that children are unlikely to "turn off the program if it offends them." She doubted children had developed sophisticated, critical viewing skills and knew they were watching a good deal of television without parent supervision.

Terry Rakolta's letters to chief executive officers (CEOs) of the companies advertised on *"Married...With Children"* brought a range of responses: Several apologized and said they would withdraw their ads; others hedged, claiming they were reviewing the situation. No one appeared to ignore her accusation that the networks provide too much gratuitous violence and sex during prime-time television.

Terry Rakolta's letter to the CEO of the Coca-Cola Company and his reply follow. A similar letter from Rakolta was sent to all corporate sponsors of the January 15, 1989, episode of *Married...with Children.*

*January 17, 1989*

*The Coca-Cola Company*
*P.O. Drawer 1734*
*Atlanta, GA 30301*

*Attention: Mr. Donald R. Keough*
*President*

*Gentlemen:*

*I am sitting down, writing the first letter to an advertiser I have ever written. I can honestly say I am as offended and distressed as I have ever* been over a prime time TV show. This should immediately alert you because of the already questionable and offensive content on television.

On January 15, 1989 at <u>8:30</u> p.m., I joined by three young children (ages 8, 9, and 10) in our family room to watch television and walk on my treadmill at the same time. We were watching Channel 50 and a situation comedy called "Married, with Children" came on. I thought, "Great, something for the family to watch together!" To make it easier for you to understand what I saw and heard, I will be brief and itemize what I saw.

1) The whole show was about a very attractive, buxom woman whose husband was going around trying to find a discontinued bra she wanted for her birthday.

2) The man and his friend went to Frederick's of Hollywood-type store where they fondled nude mannequins.

3) They watched pornographic movies and walked around bent over because of an erection.

4) A young girl walked out of a dressing room in only a garter belt and bra and then proceeded to remove her bra for the strangers and asked how she looked.

5) A male employee in the store walked around in a garter belt.

6) They talked about homosexuality.

7) A male stripper stripped down to a G string while two women behind him were touching his bottom.

8) The women and man talked about vibrators.

Etc., etc., etc.

*I sent my children out of the room after five minutes of this trash, but unfortunately I was in the middle of my treadmill program so I decided to watch and see what kind of low class advertisers would support this type of program. When I saw "Diet Coke" as one of the sponsors, I was shocked and might add, bitterly disappointed in your lack of judgment, integrity and loyalty to your consumers. I have always felt that Coca-Cola was associated with quality and somehow a "wholesomeness uniquely associated with Americans and their families. You have let the American viewing public down, the loyal Coca-Cola consumers down and most of all, your own image has been tainted by pandering to and supporting what could be called, at the very least, soft pornography in the selection of your programming material.*

*It is very difficult to raise children in a moral and wholesome environment today with all the outside pressures operating against us as parents, and now [it's] obvious your company feels the need to join the "sleeze factor" in today's TV programming. I feel as if I have lost a "friend" in the advertising world, and you have lost a friend in the American family.*

*On Monday, January 16, 1989, after a sleepless night, I started to make phone calls regarding this show. I called Channel 50 in Detroit. They told me to call Fox Broadcasting in Los Angeles, CA, who in turn gave me the number of the producer of "Married with Children." At approximately 5 p.m., Eastern Standard Time, a woman named Marcie Vosburgh from Los Angeles called me back and identified herself as one of the producers of the show. She wanted to know*

the nature of my complaint. I told her how offended I was with her show, and she told me in
no uncertain terms and I quote her words:

1) Our show pushes the limit as far as we can
go.

2) It is a "body" show.

3) We are very specific.

4) Our target audience is "beer-drinking" males
between 18 and 35.

Her last comment to me which she repeated at
least four times, was that I should be my own
best censor by getting up and changing the channel, and also maybe it would be a good idea for
me to watch NBC instead of her show. Another
thing that really perturbed me was a comment
she said, to quote her own words against, "Just
as there is an anti-Christ, we want to be the
anti-Cosby show. We want to be exactly opposite
of everything The Cosby's stand for." Is it a fair
question to ask if the Coca-Cola Company feels
the same way? Do you want to stand for the ex-
act opposite of everything the American family
stands for!

On January 16, I also talked to Mr. Whyman
Roberts, Director of Marketing of Red Lobster Inn
(which is owned by General Mills), who advertised on the January 15th show along with you.
He told me that he had watched the show that
night, and he was personally embarrassed to be
an advertiser. He also told me that his company
had decided that afternoon not to advertise on
the show again because of its offensive content. I
hope to take Mr. Roberts' lead to "Stand up and
be counted: and tell you loyal consumers that

*you stand for quality and integrity and won't be a part of the moral decline in television programming. The saying goes, "If you're not part of the solution, you're part of the problem."*

*Now that you know my feelings and the feelings of the producers of the show you choose to support, I would greatly appreciate it if you could contact me and tell me your advertising philosophy in regards to the blatant exploitation of women, sex, and anti-family attitudes this projects on prime-time television. If you indeed support this type of programming message and continue to use this medium to sell American families your products, I will be obligated to take the next step and start a boycott of all your products beginning with my family, friends, church guilds, school P.T.A.s and the various groups I am affiliated with. You leave me no choice but to join the swelling ranks of consumer activists dedicated to making this world a better place for our children and grandchildren. I am willing to commit myself and my numerous resources to achieve this goal. All I can advise you to do is not set yourself up as a consumer "target." A company of your size and reputation should "set the pace" and help American families create a better moral climate and not to do as Ms. Vosburgh from "married with Children" suggest and "push the limit as far as it will go" thereby, creating "new lows" in TV viewing.*

*I, for one, have finally been pushed too far by the Ms. Vosburgh's of this world and the people who help support her message. I plan to fight back and possibly with your help and the help of people like Mr. Roberts', from Red Lobster, we won't*

*have to be embarrassed in front of our children*
*when we turn on our television sets to watch*
*them together.*

*Waiting for a reply,*

*Mrs. John Rakolta, Jr.*

*cc: Channel 50 TV Director of Programming*
    *Channel 50 TV President, Dwayne Kell*
    *Red Lobster Inn, Director of Marketing,*
    *Mr. Whyman Roberts*
    *Coca-Cola Chairman of the Board,*
    *Mr. Roberto C. Goizueta*
    *Coca-Cola President, Mr. Donald R. Keough*
    *Coca-Cola Board of Directors*
    *Coca-Cola Director of Marketing, Don Lenahan*
    *Coca-Cola Sr. Vice President, Clause Halls*
    *Fox Broadcasting Co. President, Jamie Kellner*
    *Fox Broadcasting Co. Vice President,*
    *Robert Mariana*
    *Lintas Agency Account Executive,*
    *Robert Painter*

The reply from the Coca-Cola Company does not indicate that it also owned Columbia Pictures the producer of the show. Rakolta felt the Coca-Cola Company had an obligation to review the creative content of the program and did not. While an apology is offered for the appearance of a commercial for their product, their deeper involvement with the series, financial and creative, is omitted.

*January 27, 1989*

*Mrs. John Rakolta, Jr.*

*Dear Mrs. Rakolta:*

*Thank you for taking the time to write about the*

*commercial you saw on "Married... With Children."*

*Subsequent to receiving your letter, I and my colleagues reviewed the episode to which you refer, and spoke with the President of Embassy TV, the program production company responsible for "Married... with Children."*

*We were told by Embassy Productions that the point of view expressed to you by the production office employee did not reflect the corporate policy relative to the program. However, you should know that we have scheduled further meetings, both with Embassy and the Fox Network, to be certain that the representations on this matter are accurate.*

*Mrs. Rakolta, I must tell you I am corporately, professionally, and personally embarrassed that one of our commercials appeared in this particularly unsuitable program episode.*

*There is no real excuse I can give you except to say that our system for pre-screening all our TV shows failed in this case.*

*We contract with a company in New York to review all programs in which Coca-Cola Company commercials might appear. If there are any questions on content, these are referred to our advertising agency, who in turn communicates with the appropriate people at Coca-cola for a final decision on whether or not the commercial will run in the show. Over the course of the year relative to the over 4,000 commercials we place nationally, we make approximately 150 program content decisions. Sometimes we decide to leave our commercials where scheduled. Other times, we decide to pull the commercials from the program entirely.*

*In this case, the system failed, and the
advertising agency made a judgment without
notifying the company. Had the proper
notification been given, there is simply no way
that one of our commercials would have appeared
in that program episode.*

*I hope that you will accept not only the apologies
of The Coca-Cola Company, but myself personally
for what was, in truth, an error on our part.*

*We spent a great deal of time, effort, and money
to build our image and gain goodwill with
families such as yours throughout the United
States. To have that image and goodwill
damaged inadvertently is not the way we want
to do business or be viewed.*

*Again, I hope you will accept the apologies of The
Coca-Cola Company for any embarrassment we
may have caused you.*

*Sincerely,*

*Ira C. Herbert*

*P.S. I hope this coupon good for a case of Coca-
Cola Classic in some small way helps us back
into your good graces.*

Terry Rakolta's one-woman campaign received immediate attention in the media themselves, and, by the
spring of 1989, not only had Rakolta appeared on ABC's
*Nightline* and *Larry King Live!*, but the *New York Times*
had printed an article on her campaign. At a press
conference in May 1989, the Michigan mother announced the formation of her group, Americans for
Responsible Television, a grass roots movement Rakolta
expects will reach one million in memberships by 1991,

at which time she plans to open an office, either in Washington, D.C., or New York City.

### Speaking to the Grass Roots

In a statement read at a May 3, 1989, press conference announcing the formation of Americans for Responsible Television (ART) Rakolta drew the battle lines.

> "This organization will NOT be liberal or conservative, Democratic or Republican. This issue cuts across ideological and political party lines. And we are not calling for government control or censorship. Our emphasis at the present time will be to promote private, voluntary efforts by the advertisers and the networks to raise the standards on network television. Simply put, we want to exercise our First Amendment rights, and we want the major advertisers to exercise their rights. First Amendment rights extend beyond simply turning off the television, or turning the channel. They include the right to voice our objections to the advertisers about the sex and violence being dumped into our homes every night. We are asking the advertisers and the networks to give the American family a break from this escalation of sex and violence.
> Just as advertisers have their right to place their commercials on any programs they want, we have the right to choose any product we want. I think it would be helpful to think of our organization as a group of television consumers with a direct economic relationship to those companies that advertise on network television. After all, we buy the products that make the programs possible.
> Our first goal is to encourage the readoption of "family viewing time," by the network, in which at least two hours of nightly prime time viewing is set aside for entertainment for all ages.
> Another project will be to survey the top one hundred

advertisers responsible for buying 76 percent of all network time to find out which companies have written
policies concerning acceptable television programming.
We will publish the result in a newsletter to our
members.

The opposition to the movement is similar to that
encountered by others: corporate and media elite who
want what's good for business.[15] For example, as of
November 1989, *Married...With Children* fully sold ads
for each episode. The initial worry of a boycott is behind
them.[16]

According to an October 5, 1989 article in the *San
Francisco Examiner*, *Married...With Children* hardly
suffered when Michigan housewife Terry Rakolta complained to advertisers about the show's sexual; content
and scatological bent. Both locally and nationally, the
series jumped in ratings when Rakolta's story hit the
headlines.

"Far from being frightened away from the show, Bay
Area advertisers are clamoring to pay $18,000 to $20,000
for a thirty-second slot on *Married...With Children*."[17]
The show is one of the Fox Network's hits and it consistently receives top numbers in Nielsen's ratings. In the
San Francisco Bay area, it got the highest rating of all
shows. The article continues, "In a nutshell, more than
one-fourth of the TV sets turned on at 9 p.m. Sunday
nights are turned in to Fox.[18]

Whether this movement will grow is uncertain, but the
initial grass roots response indicates that many Americans share Rakolta's concern and campaign goals. By
spring 1990, ART was announcing impressive accomplishments in several areas. Substantial support for
boycotting the products of advertisers who sponsor ob-
jectional programs was gaining despite initial reaction to
*Married...with Children*. According to the *Wall Street*

*Journal*, Mars, Exxon, and Hardee Foods gave their advertising agencies lists of programs they refuse to sponsor. And Chrysler Chairman Lee Iacocca told the Hollywood Radio and Television Society, "Help me and every other sponsor out of the censorship business. We don't want the job. Don't write off those who send angry letters as a fringe group. They've found out they have clout and they're going to use it."[19]

ART launched a direct mail campaign in 1990 to raise funds for its grass roots program. An advisory board has been named, and membership continues to grow. Terry Rakolta credits the success. "It is because grass roots America is frustrated in their attempts to raise their children with values and social responsibility against the tremendous influence and pressures of the entertainment community that glorifies drugs, sex, and violence."

### Grass Roots Media

*The Liberator* is a model for grass roots groups to follow. William Lloyd Garrison said he would be heard, and he was. While getting on the network news today carries certain advantages, such as reaching a mass audience, instant and simultaneous presentation of the message, and visuals to accompany words, grass roots groups must produce their own message and do it forcefully and well. To rely on commercial or public media alone places the movement in the dubious position of being written or pronounced about without having the capacity, or power, to select or depend upon the messenger. A group without its own communication channels is a group without power. If a grass roots group does get good free mass exposure on television and in the press, that's a bonus.

Never underestimate the need to communicate with the membership regularly and clearly. Informed and dedicated members and supporters are key to any action the group may take to achieve its objective. When the grass roots group is completely local, telephone calls provide a quick way to inform and mobilize the membership, and community meetings can be effective. The printed word is essential, even among loosely organized groups with virtually no structure. Some grass roots groups, including PETA and CCHW, use the telephone tree—a list of phone numbers of members and supporters—to alert people when a group action is required, such as forming a picket line, demonstrating at a shopping mall, or attending a rally at city hall or meeting with the opposition.

Many grass roots groups begin with a neighborhood or community and, ultimately, become national in scope, and that requires a system of regular communication with a far-flung constituency. All but two grass roots groups discussed in this book make a national newsletter or journal available to their members. However, ACT UP, an intentionally unorganized string of autonomous local groups with no national office, provides no systematic communication among its members and encourages a low profile for its activists while seeking high visibility for its protests. Reporters have a difficult time finding a local spokesperson for ACT UP.

Many local groups affiliated with a national office produce their own local newsletters or memos that concentrate on local issues and provide recognition and visibility for their community leaders, workers, and opponents. These newsletters are frequently typed by a member, duplicated, and distributed, either at regular intervals or when there is a need to call attention to a specific meeting or activity.

Two organizations' newsletters are particularly well

produced. *Everyone's Backyard,* the organ of the Citizen's Clearinghouse for Hazardous Wastes, and *PETA News,* the glossy bimonthly magazine of People for the Ethical Treatment of Animals, present a detailed discussion of their respective organization's programs.

## Everyone's Backyard

In the spring of 1989 issue of *Everyone's Backyard,* the Citizen's Clearinghouse writers present a series of topics and update activities. In the lead article, "Women Movers: Reflections on a Movement by Some of Its Leaders," five women from local groups stretching from Emelle, Alabama, to North Huntington, Pennsylvania, discuss grass roots activism. An Oklahoman, Jessie Deer-on-Water, says, "I love a challenge. I'm half Irish and half Native American and those are two races that have been struggling against great odds for hundreds and hundreds of years. I just feel like everybody should do their part. We're constantly working on a way to get people to kick soap operas and get involved. Look, you're living this, folks." An update on CCHW's "McToxins: Sent It Back" campaign provides a sample cutout label for those wishing to return styrotrash, as they call it, to McDonald's. A large photograph depicts a woman with a sign: "Fairview Parents Say Make This Neighborhood Safe for Children."

"Organizing Toolbox," a regular column written by Will Collette, instructs grass roots leaders on how to take a stand and set goals. Collette writes, "Unless you know where you're going, it's hard to know when you've gotten there. That's why we advise citizens to develop a 'platform,' or a statement of principles. Put simply, what does your group stand for? What do you want?" Collette provides guidance on how to write a statement of principles.

"The Legal Corner," another regular column, written by attorney Ron Simon, discusses how to handle criminal charges in acts of civil disobedience by pleading self-defense. Simon writes, "People who have blocked the entrance to dump sites or other hazardous facilities have been successful in defending against criminal charges based on the theory of self-defense. In order to wage this defense successfully, you need to be aware of the legal elements of the defense. I will describe them in general; the specifics vary from state to state, and you should check them out with a local criminal lawyer."

A column entitled "Baffled by Terms" is contributed by Paul Connett, who humorously defines terms such as "acceptable risk" "radical," and "resource recovery." Finally, an article, "The Use of Science in Government: Don't Bother Me With the Facts," rounds out this volume. Connett concludes the piece with this advice, "The 'facts' are not important. How you play the politics of the 'game' is what matters. Apply enough pressure on the right people and you'll get your site cleanup. Spend your time digging for the 'facts' and you're playing right into the hands of your opponents, because they already know the 'facts.' Government won't be convinced by any facts you come up with unless you back up your facts with well-focused, well-organized political pressure. That's how the residents of Love Canal won. That's how communities all across the country are winning."

These words come from grass roots leaders on the front lines in community actions confronting environmental hazards. Generously sprinkled with photographs of activists, this folksy newsletter documents citizen participation while it challenges and informs the reader.

## PETA News

The full-color cover of *PETA News* depicts a red lobster with this caption: "Caring Not Who Suffers, But

How...Even Lobsters." The 20-page July-August 1989 issue of *PETA News* tells its readers to look inside: "Activists Who Spoke Out,Stood Up, Barged In, and Lay Down for Animal Rights." *PETA News* reaches 250,000 members, and this issue documents the progress of various campaigns, celebrates individual instances of activism, and includes photographs, a message from its founder, cartoons, graphics, as well as special reports entitled "The Fur Trade Fizzles," and "No Holiday for Animals" (about animals used to amuse tourists.).

In the "Getting Results" spread, PETA tells its readers about the organization's successes. Here are a few:

- A $50,000 civil lawsuit brought against PETA by a fur company investor for punitive damages has been dropped.
- The motion by the National Institutes of Health to dismiss PETA's case to move the Silver Springs monkeys to a sanctuary was thrown out of court.
- PETA joined a group in Seattle and others in a cooperative effort to stop the U.S. Navy from using dolphins to guard Trident submarines in Puget Sound.
- The NIH is awarding $340,000 to the University of Oregon to experiment with owls, placing them in metal grips while electrodes are attached to their brains. PETA is documenting violations of federal and state animal protection laws at the University of Oregon.
- NIH is discontinuing the practice of "toe clipping" as a means of identification of rabbits and rodents following PETA's successful protest campaign to halt this practice.
- PETA reports that more than 200 cosmetics and household product companies *don't* use animal tests, a direct outcome of PETA's "compassion campaign."

In an article on the "Fur Is Dead" campaign, PETA reports on their protest at the spring 1989 furriers' convention in Las Vegas. On hand to help with the protest were a number of Hollywood stars. Belinda Carlisle, a pop singer, said, "The dark age of animal cruelty seems to be fading at least," and Rue McClanahan from *The Golden Girls* added, "Let's push it out fast!"

In its piece on "Activism in America," PETA notes these media actions:

- A San Mateo, California, high school student taped a television free speech message concerning students' rights to refuse to dissect animals and it was aired on five television stations.
- An activist was denied entry to Emory University's animal laboratories when she came to deliver toys and treats to incarcerated animals. Television cameras filmed the event and it got widespread local coverage in Atlanta and surrounding areas.
- A photograph shows Elvira, television's "Mistress of Darkness," standing by her black Mercedes with a BAN FUR license plate.

This publication documents the wide-ranging extent of PETA's animal rights campaign. Photographs are large, and the stories mimic tabloid journalism's hard-hitting, provocative style.

*   *   *

These two periodicals demonstrate the value of a grass roots group's ability to communicate with its membership and others as well (PETA also publishes a separate newsletter written especially for young people). For grass roots groups, having control of their own communications is important. If they learn how to reach the public with their message, they are in control of the message. While mass audiences are reached with commercial media, grass roots leaders need to ensure that they loyal supporters also are kept abreast of their movement, are encouraged by its successes, and can be easily mobilized when action is required or requested.

Sociologist Todd Gitlin summarizes the importance of media for grass roots organizations in his book *The Whole World is Watching:* "The cultural industries, including the news organizations, produce self-contradictory artifacts, balancing here, absorbing there, framing and excluding and disparaging, working in complicated ways to manage and contain cultural resistance, to turn it to use as commodity and to tame and isolate intractable movements and ideas. In the process, they may actually magnify and hasten...change."[20]

# 5

# Inside the Organization

To correct a shared, perceived wrong requires an effective organization formed by dedicated, ordinary people. Through group actions, they bring political, economic, and social pressure to bear upon those they oppose. However passionate activists may feel, without a systematic plan to guide the group's intent, they are unlikely to bring about major changes. Actions of more than a dozen grass roots groups are analyzed in this book, both their tactics to reach their goals and the efforts of others who oppose them. Now, a look inside these organizations provides an opportunity to examine their successes and failures from another perspective.

The following account of the collapse of the National Federation of Parents for Drug Free Youth, a grass roots movement started by parents, illustrates the importance of a sound organization and the consequences when things inside go awry.

## Doors Close on Parents

In 1988, the National Federation of Parents for Drug Free Youth (NFP) closed the doors of its Washington, D.C., national office after eight years of grass roots activism. Their cause is not lacking in appeal and substance—parents are troubled over their children's rampant drug use; rather, organizational problems caused the group to fail. An examination of this national grass roots crusade is instructive because almost every organizational issue discussed in this chapter arose as NFP attempted to change "the permissive, drug-oriented society their young people inherited and perpetuated."

Upon learning about the success of the first parent group in Atlanta, which is documented in chapter 1, other parents began to organize. By 1979, the rate of drug abuse among the young was accelerating: 11 percent of high school seniors admitted to daily use of marijuana, and 41 percent said they drank alcohol to get drunk at least once a month. In their parent groups, members shared the frustrations that arose as they encountered the intransigence of the young drug culture and the new power their grass roots groups afforded. By 1980, at least one hundred local parent groups worked in their respective communities to convince the schools, their neighbors, and PTAs that drugs were easily available to young people, that their use was glamorized by the media, that the crisis was growing, and that parents were the front line of defense in this crisis.

In 1980, a group of active parents met in Washington, D.C., with officials of the National Institute on Drug Abuse and decided they needed a national federation, free of government funding, to support and encourage this emerging grass roots response. Parents were con-

cerned with promoting the family's role and responsibility to reverse the spiral of drug use, especially
marijuana, by children and with the need to confront the
predominant drug culture in America that promotes the
do-drugs message. They lamented the lack of cooperation
by schools, the resistance of professional drug counselors, the widespread sale of drug paraphernalia, inadequate information about the effects of illegal drugs on
young people, and the government's failure to provide
credible scientific information about the subject. Further, they wanted other parents to set rules with sanctions within their homes barring drug use for all
children. This pioneering group made tentative plans to
invite grass roots parent leaders and key supporters to
Atlanta in 1980 to plan and launch a national federation.

By May 1980, the National Federation of Parents for
Drug Free Youth was announced with fanfare on Capitol
Hill. Federation officers were elected and introduced to a
national gathering of concerned parents who learned
about the federation and declared their intentions to join
the movement by launching a parent group in their own
community and becoming a member of the NFP.

From the beginning, the NFP encountered problems in
organizing, and, five years into the movement, the seeds
of collapse wee growing. The personalities of the original
founding group presented a major problem: they were
strong-willed, individualistic, combative, and articulate.
(Ironically, these precise qualities had allowed them to
emerge as leaders in their local groups.) For the federation's guidance, they decided upon a large board of
directors—forty activists who often espoused different
causes and advocated vested interests that were influenced by a variety of unique factions in their own
communities. This mix of strong-willed leaders never
jelled into a cohesive, cooperative group.

The lack of consistent financial solvency was also a

problem that haunted the NFP throughout its eight years. With a small, start-up contribution from an industrialist, they began the organization with no full-time paid executive staff. The volunteer president ran the organization from his office and home in Florida.[1] Later, a part-time executive was hired and an office was opened in the Washington, D.C., area. At one point, NFP did receive a few sizable donations, one amounting to $500,000 from former First Lady Nancy Reagan (who awarded this donation as a gift to her from the sultan of Brunei to be used for her favorite charity). Mrs. Reagan took an interest in the NFP and the movement's thrust but abandoned it in its last year. Her contribution and others, plus membership fees and sales of publications, allowed the Washington-based staff to number more than twenty during 1985–86. However, serious retrenchments in staff and operations plagued its last two years.

The National Federation of Parents was often at odds with other strong, established groups, such as the National Parent Teachers Association, over positions this established organization took on how to solve some drug problems. The NFP and the National Parent Teachers Association never worked out a harmonious, consentual relationship on the role of parents, teachers, school curricula, or school policies. The NPTA was seen as soft on responsible use and strong on individual decision making and the right to choose whether to use drugs or abstain.

Many state and local drug officials and their staff found themselves in disagreement with NFP's heavy emphasis on drug paraphernalia. NFP's attacks on certain types of drug education curricula, particularly those that stressed values, and affective, and humanistic education, were often strident; and if a particular curriculum did not pass their litmus test, it was black-balled by an NFP review committee. Any curriculum that

promoted responsible use of illegal drugs was immediately targeted, in keeping with the federation's total
abstinence position: Teaching responsible use of dangerous, illegal drugs was the equivalent of teaching
responsible shoplifting. Some of the NFP board members' attacks on secular humanism aroused counteraction from educators and university researchers.
However, the NFP made inroads into drug education and
other aspects of school life. For nearly a decade, they
worked to stop drug use on campus by asking school
officials to enforce clear, firm school policies and legal
intervention. This position was adopted by William Bennett, the first Bush administration "Drug Czar," in 1989
as part of his War on Drugs strategy.

Within the NFP factions and alliances emerged, reflect-
ing splits or dissatisfactions over issues and approaches.
Some members proposed the Red Ribbon campaign to
commemorate a drug-free America. NFP's leadership initially rejected the campaign, but some state groups
conducted it nevertheless. Youth-To-Youth, a teen program initiated by parents in Ohio, was never fully accepted by the national leadership, which pushed its own
youth program, REACH AMERICA. Some battles were
simply personal in nature. These personal and ideological differences were never resolved; rather, they became
more pronounced as the end of the organization approached. The NFP factions aired their differences in
public, and a few groups defected. Letter-writing campaigns between members were often contentious, and
copies were mailed to key people inside NFP as well as
outside the organization.

The NFP directed much attention toward groups, publications, and activities it particularly disliked: the National Organization for Reform of Marijuana Laws
(NORML); High Times magazine; the media; Opium, a
perfume produced by the Squibb Company; rock music

concerts; and research on marijuana and other drugs performed or funded by the National Institute on Drug Abuse and some university researchers, particularly those at Harvard, Columbia, and UCLA. The strident positions taken by a few members and the invectives of some leaders gave NFP a reputation in some circles as right wing, and conservative; however, to a large following, their battle with the youthful drug culture was a blessing.[3]

Even though NFP tried to reach minority parents, such efforts were called token by minority leaders in the drug field. Minority parent group membership was minimal throughout NFP's lifetime, within local community groups, among state networkers, and in the national office. The parent movement was composed primarily of middle-class, white women whose older children may have experienced varying degrees of problems with alcohol and other drugs. This educated constituency was able to mobilize local institutions such as the schools, police, city hall, local media, the business community, and parks and recreation departments to join them in working toward a drug-free community. The NFP did not serve many parents and youth from the ghetto, the barrio, or Indian reservations. Some of these parents from poor communities tried to cope with this overwhelming problem as solitary voices. Others gave up.

In spite of the criticisms from outside and early problems within, the NFP made several substantial contributions as a grass roots movement. The NFP focused national attention on a problem that was ignored or trivialized by most of the nation throughout the 1970s— an alarming rise in the use of dangerous drugs by children, beginning at increasingly young ages. While drug abuse has been called a national problem beginning from the days of the Nixon administration, a grass roots response was never encouraged or supported until 1979, when the parent movement emerged to shake a complacent nation that was allowing drug use to become normal, even glamorous, among its young people. The NFP helped to reverse a trend in which the norm had become alcohol and other illegal drug use among high school students in America.

In addition to alerting the nation to this problem, the NFP, with two effective volunteer lobbyists, worked Capital Hill. Supported by an active nationwide constituency of parents, they influenced legislation and the appointment of persons they wanted for drug policy positions in the White House and in federal agencies. They educated congressional and state leaders about the drug problem and won allies and made enemies. They succeeded in getting funding for more research that examined children and drug abuse. They changed the focus of the message from "responsible use" to "drug free." They worked to remove drug paraphernalia from record shops and convenience stores, and they were successful in closing some "head shops" that sold to minors. Few public officials endorsed positions contrary to NFP's general goal: society must declare that children cannot use illegal drugs safely and without consequences.

The major television networks adopted standards and practices to demystify drugs and portray use as dangerous, illegal, and without humor. Television executives were forced to examine the messages they presented to their vast audiences, which include a high proportion of the nation's youth. The NFP were less successful in their campaign with the motion picture and music industries, although they made their presence known to both groups.

The NFP was never entirely successful in coping with the concern that originally mobilized parent groups— their children's attitudes toward and use of drugs, and how to actively engage the children in solving the problem. They did mount a youth program entitled REACH AMERICA (Responsible, Educated Adolescents Can Help America), a largely didactic curriculum that required an intensive crash course on Marijuana and other drugs. While some teenagers did participate, the exclusively academic focus of the program gave them little to do after they learned the facts. Not enough emphasis was placed on skills building, peer refusal, youth leadership, or the helping processes. Few youth follow-up groups developed after the course, and the program was rarely attempted in minority communities.[3] NFP never developed a program for elementary school children. Their National Federation of Youth included high school students and was not as popular as several other competing youth groups such as PRIDE AMERICA or Youth-to-Youth.

The 1987 PBS documentary, "Stopping Drugs," produced in the Boston WGBH studio, portrayed the parent movement at war with teenagers, focusing on the conflict that resulted when parents imposed their non-use position and firm code of behavior on a reluctant and rebellious band of high school students. The PBS special trivialized the parent movement, never delving into its root causes or its serious prevention strategies and programs. One conclusion of the PBS documentary was that the Reagan administration was conducting a war on drugs without adequate funding or commitment. Few people argued with that conclusion, but the PBS special shed little light on the youth drug problem and never came to grips with the NFP's grass roots attempt at a solution.[4]

One effective aspect of the NFP was the establishment of the State Networkers program. In some states, able and charismatic leaders emerged and they were assembled in an alliance that enabled state and local groups to carry out lobbying, prevention campaigns, education, and pressure where needed to promote drug-free programs. In almost every state, a person was assigned to serve as legislative contact with responsibility to monitor legislation and ensure that lawmakers were aware of the parents' concerns. These networks provided the most important NFP contact with local parent groups and bridged the gap between the national office staff and their grass roots constituents. The networks provided an opportunity for strong leaders to emerge and grow. However, these strong-willed leaders were often at odds with each other over program content; the seeds of conflict grew, and internal divisions ruptured the national organization.

## The Final Collapse

The National Federation of Parents began to unravel in late 1986, when a strong faction in the board of directors sought to remove the executive director and two other high-level staff members. A bitter feud over the leadership of NFP paralyzed the organization when one faction gained enough power to remove three top officials. These three deposed leaders filed civil suits charging discrimination and unfair labor practices. A bitter, protracted legal struggle became public and the already shaky funding base crumbled. Some of the original impetus for the grass roots movement was lost in this organizational crisis and, in the summer of 1988, the National Federation for Drug Free Youth closed its national office in Washington, D.C. At the end, they asked for help from the White House and were refused. Some grass roots parent groups, both state and local, continue today, but their peak of influence on the national scene was reached in the early and middle 1980s and has subsided since then.

## Organizational Issues

The following sections discuss primary organizational concerns of grass roots movements.

### The Structure

Three primary grass roots organizational structures are presented in this analysis: a local, autonomous grass roots group; a national organization with affiliated local groups; and a national organization with no affiliated local groups. (However, every grass roots effort originates with individual activism, stimulated by a local event or shared national concern)

***Fernald Citizens: An Example of a Local Group:*** Fernald Residents for Environmental Safety and Health was formed by citizens in this Ohio town near Cincinnati, and its mission was reached when 14,000 plaintiffs filed a class action lawsuit against National Lead of Ohio, the operator of the U.S. Department of Energy's Feed Materials Production Center. This citizens' grass roots group was organized when residents near the nuclear plant learned that the federal government knew of safety violations by the plant's contractor and did not make this information public. In their class action suit, the grass roots group asked for compensation for damages caused by lowered property values and the emotional trauma created by living near the nuclear plant. In July 1989, the Energy Department promised to pay $78 million to settle claims by local residents. The settlement will finance long-term studies to determine the extent, if any, of illnesses caused by exposure to uranium, asbestos, chlorides, and barium that were released for decades into the area's water, soil and air.[5]

The Fernald group has local leaders, local membership, and no national affiliation. This model is found among most local groups concerned about hazardous waste disposal and was also popular in the early days of the parent groups concerned about their children's drug use. These local groups usually have a small office, perhaps in a member's home or in donated space; the staff is usually volunteer; and meetings are held sporadically. Local groups usually disband after they reach their objective, or membership drops off.

The Fernald group used litigation as its primary tactic. Their effort drew national media coverage because of the widespread failure of nuclear plants throughout the country and the defense used by the contractor,[6] National Lead of Ohio, that it could not be held liable because it was following government orders. This local grass roots group will probably continue to function to ensure that long-term health studies on the residents, particularly children, are conducted. Also, new lawsuits may be filed if evidence points to a future connection between cancer, genetic defects, and other physical defects and the hazardous substances released by the plant.

*Local Grass Roots Groups Affiliated With a National Organization:* Local Rainforest Action Groups (RAGS) are affiliated with the Rainforest Action Network, their parent body. These groups, mostly located on college campuses, are basically autonomous in their operations but receive guidance and materials from RAN in San Francisco. Local groups are informal, with changing membership and few requirements and activities.

Another example is the system of local chapters of Mothers Against Drunk Driving (MADD). These local groups follow the charter of the National office in Hurst, Texas. They use materials produced by that office in

Hurst, Texas, and receive some financial assistance from their parent body.

Another example, Mothers and Others for Pesticide Limits (MOPL), is unique in one important way: its local chapters are endorsed by the National Resources Defense Council (NRDC), which is not a grass roots organization. The chapters receive program support, research, legal advice, and scientific materials from NRDC, but their local structure is based on the model used by Mothers Against Drunk Driving. Most MOPL local chapters have wide discretion in how they operate, usually from a parent's home, and in selecting the local issues they pursue.[7]

These groups depend upon local leadership and local members. Occasionally, in response to unique local issues, they operate with wide latitude.

***National Organization Without Affiliated Organized Local Groups:*** People For The Ethical Treatment of Animals has a national office in Rockville, Maryland, with no affiliated local groups. Their membership roster is national, and individual members receive PETA publications, campaign alerts, and other communications. The national office is able to mobilize its members and supporters for local events and relies on phone trees, local contacts, and mailings. The centralized staff is assigned to special projects, departments, or campaigns. A publication unit prepares *PETA News* and reports on activists and other groups concerned with animal rights issues. PETA enters into coalitions with others. Their operation from a national office, without local membership chapters, allows them to avoid complicated organizational issues. Their staff energies and resources are concentrated on specific actions: the compassion campaigns, boycotts, and litigation.

The organizational structure of the Citizen's Clearinghouse for Hazardous Wastes differs from those of other national organizations without affiliated groups. CCHW serves the national grass roots movement for environmental justice through its national office in Alexandria, Virginia, and four regional offices. These offices provide training, materials, and consultation to thousands of unaffiliated local grass roots groups. The hold a national Grass Roots Convention every five years and unite local leaders with national leaders. No other currently operating group conducts a national convention.

In summary, organizational structure is important. If it concentrates on building a national reputation at the expense of a local base of support, the result may be disastrous. Most actions occur in the local community with ordinary people

## Constituency

Obtaining and keeping an active membership and following is a primary task for a grass roots group. The potential membership pool is obvious in some cases: for example, people living within an area surrounding a hazardous waste site or nuclear plant. Geographic and interest boundaries enable organizers to attract the attention of concerned neighbors who share a common, visible problem. Lois Gibbs, though at first reluctant to approach her neighbors in Love Canal, found they shared health and property concerns and were eager to join forces.[8]

Thousands of parents who have lost children or have had them injured in alcohol-related accidents are bound in mutual concern and participate in MADD or similar groups. The MADD and RID constituencies, tragically brought together, gain new members daily.

Vietnam Veterans of America had problems mobilizing and maintaining a large membership for several reasons:

the servicemen and women served in an unpopular war, and in the years directly following that war, they were rejected by traditional veterans' groups such as the American Legion and Veterans of Foreign Wars. Many potential members were young, belonged to minorities, and were unaccustomed to social action. While Vietnam Veterans of America did manage to rally some veterans to fight for recognition of Agent Orange as a health hazard and for a different approach to counseling and health care, it found sustaining a large grass roots membership to be difficult. The height of veteran involvement came when the American hostages were released in Iran in 1981 and when the Vietnam Veterans' Memorial was unveiled in Washington that same year. Vietnam veterans were angered by the hero status given to 450 hostages released by Iran during the 1981 presidential inauguration, while they had been rejected by the American public and had received no public outpouring for their long and dangerous careers in Vietnam. In that same year, the unveiling of the Wall moved them, and they traveled to stand before it and leave mementos. Their grass roots leaders say these two events helped change their self-image. However, except for a few actions, such as supporting congressional candidates sympathetic to their cause, the grass roots activism is missing.[9] Their national office staff in Washington, D.C., is concerned with legal issues, lobbying, and monitoring the Department of Veterans Affairs, to name a few activities.

College campuses have provided grass roots groups with members and public activism. PETA and In Defense of Animals have large followings at universities. Ethical issues concerning the use of animals in laboratory experiments were first debated in philosophy courses, not schools of religion, and many students were drawn to animal rights and animal liberation groups.[10] Most of the

Rainforest Action Groups (RAGS) are located on campuses and have students as leaders and members. ACT UP has a strong following on some college campuses and tends to reach young, militant gays and their supporters.

Regardless of the issue that prompts the beginning of a movement, most of those who participate are white, middle-class, educated, and economically secure. The three major exceptions are those concerned with hazardous waste disposal, drinking and driving, and crack cocaine. These three issues attract large followings in minority and blue collar communities because the sites for waste disposal, chemical plants, and nuclear facilities are located in their neighborhoods, and the health of their families is endangered. The arrival of crack cocaine on the streets during the past six years has sent shock waves through inner cities. Recently, even rural and suburban Americans have become frightened about this insidious drug. Some neighborhood groups work to remove pushers from the ghetto and to make the area safer for their children and the elderly, using any confrontational tactics that work. Many members of Remove Intoxicated Drivers (RID) are low-income, rural, factory workers, and single parents. RID requires no membership fee if an active group member cannot afford to pay. While other grass roots movements may seen remote, esoteric, and job-threatening to minorities and blue collar workers and their families, their principal worries are safety, economic security and health. When these issues are directly at stake, many join their neighbors in protest. Reaching out to bring in these two groups is a priority for some movements as they continue to broaden the net.

### Turf and Proliferation

Conflicts, largely political, have plagued grass rots groups since the nineteenth century. Abolitionists feuded with those advocating colonization, the practice of sending free Negroes to Africa or the Caribbean to live in planned colonies. Very few slaves were relocated, and abolitionists slowly gained support for their goal or a slave-free America. The struggle for funds and public support kept these groups apart for years.[11]

Various groups sought prohibition and fought with each other, trying to reach the public conscience for their approach. The Prohibitionist Party, the Women's Christian Temperance Union, the Anti-Saloon League, and Carry Nation's Home Defenders engaged in turf battles with each other while they struggled to sober a nation.

The grass roots landscape today is strewn with conflicting and competing groups within movements as each tries to obtain leadership, followers, finances, and public support. Turf battles and personal jealousies are common, even within local grass roots groups. Most movements survive these divisions. In fact, duplication of groups and proliferation of organizations are healthy in some respects because they allow more people to lead and to participate actively than would be the case in a single organization. That there are at least fourteen major environmental groups with large memberships is a good thing. That there are ten major animal rights groups active today enriches the field and gives more ordinary people a chance to be active. Rather than pressing for consolidation or elimination of groups, grass roots activism should celebrate the array of organizations pushing for similar objectives.

Not everyone troubled by the AIDS epidemic endorses or feels comfortable with the militancy of ACT UP. Some AIDS activists are chagrined at the slow pace or direction of other groups. Instead of fighting each other, they are beginning to strive to understand and accept the other. Enough remains to be done for everyone amidst public apathy and denial.

The early altercations between leaders of Vietnam

veterans groups and the American Legion and Veterans of Foreign Wars have subsided and they work for all veterans' rights now, most of the time.[12]

Some established environmental groups are put off by the militant tactics of Earth First! and Rainforest Action Network, while others note that the movement needs both ends of the continuum. That there may be four different groups lobbying for the end to acid rain, for the end of the destruction of the tropical rain forest, or to save an endangered species is positive. They make the issue more visible; more people become involved; and the opposition is confronted by more groups. Having only one grass roots group or one national organization to tackle a social issue makes it possible for the opposition to focus its tactics on only one target. The opposition learns quickly that it's easier to compromise and immobilize a single group than many. If the environmental movement was composed of only the Audubon Society and the Natural Resources Defense Council, the movement would be drastically weakened. At this juncture, more is better.

## Coalitions

Established environmental groups have succeeded in joint action, usually litigation, to accomplish the intended result. Coalitions among grass roots groups that result in planned confrontations are less likely. Coalitions provide an opportunity to intensify the action against a target.

Grass roots activism conducted by members of divergent movements has resulted in some actions. Earth First!, Rainforest Action Network, and Greenpeace pooled their resources to conduct a demonstration at World Bank headquarters in Washington, D.C., in 1986. At the annual Bankers' Convention, activists from the three groups conducted a surprise guerrilla theater in which they gained widespread media exposure. "Greenpeace designed and paid for a huge banner, emblazoned with a growling jungle cat, that read: 'World Bank Destroys Tropical Rainforests.' Mike Roselle, one of the founders of RAN, traveled east to coordinate the logistics. Under his tutelage, RAN activists climbed the fire escape of an adjoining building, raced across the rooftop, rappelled down the World Bank, and unveiled the banner just as the bankers were pulling up their limousines"[13] These three grass roots groups, joined by others, have continued to apply pressure on World Bank officials to consider environmental impact concerns when making loans in the Third World.

In A September 11, 1989, article, the *Los Angeles Times* reported a disclosure of a confidential document prepared by the World Bank that "concluded that predictions of worldwide global warming are too uncertain to justify limiting loans for development in Third World countries on environmental grounds alone." The *Times* article further said that the Bank was under mounting pressure "to use its financial leverage to help direct economic development projects that do not harm the environment." This confidential document was leaked by the Natural Resources Defense Fund. In accord with the coalition of the three activist environmental groups that demonstrated a few years earlier at the World Bank headquarters, the NRDC charged that the document "makes little mention of the importance of reducing deforestation."

In August 1990, San Francisco's ACT UP formed a coalition with Bay Area Advocates for the Homeless and Peoples with AIDS. Their aim is to combat what they call a "political war on the homeless and the poor." The coalition agreed to launch a three-part campaign: legal actions, mass appearances at public hearings, and guerrilla street theater. The coalition was created to counter state budget cuts in social services that will affect the homeless, with or without AIDs. They also protest the enforcement of the state Vagrancy laws. The coalition is called Homeless Action Alliance.[14]

A final example of a coalition of diverse groups occurred in San Francisco in 1988, when, during the Hamburger Connection campaign against Burger King, members of Rainforest Action Network and In Defense of Animals held a joint protest. RAN was demonstrating against the slash-and-burn policy in the Amazon that creates nonsustained cattle ranches and destroys its ecosystem, and the animal rights group protested the use of factory farm techniques that slaughter cattle. Animal rights groups advocate a way to halt world hunger—discontinue grain-intensive livestock production and save the grain to feed the hungry. People for the Ethical Treatment of Animals charged that "in 1984, 40 percent of the world's grain was fed to animals going to slaughter. If the same grain was fed directly to human beings, there would be more than enough to feed the world.... In Central and South America, the meat industry is involved in the wholesale destruction of the rainforest, which is cleared, then planted with grazing grasses to create the cheap hamburger."[15] The two groups were compatible and complementary in this successful campaign.

### Funding

Local grass roots groups can operate on a small budget that covers the costs of telephones, mailings, office space (if not donated), and supplies. Parent groups and those contesting hazardous waste sites do operate within tight financial constraints.To met their budget needs, they raise funds from simple events such as bake sales, car washes, walkathons, and selling tickets to entertainment events. Some sell T-shirts and other items. Contributions come from local businesses and service organizations or from other concerned citizens. A few groups assess membership fees. Being free from the worry of meeting a payroll or operating a costly program allows the volunteer members time to pursue their primary goals—putting pressure on the targeted opposition and raising community awareness and support.

The ordinary people who start these movements usually have had no management experience.They pursue their cause because they fervently believe in it. Without a management background to guide them, they need to keep their organization simple and inexpensive. If the trappings of a large organization are suggested or imposed, grass roots leaders should seek assistance and develop the organization as proposed by those who are familiar with management.

**Shedding the Grass Roots:** "MADD is no longer a bunch of people standing outside the courthouse with signs," said Andy Dricoe, who is the organization's national public information director. "Right now, we are a group trying to achieve legislative progress by filing briefs instead of standing in the streets. We have had a positive effect on more than 1,000 pieces of anti-drunk driving legislations on the state and federal level."[16]

Calling these remarks a big put-down for volunteers, Doris Aiken (Remove Intoxicated Drivers) the founder of RID-USA), wrote a letter to the editor of the *San Francisco Chronicle* on March 23, 1990.

> It takes a lot of nerve and dedication to stand outside a courthouse with signs—much more than to hire a lawyer to write legal briefs, although that is something most activist organizations do.

When the day comes that there is no one to stand
outside courthouse or legislative buildings, with signs
to promote the rights of victims, or anything else, then
the most powerful expression of public will and caring
will be gone. I hope there will always be those willing to
brave public scrutiny, and, yes, scorn on behalf of the
rights of others. The value of a charity is not equitable
with the amount of money it raises, but by the quality
of services rendered. When Basic advocacy services performed by volunteers, many of them victims, become
unimportant, then the purpose, and quality of that
charity is greatly eroded. I take my hat off to anyone
caring enough about their community, to stand with
their banner, for all to see. Without these people, we'd
still be fighting in Vietnam, or paying taxes to Queen
Elizabeth.

The transition from MADD's original impetus of dis-
traught parents who lost a child in an automobile accident in which the driver was impaired by alcohol or
drugs to a national organizations with an annual budget
or more than 30 million dollars has created dissension
within. Some parents prefer the original approach. "I'm
still working in a grass roots situation. It's the grass
roots that gave MADD its strength, and it's the grass
roots that will, in the long run, eliminate the terrible
problem of the drunk driver." This is the opinion of Pat
Baird, who broke with MADD to form the first Northern
California Chapter of RID. From the beginning, unpaid
volunteers have agitated for stiffer penalties and increased aid to victims of alcohol-related accidents.

Problems within the rank and file MADD membership
were first publicly noted in NBC's April 27, 1989 episode
of *Inside Edition*. In that NBC special, MADD's fundraising approach and its use of funds—building a large
national office, staff, and maintaining a bureaucratic
structure of regional, state, and local offices with rigid
controls over member activities—were questioned.

MADD'S national office in Texas routinely raises millions each year and has a large professional staff with corporate officials sitting on its board of director.Beginning in 1985, MADD's national office has been criticized for its fundraising efforts by the Council of Better Business Bureaus and the National Charities Information Bureau. As recently as May 1990, the report of those two private organization states, "Mothers Against Drunk Driving does not meet the standard calling for solicitations in conjunction with the sale of goods, services, or admissions to identify at the point of solicitation the actual or anticipated portion of the sales price to benefit the organization or cause"[17]

MADD's national fundraising campaign that touched off the largest protest from local chapters is called Coupon Power and is conducted by the Pennsylvania-based Reese Brothers firm. According to an article in the May 2, 1989, issue of *The Chronicle of Philanthropy*, annual revenues for MADD grew from $13 million in fiscal 1985 to $32 million in 1989. "Most of the increase can be directly attributed to the Reese Brothers. Total revenue from their MADD solicitations increased from $3.1 million in fiscal 1986 to about $19 million in fiscal 1988."[18]

The controversy over using Reese Brothers created deep division among Alabama's local MADD chapters in 1989. "MADD's financial records show Reese Brothers received about 75 percent of the $400,000 it raised in Alabama in 1988."[19] Discontent over the emphasis on national fundraising was expressed by a former MADD Alabama chapter founder and president who said, "MADD's focus went from raising hell to raising money."[20] Another observed, "When MADD was founded by Candy Lightner, its goal was to assist victims, not make money or get power. It was to help victims."[21]

Over its first stormy ten years, internal conflict has persisted, and power struggles, ideological disputes, and allegations of financial mismanagement grew. In three

states in particular (California, Texas, Alabama), as local
MADD chapters disband, they often reorganize as RID
chapters, an organizations they say maintains its grass
roots origin.

### Build The Business

Contrary to the impression generally held by the public, the former first lady Nancy Reagan did not initiate
the original "Just Say No" clubs. This grass roots movement began in Oakland, California, in 1985, (when two
black parents, Joan Brann and Linda Wiltz,) three young
black children under ten years of age, and a couple of
interested principals launched the clubs at Peralta Year
Round School and Allendale Elementary School. The
parents wanted the clubs because they knew that strong
pressures to use drugs began while the children were in
elementary school. The children wanted the clubs because they did not use illegal drugs and they wanted to
associate with like-minded friends. Together, the children could resist the constant pressures to use drugs in
their inner city.[22]

From the beginning of this grass roots movement, I
worked closely with Oakland parents and children, and
together we began the Just Say No Foundation in 1986.
Parents and teachers supported the clubs' members, and
together they began to meet as separate clubs and
engage in prevention activities. The movement spread to
other minority communities in mind-1985. Eight-year-
old Angel Wiltz, one of the original founders, wrote a
letter to Dear Abby about the clubs, and when it appeared in Abby's syndicated column, the responses from
across the nation numbered more than ten thousand.

On October 1985, NBC aired a *Punky Brewster Show*
that was seen by millions of young children. In that
episode, Punky and Cherie, the lead characters, showed

children how to resist peer pressure from older children. They refused to join the "Chicklets," a club composed of older popular girls, when they discovered that the girls used drugs and wanted Punky and Cherie to join them. The older girls were thrown out of their meeting room in Punky's tree house in the backyard. The final outcome of the episode showed Punky and Cherie starting a "Just Say No" club. In actual life, these two young television celebrities (Soliel Moon Frye and Cherie Johnson) traveled thousands of miles to cities and small towns over the next three years to promote the formation of these clubs, and hundreds of thousands of children responded in every type of community.

I told the first lady's staff about those clubs and this novel prevention program that embraced children ages five to fourteen. She invited the Oakland club's three young founders, myself, and some other adult supporters to the White House. Later, she began to actively support the concept. Overnight, the words "Just Say No" became easily recognized by the public and identified with Nancy Reagan. Unfortunately, the slogan became synonymous with the Reagan administration's War On Drugs. Critics expected the "clubs" to stop drug addiction, remove cocaine from our nation, take violence from the drug deals, and cure all of the nation's drug ills. In reality, the movement was simply for children who did not want to use drugs and who believed they could help each other resist even experimentation. Unfortunately, the media's identification of "Just Say No" clubs with the Reagan administration's drug efforts trivialized this children's movement, the only grass roots movement in the nation's history that was begun by and spread by children. Nancy Reagan's image was enhanced, while the program's intent was never communicated properly.

With the widespread popularity of the slogan "Just Say No," many corporations rushed to associate their products or services with the catchy slogan and the White House's involvement. The following correspondence sent to me reveal how one giant corporation, Procter & Gamble, used this children's prevention program to sell their products and "build the business." Supporting drug-free children was secondary to them.

THE PROCTER & GAMBLE COMPANY
*Advertising Department*
*1 Procter & Gamble Plaza, Cincinnati, Ohio 45203-3315*

*March 23, 198*
*Mr. W. T. Adams*
*1777 North California Blvd.*
*Suite 500*
*Walnut Creek, Cal 94596*

*Dear Tom:*

*In light of the many corporations, organizations, etc., jumping on the drug prevention campaign bandwagon, I want to reiterate Procter & Gamble's position on continuing support of the JUST SAY NO Foundation.*

*As you know, we are planning a multi-million dollar action-oriented and response-generating promotion in support of the JUST SAY NO Foundation's Back-To-School Pledge Campaign. While we are excited about the opportunity to teach kids to stay drug-free, we remind you that our primary objective is to build the business. Our JUST SAY NO Pledge Campaign will only work for JUST SAY NO if P&G sales and P&G customers become excited about the opportunity to get involved and help! To accomplish this, our* relationship <u>must be exclusive</u> in the packaged goods industry. If the event smacks, even a little, of "we've heard this before" or "so what's so special about this one?" our sales personnel and customers will not be moved to support our goal—lots of activity, pledge and product.

We have discussed the executional pieces necessary to make this event happen right and happen big. Tom, we share a dream—to use P&G's product reach and promotion strength to get 10,000,000 kids to say "NO" to drugs. Please help us prevent our dream from becoming just another anti-drug promotion. The Foundation must actively identify possible areas of promotional conflict and <u>prevent</u> them from becoming areas of conflict. Our contract, as you have agreed, will define exclusivity as in the attached. Any breech of this agreement will preclude P&G's interest in supporting JUST SAY NO in years to come. The Foundation must continue to eliminate "competitive" JUST SAY NO activity like Hill's/Mr. Big paper towels and do everything to minimize the presence of the already planned "Ziplock" sandwich bag promotion (e.g. eliminate television advertising and use of shelf talkers).

We suggest you have Tom Sharritt create guidelines, clearance procedures, and approval requirements for all partners', organizations', corporations' association with JUST SAY NO. Tom can help you define fund-raising opportunities as well as "protect" the JUST SAY NO Club and Foundation name, activities, and partner relationships.

Tom, please confirm what specific actions can/

*will be taken. Let's make sure we do everything
we can to move millions of Americans to sign
pledge cards and buy P&G products.*

*Sincerely yours,*

*P.H. Goldman
Promotion Manager*

The message in this Procter & Gamble letter is clear:
the company wanted exclusive use of the "Just Say No"
logo and program in order to enhance its sales. Incidentally, if young people happened to remain drug-free, P&G
would take credit. From the beginning, Procter & Gamble's involvement was dependent on having Nancy
Reagan heavily involved in this corporate venture with a
fledgling grass roots movement. They decided upon a
pledge campaign to sell their products and used the first
lady's name to do it, even though White House policy
forbade this commercial use. On many previous occasions, requests to use the White House names had been
rejected if the request involved raising funds or endors-
ing a product.

The April 17, 1987, Procter & Gamble letter to Mrs.
Reagan's chief of staff demonstrates the extent of collab-
oration between the multinational corporation and the
White House.

*April 27, 1987*

*Mr. Jack Courtemanche
The White House
1600 Pennsylvania Avenue
Washington, DC*

*Dear Jack:*

*Thanks for taking the time on Friday to talk
about our plans to support the Just Say No Back-*

to-School *Pledge Program. This letter will serve to confirm the points we discussed.*

*As I mentioned, I believe that a well executed program, designed to achieve broadscale awareness of the Pledge Program, could significantly enhance support for Just Say No and move a large number of people to show their support by signing the Back-to-School Pledge. In addition, this project will provide an opportunity to achieve support from a large number of companies whose access to millions of households can really make this Just Say No program impactful. The elements we discussed are all aimed at enhancing the possibility of really largescale participation in the Back-to-School Pledge Program during the first two weeks of September. Specifically, we agreed that:*

1. *The signed pledges will be addressed to Mrs. Reagan as "Honorary Chairperson of the Just Say No Foundation." Arrangements will be made to ensure that the mail does not have to be handled by the White House staff to avoid any logistical programs, etc.*

2. *Mrs. Reagan will host a meeting at the White House with "a panel of advisors" for the Back-to-School Pledge Program. She will invite these key industry leaders to participate in a program designed to get their support for the project and solicit their ideas on involving the entire retail industry. A key here is to agree on a date as soon as possible so that we can ensure participation by those most likely to be effective. As we discussed, a meeting in mid-July would appear to be appropriate. In any case, it is desirable to have invitations*

issued as early as possible so that we can build interest in the project.

3.   Mrs. Reagan will write a letter to Tom Adams indicating her support for the pledge campaign. As we discussed, I have attached a draft of a letter that would be helpful in obtaining support from key industry contacts. Importantly, it would be extremely helpful if we could have a copy of the letter in time to meet our April 29 release date.

4.   Consistent with your on-going plans, the White House will undertake publicity efforts to publicize the Pledge Program. Here, it is important for us to focus as much publicity on the early September period as possible. In addition, we would hope to have a coordinated effort between the public relations activities which we will initiate and those of the White House.

5.   Following the campaign, we would expect to provide special commendation or recognition for approximately 50 industry contacts who provided unusually positive support. In addition, we would ask that there be some kind of certificate developed to thank participating retailers so that we can have a better chance of achieving their support in the future.

Jack, I appreciate your willingness to undertake these initiatives. As I said, I believe this effort can mark the beginning of a significant annual support project for the Just Say No Foundation. If you have any additional questions or if I can be *of any assistance in helping to move this project ahead, please let me know.*

Sincerely,
H.R. Wietzen
Manager
Promotion & Marketing Services

cc: Mr. Tom Adams
Ms. P. H. Goldman.

# *DRAFT*

Mr. W. T. Adams
Just Say No Foundation
1777 N. California Boulevard
Suite 200
Walnut Creek, CA 94596

Dear Tom:

*I wanted to let you know how pleased I am with plans to conduct a Just Say No Back-to-School Pledge Program.*

*Having had the opportunity to review the Back-to-School Pledge Program, I am excited about the potential impact of this innovative project. Just think, there is the possibility that we can have 10 million families join in our effort to have children say No to harmful drugs and Yes to a stronger brighter America. A successful program will certainly make for a great beginning of the upcoming school year.*

*I am also pleased about the opportunity to involve many of our country's businesses in this effort. With their assistance, it will be possible to get the message about the Back-to-School Pledge Program into every home in America just before school starts. If everyone joins in, the first two weeks of September could be the most successful in Just Say No's exciting history.*

*I look forward to helping you make the Back-to-School Pledge Program a huge success!*

*Sincerely yours,*

*Mrs. Nancy Reagan*
*Honorary Chairperson*
*Just Say No Foundation*

The First Lady's name and the White House emblem were used prominently by Procter & Gamble in the 1987 and 1988 pledge campaigns, and many products were sold, enriching the corporate coffers. No other corporation was given this kind of specialized treatment by Mrs. Reagan's staff. The primary interest of Procter & Gamble was to make a profit, as was clearly stated in the March 23, 1987, letter sent to me by a P&G marketing executive.

The relationship between the White House and Procter & Gamble grew stronger over the course of the two pledge campaigns. On two occasions—March 12 and May 6, 1987—I was invited, as president of the Just Say No Foundation, to the office of the First Lady of the United States to attend ceremonies related to drug abuse prevention programs. At the first event, two foundation executives were honored for their educational contributions to "Just say No" clubs and, at the second, a donation was presented to the Just Say No Foundation by a professional athlete. On both occasions, Nancy Reagan asked me to accompany her to an adjoining room and privately requested that a Procter & Gamble employee be hired to assume major management responsibilities in the foundation. Mrs. Reagan's chief of staff, Jack Courtemanche, followed up with telephone calls encouraging my speedy action on her request. Procter & Gamble staff were contacted to name a candidate for the new position.

On May 6, 1987, in the second private meeting at the White House, Mrs. Reagan expressed annoyance that her request had not been met. She stated that if her request was not satisfied immediately, she would withdraw her support for the Just Say No Foundation. At that time, Mrs. Reagan's support was critical to the success of the foundation's objectives. Accordingly, on May 18, 1987, a former Procter & Gamble employee was hired as executive director of the foundation. When Mrs. Reagan was told of this hiring, she subsequently wrote a letter and encouraged the foundation "to use the extra help."

## THE WHITE HOUSE
## May 18, 1987

*Dear Tom:*

*What a wonderful rally last week in Los Angeles! Judging from the exuberance of the children who took part in it, I think it was a great success! Thank you very much for all your hard work.*

*As always, I'm very encouraged at the progress being made in the area of substance abuse prevention, especially when I see the success of the "Just Say No" clubs. I know how much we owe you, Tom, for your outstanding contribution. All I*

*can say is please keep up the good work!—and*
*use the extra help!*

*With warm best wishes.*

> *Sincerely,*
>
> *Nancy Reagan*

*Mr. Tom Adams*
*"Just Say No" Foundation*
*1777 North California Boulevard*
*Walnut Creek, California 94596*

In late 1987, White House staffer Jack Courtemanche asked the Just Say No Foundation to appoint a senior official from Procter & Gamble to serve as chairman of its board of directors. In early 1988, Wallace Abbott, at the time vice-president of marketing for Procter & Gamble, was named the foundation's chairman. The foundation was experiencing financial problems due to two unsuccessful fundraising events and a rapidly growing staff required to meet the demands placed upon it by its highly visible programs.

The direction the Just Say No Foundation should take became an issue between the new chairman from Procter & Gamble and several of the principals in the foundation. Abbott wanted the Just Say No Foundation to recreate Procter & Gamble's Special Olympics sponsorship program. The wisdom of his replacing a grass roots approach with two levels of bureaucracy (a state office with local committees) was adamantly opposed. He was determined to alter the basic structure of this primarily volunteer movement in order for Procter & Gamble to have greater access to the clubs and their supporters through these state and local offices in order to "build the business"—his company's primary goal.

In May 1988, Abbott called together members of Procter & Gamble's marketing services to decide the fate of this struggling foundation. With little or no concern for the basic principles of this spontaneous children's movement, the Procter & Gamble marketing group met to devise a plan. No one from the foundation was asked to give advice or information except the former Procter & Gamble employee who was serving as the foundation's executive director. The following plan was submitted to Wallace Abbott:

*May 31, 1988*
*R/L: 5/89*

*Mr. W.W. Abbott*

*SUBJECT: JUST SAY NO FOUNDATION*

*This responds to your request for some thoughts on how the Just Say No Foundation might proceed to develop a more viable national organization. As I perceive the current Just Say No "situation," I believe that the intermediate term objectives for its organizational development should be as follows:*

| *Objectives* | *Action Plan* |
|---|---|
| *1. To develop national management capable of establishing the organization as a nationally effective entity with adequate long-term funding, strategic planning, and innovative programming.* | *1. The national/regional management structure of the Just Say No Foundation needs to be reorganized as soon as practical. The elimination/reduction of the Washington and Oakland office activities* |

would result in a re-
duction of current
case demands.

The Foundation
should recruit an ex-
perienced and sea-
soned manager to
oversee the Founda-
tion's development as
an on-going entity.
The Board should
provide a clear de-
scription of the role of
the current manage-
ment positions and
set specific near-term
objectives so that
there is a clearer
understanding of the
Foundation's near
term objectives as
well as a vision for
the future.

2. To develop a national
   infrastructure capa-
   ble of facilitating
   communication,
   fund-raising, pro-
   gram development,
   and program
   expansion.

2. The long term
   viability of the move-
   ment depends on the
   development of local,
   regional, and na-
   tional infrastructure.
   A detailed plan
   should be developed
   immediately. Such a
   plan might include
   the following:

   a. Hire a manager ca-
   pable of organizing

*existing Just Say No volunteers into local or regional organizations.*

*b. Identify 20 major metropolitan areas currently having strong Just Say No clubs. These metropolitan areas or regional clubs would be organized into separate coordinating committees and might even incorporate. Eventually one organization in each state would be developed with an independent Board that was "licensed" to coordinate the Just Say No activities within the state.*

*c. Over time additional target cities would be identified until each state has functioning regional entities, as well as one state-wide coordinating body.*

*d. The national headquarters would continue to operate training programs,*

develop policies, and
establish operating
guidelines for the
state organizations.
Additionally, the
Foundation head-
quarters would con-
duct fund-raising
activities to supple-
ment the fund-raising
of the local and state
organizations.

3. To provide adequate
   long term funding for
   present programming
   as well as the fund-
   ing of expanded pro-
   gram activities.

3. The national head-
   quarters should im-
   mediately develop
   federal or Foundation
   grants aimed at fund-
   ing projects which
   would have as their
   goal the development
   of the state based in-
   frastructure de-
   scribed above.

   The Foundation
   should continue to
   seek Foundation and
   Corporate support to
   pay for all materials
   being developed and
   forwarded to the
   clubs. No unfunded
   projects should be
   undertaken.

   State and local Foun-
   dation funds (rather
   than national

*sources) should be
sought to establish
the metropolitan
area operations pre-
viously described.*

*The national Founda-
tion should develop
fund-raising guide-
lines and suggestions
for Just Say No clubs,
as well as local coor-
dinating committees.*

*The above plan assumes that the organization
can raise sufficient funds from Federal and
individual sources to maintain a headquarters
operation over the next six months. Given the
current financial situation, the immediate
restructure described above, as well as the
acquisition of transitional funds must be an
immediate priority.*

H.R. Wientzen
Manager
Promotion & Marketing Services

HRW:vlc
(588:028)

cc: Mr. R.L. Wehling
Mr. Tom Collins
Mr. V.O. Hamilton

During June 1988, Wallace Abbott met with the Just
Say No Foundation officials to announce that he would
expedite the plan developed by Procter & Gamble's marketing division. Abbott denied any conflict of interest
when it was pointed out that a large corporation was

taking over a nonprofit foundation and was using this children's program for its own plans to "build the business." Abbott closed the inner city Oakland office, the birthplace of the movement, closed the Washington, D.C., office, and asked me to step aside as president and become a consultant. I refused and resigned in August 1988, as did Joan Brann, the parent/founder who served as JSN's vice president.

This matter of a corporate giant taking over a nonprofit foundation was brought to the attention of Charles B. Rangel, a member of the U.S. House of Representatives. At an August 12, 1988, press conference organized by Charles Rangel's staff and conducted at the United States Capitol, the incident and supporting documents were released to the press.

RANGEL REVEALS THE ABUSE OF
"JUST SAY NO" BY PROCTER & GAMBLE

STATEMENT BY REP. CHARLES B. RANGEL
AT NEWS CONFERENCE
FRIDAY, AUGUST 12, 1988

IT IS WITH THE DEEPEST SADNESS THAT I COME BEFORE THE MEDIA TODAY.

FOR THE LAST EIGHT YEARS, WHILE I HAVE CRITICIZED THE REAGAN ADMINISTRATION ON DRUG ABUSE POLICY, I HAVE ALWAYS LAUDED THE FIRST LADY AND SUPPORTED HER ANTIDRUG EFFORTS. NANCY REAGAN HAS SYMBOLIZED THE DRIVE FOR A DRUG-FREE SOCIETY. SHE HAS REACHED OUT TO YOUNG PEOPLE. SHE HAS ENLISTED THE VOLUNTEER EFFORTS OF PARENTS, ENTERTAINERS, MOVIE PRODUCERS, ATHLETES AND OTHER SEGMENTS OF THE PRIVATE SECTOR IN HER "JUST SAY NO" CAMPAIGN. SHE HAS CALLED MEETINGS OF FIRST LADIES FROM NATIONS THROUGHOUT THE WORLD TO FIGHT DRUGS. SHE HAS RAISED THE CONSCIOUSNESS OF AMERICA ABOUT OUR NUMBER ONE PROBLEM—THE SCOURGE OF THE POISONS CALLED DRUGS DESTROYING OUR YOUNG PEOPLE. NANCY REAGAN HAS MADE 'JUST SAY NO' A NATIONAL CRUSADE.

THAT IS WHY I AM GRAVELY CONCERNED BY EVIDENCE THAT
APPEARS TO INDICATE THAT THE GOOD NAMES OF THE FIRST
LADY AND THE 'JUST SAY NO' FOUNDATION SHE HAS SO ARDENTLY
SUPPORTED ARE BEING ABUSED AS A SALES PROMOTION, FOR
PROFIT, BY ONE OF AMERICA'S LARGEST CORPORATIONS, PROCTER
& GAMBLE (P&G).

WITH ME TODAY ARE TOM ADAMS AND JOAN BRANN, WHO UN-
TIL LAST WEEK WERE THE PRESIDENT AND VICE PRESIDENT OF
THE 'JUST SAY NO' FOUNDATION. I WISH TO THANK THEM FOR THE
PIONEER WORK THESE TWO HAVE PERFORMED OVER THE YEARS
IN DRUG ABUSE PREVENTION. JOAN BRANN FOUNDED THE 'JUST
SAY NO' PROGRAM, IN OAKLAND, CALIFORNIA. TOM AND JOAN TO-
GETHER, WITH THE SUPPORT OF NANCY REAGAN AND VOLUN-
TEERS THROUGHOUT THE COUNTRY, EXPANDED THIS GRASSROOTS
PROGRAM NATIONWIDE. THEY RESIGNED A WEEK AGO YESTERDAY
AND ARE JUST STANDING WITH ME TODAY TO PROTEST THE COM-
MERCIALIZATION OF THE 'JUST SAY NO' PROGRAM.

I HAVE DOCUMENTS AND EVIDENCE OF PROCTER & GAMBLE'S
INTENT TO USE THE FIRST LADY, THE WHITE HOUSE, THE 'JUST
SAY NO' PROGRAM AND FOUNDATION, THE VOLUNTEERS THAT
HAVE HELPED THE 'JUST SAY NO' PROGRAM TO GROW, AND OUR
NATION'S YOUTH TO INCREASE SALES OF PROCTER & GAMBLE
PRODUCTS.

THESE DOCUMENTS INDICATE THAT PROCTER & GAMBLE MADE
ITS CONTINUED SUPPORT FOR THE FOUNDATION CONTINGENT ON
THE COMPANY HAVING A RELATIONSHIP WITH THE PROGRAM "EX-
CLUSIVE IN THE PACKAGED GOODS INDUSTRY."

IN MARCH 23, 1987, LETTER TO THE FOUNDATION FROM PROC-
TER & GAMBLE DISCUSSING THE COMPANY'S SUPPORT FOR A 'JUST
SAY NO' BACK TO SCHOOL DRUG-FREE PLEDGE CAMPAIGN, PROC-
TER & GAMBLE INSISTED THE FOUNDATION "ELIMINATE 'COMPETI-
TIVE' JUST SAY NO ACTIVITY" BY OTHER RETAILERS. "ANY
BREECH OF THIS AGREEMENT," THE LETTER SAID, "WILL PRE-
CLUDE PROCTER & GAMBLE'S INTEREST IN SUPPORTING JUST SAY
NO IN YEARS TO COME.":

THE SAME LETTER ALSO SAID, "WHILE WE ARE EXCITED
ABOUT THE OPPORTUNITY TO TEACH KIDS TO STAY DRUG-FREE,
WE REMIND YOU THAT OUR PRIMARY OBJECTIVE IS TO BUILD THE

BUSINESS." THE LETTER CONCLUDED, "LET'S MAKE SURE WE DO EVERYTHING WE CAN TO MOVE MILLIONS OF AMERICANS TO SIGN PLEDGE CARDS AND BUY PROCTER & GAMBLE'S PRODUCTS."

THESE DOCUMENTS ALSO INCLUDE A LETTER FROM PROCTER & GAMBLE TO THE FIRST LADY'S STAFF, ALLEGEDLY CONFIRMING PLANS FOR MRS. REAGAN'S INVOLVEMENT IN THE BACK TO SCHOOL PLEDGE PROGRAM.

IN FACT, PROCTER & GAMBLE SENT OUT A MASS COUPON MAILING LAST YEAR, AND A SIMILAR MAILING THIS YEAR, PROMOTING THE PLEDGE PROGRAM. THIS YEAR'S MAILING INCLUDES A COVER SHEET SAYING "HELP US HELP KIDS 'JUST SAY NO': THE 'JUST SAY NO' FOUNDATION, NANCY REAGAN, HONORARY CHAIRMAN". INSIDE A PLEDGE CARD IS INSERTED TO LEAD A DRUG-FREE LIFE." NEXT TO THAT CARD IS A GREEN AND YELLOW SUN BUBBLE SAYING "COUPONS INSIDE WORTH OVER $4.00." AND THE REST OF THE MAILING IS ADS FOR PROCTER & GAMBLE PRODUCTS.

IN ANOTHER LETTER TO THE FOUNDATION, PROCTER & GAMBLE COMPLAINED ABOUT THE ASSOCIATION BETWEEN THE FOUNDATION AND ANOTHER COMPANY, TEXIZE, AND ASKED HOW THE USE OF THE 'JUST SAY NO' LOGO BY TEXIZE "FIT WITHIN OUR EXCLUSIVE CONTRACT DISCUSSION.".

I WANT TO ASK TODAY WHAT RIGHT DOES PROCTER & GAMBLE HAVE TO DEMAND AN EXCLUSIVE FRANCHISE TO THIS VOLUNTARY DRUG PREVENTION THAT BELONGS TO THE AMERICAN PEOPLE? WHAT RIGHT DOES PROCTER & GAMBLE HAVE TO SUGGEST THAT THE FIRST LADY AND THE WHITE HOUSE APPROVED PROCTER & GAMBLE'S COMMERCIALIZATION OF THE JUST SAY NO PROGRAM AND THE FOUNDATION?

CLEARLY, IT WAS NEVER THE FIRST LADY'S INTENTION TO ALLOW A SOAP COMPANY TO USE THIS PROGRAM AND THE CHILDREN OF OUR NATION FOR COMMERCIAL PROFIT. AND I AM SURE HER STAFF WOULD NOT PERMIT HER NAME AND REPUTATION TO BE USED IN A COMMERCIAL VENTURE. IN FACT, THE WHITE HOUSE WOULD NOT EVEN ALLOW THE JUST SAY NO FOUNDATION TO USE MRS. REAGAN'S SIGNATURE ON CERTIFICATES TO THE JAYCEES, CLAIMING "THERE IS A WHITE HOUSE POLICY WHICH PRECLUDES THE USE OF THE FIRST LADY'S NAME."

SO THIS IS A SAD MOMENT FOR ME. IT CLEARLY APPEARS THAT
PROCTER & GAMBLE USED THE FIRST LADY'S NAME FOR PROFIT
WITHOUT HER KNOWLEDGE OR SUPPORT. HOW COULD PROCTER &
GAMBLE BETRAY THE PROGRAM AND THE COUNTRY AND THE
FRIENDSHIP OF THE FIRST LADY? I CALL ON PROCTER & GAMBLE
TO EXPLAIN THEIR ACTIONS. I ALSO CALL ON THE FIRST LADY'S
STAFF TO JOIN WITH ME IN CALLING FOR AN END TO THE COM-
MERCIALIZATION OF NANCY REAGAN'S NAME. I CALL UPON THE
FIRST LADY'S STAFF TO COME FORWARD TO PROTECT HER INTEG-
RITY AND THE ENORMOUS CONTRIBUTIONS SHE HAS MADE TO THE
VOLUNTEER DRUG ABUSE PREVENTION EFFORTS IN OUR NATION.
PROCTER & GAMBLE APPARENTLY HAS ABUSED ITS RELATIONSHIP
WITH THE WHITE HOUSE STAFF IN THE INTEREST OF PROFIT.

THE FIRST LADY'S 'JUST SAY NO' PROGRAM WAS THE LAST RAY
OF HOPE THAT WE WOULD HAVE A NATIONAL DRUG PREVENTION
POLICY BY ENCOURAGING THE PRIVATE SECTOR TO DO WHAT THIS
ADMINISTRATION HAS NOT ALLOWED GOVERNMENT TO DO. NOW
WE SEE THAT ONE COMPANY, IN THE NAME OF PROFIT, HAS NOT
ONLY DEMANDED EXCLUSIVE RIGHTS TO THE "JUST SAY NO" PRO-
GRAM BUT ALSO APPARENTLY HAS ATTEMPTED TO MAKE THE
FOUNDATION NOTHING MORE THAN A DIVISION OF PROCTER &
GAMBLE TO SELL SOAP. I AM SHOCKED AND CRESTFALLEN TO
HAVE TO BRING THIS NEWS TO YOU.

Procter & Gamble, with assistance from Mrs. Reagan's
chief of staff, enhanced its ability to profit from a grass
roots movement largely generated by children. Their
callous disregard for those who founded and directed the
program in the inner city of Oakland was revealed by a
Procter & Gamble marketing official who scribbled "pull
the plug on Oakland" on an internal document during a
discussion on the plight of the JSN Foundation. Procter
& Gamble continues to control this program and Nancy
Reagan remains its honorary chairman.

Finally, this inconsistent application of this White
House policy affected another grass-roots group. A White
House letter dated July 19, 1988, states the policy pro-

hibiting the use of the First Lady's name in any fundraising. The group turned down by the White House was the National Federation of Parents for Drug Free Youth, a nonprofit group that boasted First Lady Nancy Reagan as its honorary chairman. In less than a month following the rejection of NFP's request, the grass-roots group closed the doors of its national office in Washington, D.C.

*THE WHITE HOUSE*
*WASHINGTON*
*July 29, 1988*

*Mr. Karl Bernstein*
*Executive Director*
*National Federation of Parents*
*for Drug-Free Youth*
*8730 Georgia Avenue*
*Suite 200*
*Silver Spring, MD 20910*

*Dear Karl:*

*As I told you in our phone conversation, Mrs. Reagan has not agreed to attend NFP's luncheon during your sixth annual conference. I must ask, therefore, that you refrain from using her name in connection with the lunch. Also, I would appreciate your attempting to correct any misperceptions regarding her attendance which may have occurred [sic] so far.*

*The attached copy of Marilyn Bryant's memorandum does not do this. For your information, established White House policy does not allow the President's or First Lady's name to be used for fundraising purposes. I am sure, therefore, that you will understand our desire to refrain from any action that could be construed as such.*

*Again, thank you for all you are doing, and for your cooperation with this matter. Mrs. Reagan joins me in sending our warm regards.*

*Sincerely,*

*James F. Manning*
*Director of Projects*
*Office of the First Lady*

National grass roots groups with popular followings are frequently approached by ambitious public relations firms or other entrepreneurs. Commercialization of the movement is always a problem that grass roots leaders must consider, particularly if they need and expend large sums of money. The temptation to compromise a program's intent in order to raise money is very real.

---

### WARNING SIGNS: SHEDDING GRASS ROOTS

The following events signal a potential
loss of grass roots activism:

- Volunteers are replaced by paid staff.

- A national office is established.

- A public relations firm or a professional fundraiser is hired.

- The original grass roots cause becomes commercialized; that is, identified with specific corporations.

- The national office becomes more important than local groups: bureaucracy is created, with regional, state, and local offices.

- Celebrities dominate the message to the public.

- The board of directors becomes dominated by male, corporate officials at the expense of activist volunteers (usually women).
- The national office raises money at the expense of local groups, resulting in inadequate sharing of revenues.
- Activities of local groups become less valued than the mission of the national organization, and controls are placed on local groups.
- The national office changes its original methods of local grass roots activism to lobbying, litigation, and legislation.

---

**Team Up With "Team Valvoline":**   In 1987, when the National Federation of Parents for Drug Free Youth was plagued with debts, the movement was approached by Valvoline Motor Oil. The deal was that if NFP would allow Valvoline to place its logo on race cars that were part of Team Valvoline, each time one of these cars reached the winner's circle in auto racing competition, NFP would receive a specified sum of money. In addition to the NFP logo that advocated a drug-free life for children, the race cars also carried the Budweiser Beer logo. The mixed message was obvious: kids should remain drug free (alcohol is a drug), but consumers should use Valvoline Motor Oil and drink Budweiser because these two corporations are helping kids remain drug free.

Grass roots groups are safe from contamination or the appearance of a conflict of interest if they rely on membership fees, sales of their own publications, unattached donations, and grants from foundations, with no strings attached to a product or service. Contributions can be accepted from businesses that genuinely want to assist, without putting a profit motive ahead of the cause or selling a product or service that is in conflict with the intent of the grass roots movement.

## Becoming a Political Party

Third parties spawned in the nineteenth century by abolitionist and prohibitionist movements did poorly in general elections. The Union Party's formation and entry in the 1936 general election was the culmination of four grass roots movements' uniting to form a political base among their vast constituencies. These groups—the National Union for Social Justice, Farmers Relief Group, the Townsend Plan, and Share-the-Wealth—had extensive grass roots support but were unable to obtain one million votes for their party's candidate for the presidency of the United States.[23] All four grass roots groups lost membership, influence, and direction following that decisive defeat by the electorate.

In European countries with traditions of multiple political parties the environmentalist Greens won elections through the 1980s, although the Green party lost all of its seats in the first national elections in unified Germany in December 1990. Their influence is being felt in local and national elections and is likely to increase if environmental issues do not receive attention from the dominant political parties.

The likelihood of a strong Green party in the United States is remote. The time, money, and organizational complexities required to form a political party are formidable and, for most grass roots groups, prohibitive. However, if the Democrats and Republicans fail to begin solving problems of hazardous waste disposal, acid rain, ozone depletion, nuclear site selection, endangered wetlands and species, rain forest destruction, oil spills, pesticides in food, and a host of other environmental problems, the environmental movement may launch a national Green party in the United States as a last resort. The Bay Area Green Party has been formed in San Francisco.

## Open or Secret

The leaders of a grass roots group may decide to adopt a closed organizational stance, either when they fear infiltration and disruption from their opponents or the federal government, or because they think secrecy necessary for a preemptive strike. However, most grass roots groups use an open, public approach. The Citizen's Clearinghouse for Hazardous Wastes encourages those local groups it counsels to put up with would-be infiltrators: "In most instances, you'll simply have to put up with them. Identify them for who they are to the audience and the other group members. Don't become a secret society yourselves. We've seen groups self-destruct, or, even more pathetic, fizzle out because they feared having their 'secrets' fall into the hands of their opponents."[24]

Operation Rescue uses surprise tactics to ensure an effective "minute man raid": an unannounced medical clinic blockage. Its members mobilize at secret locations to launch a "rescue" at a specific site known only to a few leaders. "The bottom line is we're involved in a war. The last thing a military officer wants is to let out the secrets beforehand."[25] Operation Rescue groups anticipate infiltration from pro-choice supporters.[26] Civil disobedience at Planned Parenthood offices or medical clinics often results in public confrontations between the two groups, with customary arrests and other disruptions. Most Operations Rescue groups do not list their names in local telephone directories.

The decision to be open or secret depends largely on the tactics used by grass roots groups and the degree to which they feel threatened by those who oppose their actions.

*   *   *

The organization components discussed in this chapter are developed by grass roots groups as they progress from a few adherents to large-scale organizations. When these components are neglected or improper decisions are made about them, the effectiveness of the movement is diminished.

# 6

# The Challenge and the Future

For those who may want to begin a grass roots movement, form an affiliate of a national organization, or participate as an ordinary member, the following discussion presents "how to" and "what to do," based on the experiences of more than a dozen current, important efforts and three historic grass roots groups.

## To Begin

The budding of a grass roots movement begins when a concern becomes great enough to prompt a person to take action. In some cases, it matures; in others, it fades away after an initial burst of energy. Those times and circumstances of genuine initiation are chronicled in the opening chapter. A movement does not start because of a fluke or happenstance; the grievance or wrong is shared and visible. In some instances, a grass roots movement originates in a community because people have learned about a particular problem from sources outside—perhaps far away—but the impact of the problem draws them into the fray. Rain forests in the Amazon are remote, but the dangers that will follow from their destruction are global.

### Zeal Required

Begin when zeal replaces general concern, for zeal, in its finest sense, is an eagerness and ardent interest in pursuit of something! Without it, concern can go flat, and an initial rebuff can lead to abandonment of the effort.

### What About Others?

Check out the extent of concern about the problem to determine if the grievance is shared and if others are moved to join the struggle. By simply asking friends and neighbors first, one can sense the extent of a desire to act in concert. Grass roots activism cannot be a lonely journey into an obscure cause. If others care enough to participate, solidarity of purpose will follow.

### Assessment

What is already being done to solve the problem? An assessment of the response by those entrusted to act is important. If the assessment reveals that those in charge will not pursue an acceptable solution, the need for independent action increases. Opposition to grass roots actions takes many forms, as noted earlier. When enough people encounter strong resistance, then it's time to act.

## A Clear Purpose

Fix in mind the intent of those who share the cause and come to a consensus of purpose before another step is taken. Determine the following:

- the problem
- its causes
- possible solutions
- obstacles
- results and desired outcomes

## Form Follows Function

The form an organization takes is determined by its functions. If a large membership is required and desirable, the organization must develop complex structures and systems that demand constant attention. Those grass roots groups with national, regional, state, and local chapters build a form to suit their function. Local groups require less complicated organizations; however, knowledge about form and function is invaluable to any grass roots movement.

## Build Deliberately

Without consciously realizing the value, most organizations prize grass roots support and involvement because ordinary people enable them to operate, whether selling a product, winning an election, succeeding in entertainment or sports, or governing. Build membership and the organization with deliberation. Two types of grass roots support are necessary: core members who assume organizational responsibility, and those in the general public who endorse and support the actions but do not actively participate in the operation. Both components are essential to the success of the effort, and each plays distinct roles.

### The Core

Leaders of the movement should remain in that role unless reasons to change are evident and agreeable to the group. Some type of sanction is needed to determine leadership: election, consensus, or appointment. Members function most effectively when their activities within the group match their skills, interests, and talents.

When the movement begins, those guiding it need vision and a sense of direction, as discussed earlier. As the organization grows, a consensus statement of principles and purpose should be endorsed by the membership, especially the core group that directs the movements.

### Informed to Act

Members and supporters, as well as the public at large, require information about the movement produced by those leading it. In many cases, events move quickly, and reliable, current information should be made available to the community. Group members who can write and speak with authority help keep everyone alerted to the needs of the local group. Where a national organization exists, local members need written materials to keep abreast of national trends and objectives. Telephones, leaflets, newsletters, announcements, meetings, and briefings link people.

### Meetings

One simple instruction: meet as a group only when necessary and only when the group has business to attend to. Core members should be in regular contact, but the larger group can be convened when action is decided upon, or when a special event such as a speaker, a film, or an action is scheduled. On those occasions, invite the public. For instance, victim-oriented groups such as those fostered by RID hold monthly meetings as support sessions for those who have lost loved ones to drunk-driving accidents.

### Open and Democratic

An open and democratic organization fares well in American society and builds trust among members and the public. If the cause is credible and just, the issues need to be presented and discussed in an open arena where ideas can be tested by believers as well as skeptics.A group with shared norms and goals is capable of obtaining and keeping members, and when the process of deciding upon an issue allows full participation, members' commitment to the cause grows. An intense verbal struggle over ideas, tactics, and outcomes is preferable to decisions made by a small clique and forced upon the membership. The group needs official positions that reflect the intentions of all its members.

### Alliances

Going it alone often means going nowhere. Finding common purpose and genuine support enhances a group. When an issue draws intense public concern, factions within the community will surely appear, and the grass roots group must assess those with compatible views and actions to determine if an alliance would be advantageous. A coalition can be temporary or permanent. If mutual support brings strength, attach and build from that base. The proliferation of groups is generally good, because, as more ordinary people become involved, public support and awareness expand. Carefully assess the motive for any potential alliance or coalition, however, to ensure that integrity is maintained. Groups are judged by the company they keep.

### Recruit Well and Grow

If the grass roots group is to gain support and grow, those in charge need to recruit people who can contribute to the group's mission, who work well in an organization that is growing, and who are committed to the cause. Everyone needs to grow and develop in order to fulfill the organizational demands. While most grass roots leaders have had little, if any, prior management experience, they need to acquire it or complement their skills with those of others who serve the organization honestly and faithfully.

## The Arsenal: Choosing Tactics

Those intent on making social change have a variety of tactics at their disposal. A rule of thumb: Use only those tactics with which the group members feel comfortable. Public reaction comes from both what is said and how it is said. A tactic succeeds when there is a personal commitment to using it. Some people practice nonviolent civil disobedience, while others eschew it. It's a matter of choice. Respect it.

### Know the Continuum

Tactics used by the groups analyzed in this book range from writing a letter or making a telephone call to sabotaging a logging truck or vandalizing laboratory equipment. Grass roots leaders should learn about the tactics at their disposal and discuss with members what each one entails for the group as well as for individuals. Each tactic requires its own set of skills, creativity in its application, and assessment of strategic impact. Each generates a response, and some require long-term commitment of resources, time, finances, and personal sacrifice. No tactic should be employed unless the group makes a commitment to seeing it carried out in its entirety. A failed tactic is difficult to erase in public awareness or in personal frustration.

### Select a Path

Determining the methods for achieving a particular outcome, or goal, usually evolves over time and is frequently influenced by the degree of resistance encountered. Some grass roots groups decide at the outset to take a certain path. Barry Commoner refers to this decision as taking the hard or soft path. Once a group has embarked on a hard path, reversal is difficult. Operation Rescue, Earth First!, ACT UP, some local hazardous waste groups, the Animal Liberation Front, and the Rainforest Action Network are examples of groups that have adopted the hard path. Their tactics are deliberately confrontational. Many anticipate being arrested. They gamble on getting high visibility to make their point, and they usually succeed because media attention is likely to focus on the dramatic, extraordinary, and creative use of confrontation. Some groups choose the soft path because it fits their style and intention: Mothers and Others for Pesticide Limits, MADD, parents' groups, and Just Say No clubs follow the soft path most of the time. Those taking the hard path can and do use other tactics found in the continuum: petitions, letter writing, litigation, publications, and shareholder presentations. Keeping the organization flexible enough to employ any tactic acceptable to the group is important.

### Train for Success

Many tactics require skills already possessed by the membership: writing and speaking. Signing a petition or attending a meeting is easy. But some tactics require training, and the group should prepare its members before they launch an action in public. Many groups already do some type of training, while others learn through experience—a sometimes painful process.

Members should be taught that civil disobedience may result in their being arrested. They should be taught how to respond to arresting officers and subsequent court behaviors if necessary. People preparing and making presentations at shareholders' meetings need expert instruction. Launching and participating in a boycott campaign requires methodical planning. And guerrilla theater is effective only when the actors rehearse and know the essences of drama and comedy and use the element of surprise.

### Gain Public Support

One primary objective of any grass roots movement is to gain public support for its cause(s), because, without broad appeal, its tasks will be difficult to accomplish. When a group loses touch with or angers the populace, their cause risks rejection. Father Coughlin had a massive following, but his message became bitter, and he was ultimately rejected. Tactics should be chosen with the *public* in mind; if an act inflames a large populace, trouble lies ahead.

## Negotiate

Few victories are possible without negotiation, either during the confrontational phase or at the close of a struggle. Leaders need to learn negotiation skills if the opposition is powerful and antagonistic. When groups face elected officials, they need to bring a plan that allows discussion, joint decision making, and, in some cases, compromise. Even though the struggle may be bitter, intense, and seemingly irreconcilable, an all-or-none positions can prove fatal. When groups opposing a hazardous waste site confront their opposition, they often propose compromises such as recycling, waste recovery at site, prevention of waste during production, and use of nonhazardous materials in production.

If the grass roots group's position leaves no room for compromise, the group must remain committed to see the struggle through until its objective is reached. Mothers and Others For Pesticide Limits can never agree to a level of pesticide risks in foods that endangers their children's health. Groups must decide if and when to negotiate as part of their overall strategy.

## Use Affordable Tactics

Some tactics are costly to implement, for small, local groups as well as for larger and nationally based movements. The most expensive and time-consuming tactic is to carry on a legal contest by judicial process—to litigate. Unless legal services are *pro bono*, most local groups cannot afford to sue for their causes. Corporations have access to legal resources that dwarf citizens' complaints, and if they don't win outright, they drag out the legal process indefinitely to drain their opponents. However, some groups, such as People for the Ethical Treatment of Animals and Vietnam Veterans have filed suits and won. Large public-interest law firms and some of the prestigious environmental justice groups are better equipped to use litigation successfully than are struggling local groups.

Paid lobbyists are also costly. Since lobbying requires complex skills and large financial commitments, care should be taken when deciding upon using this tactic.

Finally, the production of publications, media, and other printed material is expensive.Groups should try to obtain "in kind" contributions, pool resources with other groups, or use appropriate materials produced by other sources when their budgets preclude expensive media.

### Work With the Nationals

For those grass roots groups that are affiliated with a national organization that provides leadership or for those that may aspire to become national, some activities are proposed by the parent body, and the local group decides whether to participate. When People for the Ethical Treatment of Animals announces a boycott as part of its "compassion campaign," interested citizens can choose to participate and other animal rights groups can join in, making the boycott truly national. When Rainforest Action Network announces National Rainforest Action Week, RAGS (their local affiliates) plan concurrent activities. When the National Federation of Parents for Drug Free Youth holds its annual red-ribbon campaign to symbolize the hope for a drug-free nation, local and state parent groups conduct activities as part of the campaign. By participating in the national activity, local groups draw greater attention to the grass roots cause, and their impact is intensified. Nationally sponsored walks, rallies, and demonstrations enhance public awareness and increase internal communication.

## Avoid Violence

No grass roots groups should engage in violence against living things. Edward Abbey spoke through his character Doc Sarvis, a member of the Monkey Wrench Gang, about this point. Doc says, "I hold with the consensus of the community here, whatever it may be, wherever it may lead, so long as we follow one cardinal rule: no violence to human beings."[1] Nonviolent civil disobedience is used successfully by some groups, but violence against others is never acceptable to the public.

Several grass roots groups have employed violent tactics—sabotage and vandalism—against property. They fully expect to be arrested if apprehended and engage in this extreme measure with malice aforethought. But with those few exceptions, grass roots groups eschew violent tactics used against property.

## Ordinary People versus Powerful Institutions

Never underestimate the opposition! When virtually powerless groups of people encounter big government or big business, they should consider the potential for a mismatch. However, time and again, grass roots groups have set their course to change the way things are done by their "offenders" and have accomplished their goal. The fur industry is on the ropes; disposable diapers are not as popular this year; many communities reject siting of hazardous waste in their midst; and the judicial system has become stern with those who drink and drive. People can empower themselves and achieve a redress of a grievance. Many grass roots groups that began in the 1980s are still at work, trying to move those they see as recalcitrant.

### Learn the Opposition and How It Operates

Knowing the opposition is the first step. Find out how the corporation works or which governmental body is responsible for the problem. Know where to strike within the organization with letters, petition, or demonstrations. Get to know who's responsible or who's assigned to deal with the irritant—the grass roots group. Focus the tactic at that part of the organization. To have a name and a position identified with the cause personalizes the complaint. Those in the bureaucracy wish to remain invisible, if possible.

Expect that their resources are vast. They have lawyers, public relations staff and hired public relations consultants, scientists, boards of directors, and many other resources to mobilize against the outside. Government agencies prefer to use regulations, threats, deflections, studies, inaction, and procedures to block change proposed from outside the bureaucracy. Stalling is one of their most frequently used tactics. In the beginning, be prepared to cope with arrogance from the opposition: they plan to minimize the complaint and cast disdain on the effort to move them, especially if their bottom lines— money and power—are threatened.

### Expect to Be Outspent

As grass roots groups begin to build and threaten a procedure, a practice, a product, or a plan, the opposition digs in and intensifies its resistance. The example of Procter & Gamble, the American Medical Association, and the National Institutes of Mental Health combining to expend millions of dollars to counter and discredit People for the Ethical Treatment of Animals and other animal rights groups demonstrates the extent of resources available, as well as the commitment to stop them. Most opposition groups will not reach the dimensions described, but they have resources and the will to use them. To win, the cause cannot be based on money alone to support it.

### Resist Intimidation

Intimidation comes in several forms: a threat, superior resources, the appearance of greater competence, access to the media, infiltration, and legal action. Many grass roots groups have encountered some or all of these forms of intimidation during the course of their struggles. The Love Canal Homeowners Association experienced a series of actions and counteractions for three years before it could declare victory over a coalition of government agencies and a corporate giant. The leaders and the rank and file were subjected to personal, financial, legal, scientific, and psychological intimidation. But they persevered.

### Make Tough Choices

In most cases, the grass roots group and its opponent take opposite sides of an issue. The opposition will use their resources to gain public support and put the grass roots group on the defensive. The struggle can be intense: an endangered species or jobs; convenience or pollution; medical research or animal rights; abortion or killing; pesticides or lowered production; enforcement or civil liberties. In the free market of ideas, a fair discussion of controversies should be possible; however, the deck can be stacked by those with greater resources and access to the media.

### Open Out the Organization

Having valuable information fall into the hands of those who oppose the group can be harmful only if the group attempts to conceal a secret strategy or incriminating information. That the opposition will attempt to learn about the grass roots movement is taken for granted. By keeping the organization open and democratic, concern over infiltration and surveillance diminishes. On the other hand, environmental and animal rights groups have been particularly successful in obtaining plans and materials prepared by their opponents, usually given to them by someone sympathetic within the organization.

### Avoid Diversions

A favorite tactic of the private sector when confronted by a grass roots group is to establish a local countergroup or a competing group to divert those working for change. On occasion, a bona fide group does appear, independent of any surreptitious motives or assignments. Learn about them, but do not waste valuable time and resources trying to uncover or discredit their actions. If evidence surfaces clearly exposing the countergroup as a front for the opposition, reveal it to the press and the community and proceed with plans as usual.

### Remain Vigilant

Just when it appears that success has been achieved and the group is no longer needed, a new problem may appear or the ground that has been gained, eroded.

When Love Canal residents thought they could be relocated because of the chemical hazards, the state reneged at first. Ten years after Love Canal residents were relocated, the Environmental Protection Agency concluded in 1990 that four of the seven areas were "habitable," and they approved the resettlement of Love Canal. Homes, once abandoned, were placed on the discounted market, and low-income buyers, many with children, flocked to pick up the bargains. The Sierra Club, the Natural Resources Defense Council, and other environmental organizations filed suits in state and federal courts to block the immediate sale of homes and seek new risk assessment.

When Proposition 103 passed in California, the state insurance commissioner set up one roadblock after another to confuse the situation and whittle away at the voters' intent to lower insurance rates. When parents thought they had convinced the National Institute on Drug Abuse to discard its early policy of "responsible use," another NIDA-funded study appeared with a mixed message about youth and drugs.

Less than one year after the Bush administration banned imported assault weapons, the U.S. Bureau of Alcohol, Tobacco and Firearms granted requests from gun importers to import new versions of these assault weapons. By modifying several features, the weapons were now said to be suitable for sporting purposes. A spokesperson for the Bureau of Alcohol, Tobacco and Firearms said the modified weapons no longer fit the category of semiautomatic, assault-type weapon, and the bureau had no grounds for keeping them out. Members of Handgun Control, Inc., and other groups advocating gun control protested to no avail.

When abolitionists gained public support, the Fugitive Slave Law was passed. Grass roots groups have learned to be vigilant, and they realize the opposition doesn't give up easily. Procter & Gamble tells the press it wants alternative tests that require no use of animals and then proceeds to establish a coalition of corporations to support and justify its use of animal tests on household products, presenting an illusion that the group works for animal research for medical purposes, not floor wax. Constant monitoring is required to ensure that those achieved objectives are not rescinded or compromised. It's not always over when it appears to be.

### Keep a Sense of Humor

Grass roots work is serious and time-consuming, and the issues frequently affected life, health, safety, and finances. If the group loses determination and commitment to see the work completed, the game is over. In order to keep a sense of balance and spontaneity, a little humor helps. When the founder of the first parents' group was asked, "How do you persist?" she replied, "We laugh at ourselves a lot and that keeps us going. For example, when one dad found bottles of Visine in his son's room, he thought it was a drug and had it analyzed. When he found out his son used it to clear his red eyes after smoking pot, he was amused at his own naivete. We all got a good laugh."[2] Some guerrilla theater is comic as well as sardonic. Carry Nation was burlesque but impressive. Edward Abbey was hilarious but incisive when he wrote about a desecrated West and a band of eco-radicals fighting to save it. Humor helps in the face of adversity.

### Close In on Goals and Close Out the Program

As grass roots groups gain public support, develop organizational structure and operations, and achieve their objectives, the opposition to them is likely to intensify. Within four years of its formation, People for the Ethical Treatment of Animals had begun to incur the annoyance of and counteraction by powerful forces in the public and private sector. ACT UP, in two short years, has grown and produced results, all the while being drubbed in the media, by law enforcement, and, most recently, by President Bush. Be prepared for an accelerated and intensified campaign by the opposition when the group succeeds! While it's failing, no one cares or notices.

Finally, know when to close out the program. When all objectives are accomplished and retrenchment or reversal are unlikely, terminate the effort and allow members and supporters to pursue other interests and bask in the glow of their accomplishments. Organizations that outlive their mission and attempt to diversify usually fail. Close the doors when the task is done—and celebrate!

### Making Ends Meet

Few grass roots groups escape the rigor of raising money to keep the operation solvent. The smaller and more voluntary the organization, the less need for large budgets; however, even local parent and hazardous waste groups require some money, and getting it can present problems. The following guides are suggested:

1. Plan reasonable, workable budgets and stick within them.
2. Even if affiliated with a national organization, keep local money in the local community for use by the group.
3. Never accept money that compromises integrity— turn away money from public or private sources if

the acceptance of it hinders or reflects badly on the group's mission.

4. Keep staff small and rely on volunteers where possible.
5. Seek in-kind contributions and donations when appropriate.
6. Rely on members to support the organization because, if they invest in it, they feel ownership and commitment.
7. Do fund-raising by staff and avoid using outside consultants or firms. Make solicitations identified with a particular program or campaign; for example, ask for money to fund a legal project or to be used in publishing a special report.
8. If cash is not available for staff or a project, don't incur a debt.

### Making News

The best way to approach the media as a grass-roots leader is to expect little from it. The media are owned by corporations. Chemical corporations, waste management companies, cosmetics firms, fast-food companies, and consumer product giants such as Procter & Gamble and Gillette advertise extensively in the media. Grass roots groups don't. Basically, the media can do anything they want: celebrate, support, expose, distort, trivialize, or ignore. They call the shots. On the other hand, the media are often responsive to grass roots movements because they keep a story in the public eye, even if the coverage is negative. Use the media when possible since they will use the movement. Never be surprised by good or bad coverage—be prepared. If the group wants the

public to know about it through the media, here are a few
helpful pointers:

## Be Credible and Creative

Always come prepared with the facts, well-written
press releases, and the best spokespersons, who can
handle tough and intensive questioning if the event is
broadcast live.

Use charismatic speakers and allow young people to
present only if they are prepared and sincere in their
remarks. Never rehearse a child to speak about something that's poorly understood by the child or written by
adults. A child's spontaneous truths far surpass the best
adult-written prose put in the mouths of the young.

State the purpose of the organization forcefully and
succinctly. The media do appear at events they anticipate
will provoke controversy or if the movement has been in
the floodlight recently. Since there are few opportunities
to tell the public the story, do it well—that means
prepare!

## Use Celebrities Carefully

If the media learn that a celebrity will be at an event,
chances are improved that reporters and cameras will be
there also. Animal rights activists, environmental
groups, and the homeless have large followings among
media celebrities. Brief the celebrity before the appearance to ensure that the appropriate message is
delivered. Do not expect celebrities to be authorities—
their sincerity toward the cause suffices. If the celebrity
is also well informed on the subject, that's an advantage.
Some are. Do not use a celebrity whose acceptability to
the public as a spokesperson for the cause is questionable, or whose own behavior may compromise the issue.

## Use Local Media

Rarely does a local grass-roots movement event receive prime-time national network news coverage. Concentrate on building relationships of mutual respect with local reporters and newscasters. Appear on talk shows, public message spots, and interviews with local and cable television personalities, and write articles, press releases, and letters to local newspapers. Include good black-and-white glossy photographs.

## Do Your Own Media

Frequently the most important media are those created by the grass roots groups. The most unadulterated, accurate messages are usually the ones prepared by those who can speak for the movement. Prepare newsletters that interest and stimulate the membership, and circulate them quickly and regularly to maintain interest and support.

Finally, resist letting the media cast one person in the movement as the celebrity of the cause. A cadre of able, articulate spokespersons ensures a broader appeal and less likelihood that the media can create a personality that limits the impact and depth of the issue.

## American Grass Roots Movements in the 1990s

Our society is propelled, for better or for worse, by its government's actions or inaction, by the private sector's corporate responsibility or irresponsibility, and by a large collection of private associations and organizations. Grass roots groups emerge when these institutions appear to fail and zealous leaders appeal to others to cleanse the social fabric and to right egregious wrongs. That they make an impact is irrefutable. The question is not will they grow, but how much and in what directions during the next decades?

Certain movements with unfinished agendas, large public followings, and a spirited opposition trying to suppress them will be on the American scene at least until the end of the century. Environmental issues, animal rights, hazardous waste disposal, AIDS treatments, and pesticide limits will continue to capture a grass roots following. Tom Wicker of the *New York Times* assesses the power of these movements in his description of an anti-Vietnam War protest he witnessed in 1966:

> I was... impressed by three young women, wives and mothers, seemingly typically suburban except for one thing: they each were about to go to jail for three months for having lain down in front of trucks being loaded with napalm from the plant.
>
> "What made you take that kind of risk?" I asked them.
>
> "Because we stopped those trucks from moving for eight hours," one of them replied.
>
> That was a moment of truth for me. If women like those three were willing to go to jail for their beliefs, the anti-war movement was serious—its roots were deep in the people, and they had the courage to defy the government and its war.[3]

All over America, others have spoken out, learned, petitioned, and lain on sidewalks to protest a perceived wrong, and they have been heard, just as William Lloyd Garrison was heard about slavery.

### Future Issues

In the struggle for social perfection, grass roots groups may convene around new or smoldering issues that will peak during the decade of the 1990s. Several appear already to be attracting an early following.

*Electromagnetic fields:*   A growing number of people suspect a link between disease and death and the body's sensitivity to electromagnetic energy. Paul Brodeur, the author of *Currents of Death: Power Lines, Computer Terminals, and the Attempt to Cover Up Their Threat To You,* is reported to have said, "Despite clear signs of a hazard, utility companies and the electronics industry are pretending there's no cause for concern; mainstream scientists are ignoring the evidence because their out-moded theories can't account for it; and public health officials are standing by idly."[4]

Once belittled by some scientists, concern has grown in the past five years, and recent studies have linked exposure to electromagnetic fields with an increased risk of leukemia, lymphoma, and brain cancer. High exposure to the fields can double or triple the risk of these relatively rare cancers. New studies of the effects of electromagnetic fields on cells, animals, and people are being conducted by the Electric Power Research Institute, the U.S. Department of Energy, and the Environmental Protection Agency.

People ought to know if there is a connection between leukemia, brain cancer, birth defects, childhood cancer, and the use of electric blankets, video display terminals (VDTs), microwave ovens, living near high current power lines, and occupational exposure. In December 1990, the EPA released a report linking electromagnetic fields to leukemia and brain cancer in children. It also cites studies linking occupational exposures to cancer in adults. The release of the report was delayed until early 1991 by White House officials who said they were concerned that the report would alarm the public. David Bayliss, one of the authors, commented, "What is the use of having an Environmental Protection Agency if they're going to withhold information from the public? I thought the EPA was for letting people know about health problems, or possible health problems."[5] As new evidence is found to substantiate a link, grass-roots activism may emerge if those in control do not act to remove the risks.

*Overmedicating and Mistreating the Elderly in Nursing Homes:* In 1989, a woman in Sacramento began to question openly the medication given to her father in a nursing home. She claimed to see marked changes in her father following a short stay in a home and questioned the overuse of medication by staff. She announced the beginning of a movement to monitor these homes in order to stop overmedication. In the general population, the misuse and overuse of drugs among the elderly is extremely high. Sidney Wolfe of the Public Citizen Health Research Groups says, "Most older people are taking too many drugs, and are taking doses that are dangerously high. The greatest epidemic of drug abuse in American society is among our older people."[6] While people sixty and older represent only 17 percent of the U.S. population, they account for nearly 40 percent of all drug-related hospitalizations. These figures do not specify a link among drugs, nursing homes, and the elderly, but if this concern over health care for the elderly gains a broader following, a grass roots group will emerge.

Many of those who relatives are in nursing homes are questioning whether the facilities are safe havens for long-term care, not only regarding the use of drugs, but treatment in general. Researchers at the University of New Hampshire have found a high incidence of physical and psychological abuse in these facilities. In interviews with a sample of nursing home staff, 10 percent "admitted having committed acts of physical abuse; 40 percent, one of psychological abuse."[7] The researchers concluded that "maltreatment was related to a stressful working environment, and came more often from those who viewed patients as children."

The 1990 report of the Health Care Financing Administration found that nearly a quarter of the nursing homes were guilty of improperly administering drugs. They also lacked hygiene: more than a third did not follow the rules for sanitary food preparation. In response to these negative findings, Ken Hoagland of the National Council of Senior Citizens said, "It's a sad fact that enforcement of existing regulations in nursing homes across the nation is grossly inadequate. This latest report merely tabulates some of the more egregious violations and points up the continuing necessity for enforcement of existing regulations and for enactment of stronger regulations." The more than fifteen thousand nursing homes included in this study participate in the Medicare and Medicaid programs and qualify as both skilled nursing facilities and intermediate care facilities.

"Today, some six million Americans sixty-five years or older require help in dressing, eating, bathing, and going to the bathroom. That number will swell to 13.8 million by 2030, according to an Urban Institute study."[8] With medical advances extending life, more and more will enter nursing homes and the potential for mistreatment will increase. A grass roots movement may be in the making.

*Affordable Housing and the Homeless:* Homelessness in America has haunted this nation for the past decade, and the problem has not subsided. Groups and coalitions have emerged to call attention to the visible problem, which has not been addressed by those responsible for providing care. In the beginning, the homeless were trivialized and marginalized as misfits, winos, mentally ill, vagrants, or capable of making it if they wanted to work. This negative labeling is slowly disappearing as more children live in shelters or on the streets and more people become aware that during the eight years of the Reagan administration, affordable housing began to disappear and was not replaced. Singleroom occupancy settings were removed to make room for high rises and condominiums. The authors of a study released by the Center on Budget and Policy Priorities, in Washington, D.C., found a shortage of low-rent housing units and that no one was building low-income housing any more. They further reported that government housing policy has essentially been one of cutting back on housing programs for the poor.

"Homeless advocates estimate that 3 million Americans are without housing and cite a congressional study predicting that 19 million more will face the prospect of homelessness in the next 15 years."[9]

If this prediction is accurate and lack of affordable housing continues to be synonymous with homelessness, this grass roots movement will accelerate during the 1990s.

*Repetitive Motion Disorders:* As computer technology has grown and more people use computer keyboards in the workplace, repetitive motion injuries have increased. Carpal tunnel syndrome, an injury to the hand and wrist, has emerged as the most frequent complaint. Many employers fail to respond to these complaints made by workers who use computers or computerized equipment, and few physicians detect the early warning signs of the syndrome. Many with the disorder are frustrated by the failure of employees and physicians to respond.

According to a 1989 Bureau of Labor Statistics report, 48 percent (115,400 cases) of all workplace illnesses in 1988 were recorded as repetitive motion disorders, up from 18 percent in 1981.[10]

After numerous employees of the *Fresno Bee*, a California newspaper, complained of problems associated with repeated work at video display terminals, the Bee developed a long-term safety plan to protect workers using computer terminals. The action was taken after the Northern California Newspaper Guild filed a complaint with Cal-OSHA (Occupational Safety and Health Administration). The Guild complaint and action proposed by Cal-OSHA were appealed by the *Bee* in 1989 but finally accepted by the newspaper owners. The settlement provides for new furniture, adjustable VDT chairs and support tables, and training sessions to lower the threat of repetitive strain problems caused by working at the computer screens.

No video display terminal safety standards exist, and attempts to require computer manufacturers and firms with high-volume VDT use have failed to date. A Suffolk County, New York, ordinance to provide safety standards was overturned in 1989 after business groups challenged it in court. Growing fear of repetitive strain injuries among VDT operators, labor unions officials, and occupational health specialists is motivating a grass roots response as computer manufacturers and business groups resist efforts to adopt specific standards, such as breaks, required adjustable office furniture, and training.

In September 1990, the U.S. Labor Department issued voluntary guidelines for the nation's meat-packing industry, an industry with ten times the repetitive strain injury rate of any other. However, the bureaucratic process will be lengthy. "We're not talking months; we're talking years," said (then) Labor Secretary Elizabeth Dole, in acknowledging the long process of designing and implementing mandatory standards.

**Gun Control:**  During 1989, the massacres of school-children in Stockton, California, and of employees at the Standard Gravure Corporation in Louisville, Kentucky, by mentally unstable men stirred grass roots support for the banning of military assault weapons. In response, the Bush administration declared a permanent ban on almost all foreign-made semiautomatic assault rifles in July 1989. California passed a series of tough gun-control laws, overriding the stiff opposition of the National Rifle Association (NRA), the chief opponent of gun-control measures. The NRA bases its opposition on its interpretation of the Second Amendment, which gives people the right to bear arms.

In May 1990, the New Jersey legislature approved the nation's strongest ban on assault weapons. "Manufacture, sale, or possession of the 38 kinds of assault weapons listed in the bill would be punishable by three to five years in prison and fines of up to $7,500."[11] Aggressive lobbying against the bill by the National Rifle Association failed.

Activism is spreading, particularly in California and Kentucky, the sites of the deadly massacres. "I've never been much of an activist," said Mike Campbell, one of the victims of the shooting in Kentucky. "Obviously I am for gun control now." His wife has joined him in the campaign to counter strong opposition from the NRA. "I am not a public speaker but I will support, in any way I can, legislation to ban those kinds of weapons," said Betty Campbell, his wife.[12]

Handgun Control, Inc., is led by James and Sarah Brady, who appear before groups to urge tighter controls on pistols. James Brady was partially paralyzed by a gunshot on March 31, 1981, during the attempted assassination of President Ronald Reagan. Brady was White House press secretary at the time. The couple's efforts are intensifying. In his November 1989 testimony before a congressional committee considering legislation (the "Brady Bill") that would require a seven-day waiting period between ordering and picking up a handgun and would increase the pressure to check on those attempting the purchase. Brady asked the senators, "Are you willing and ready to cast a vote for a common sense public safety issue endorsed by experts in law enforcement? Or are you going to continue to pander to the special interests that whine about a little inconvenience and other such lame-brained foolishness?"[13]

Handgun Control, Inc., based in Washington, D.C., is developing a national network of grass roots activists who work to recruit new supporters and educate Americans about handgun violence. In 1990, their membership reached one million, and the goal is to recruit an additional million over the next few years. The national office supplies press releases and financial contributions through its political action committee to candidates for federal office who support laws to keep handguns out of the wrong hands.

A 1988 Gallup poll found that 91 percent of Americans supported a seven-day waiting period for handgun purchases. However, in spite of this public support, the highly organized National Rifle Association, with its three million members, has been able to defeat all congressional legislation on handgun control. In 1988, the NRA spent more than $4 million to defeat the Brady Bill. This bill has been reintroduced in Congress and was being voted on in spring 1991. Former President Ronald Reagan now supports this legislation, after ten years of resistance and/or silence. National Rifle Association opposition is, once again, highly organized.

The National Rifle Association claims that the American people have a Second Amendment right to keep and bear arms. In most instances, they do not quote the entire amendment. It reads: "A well-regulated militia being necessary to the security of a free state, the right of the people to keep and bear arms shall not be infringed."

According to the American Bar Association, "In addition to the four decisions in which the Supreme Court has construed the amendment, every federal court decision involving the amendment has given the amendment a collective militia interpretation and/or held that firearms control laws enacted under a state's police power are constitutional. Thus, arguments premised under the federal Second Amendment, or the similar provisions of the thirty-seven state constitution, have never prevented the regulation of firearms."

Efforts at gun control have been made by groups for decades with little success because of the strong opposition forged by the members of the National Rifle Association. Activism by gun control advocates is on the increase as the new decade begins, and the issue will be hotly contested.

*The Ocean:* Although more than half the population of the United States lives within fifty miles of a coast, a strong grass roots effort to save the ocean has not yet materialized. Several movements have emerged but have not succeeded in mobilizing the nation or the world to prevent the steady pollution of the ocean. Early warnings were delivered by the Norwegian explorer Thor Heyerdahl in 1971 in his account of the RA expedition in the boat made of reeds that took him and his crew across the Atlantic:

> Next day we were sailing in slack winds through an ocean where the clear water on the surface was full of drifting black lumps of asphalt, seemingly never-ending. Three days later we awoke to find the sea about us so filthy that we could not put our toothbrushes in it.... The Atlantic was no longer blue but gray-green and opaque, covered with clots of oil ranging from pin-head size to the dimensions of the average sandwich. Plastic bottles floated among the waste. We might have been in a squalid city port. I had seen nothing like this when I

spent 101 days with my nose at water level on board the *Kon-Tiki*. It became clear to all of us that mankind really was in the process of polluting his most vital well-spring, our planet's indispensable filtration plant, the ocean. The danger to ourselves and to future generations was revealed to us in all its horror.... We must make an outcry to everyone who would listen. What was the good of East and West fighting over social reforms on land, as long as every nation allowed our common artery, the ocean, to become a sewer for oil slush and chemical waste? Did we still cling to the medieval idea that the sea was infinite?[14]

Since that prophetic cry, the ocean has suffered continued degradation from dumpings by man that include plastic, oil, toxins, chemicals, pesticides, medical waste, sludge, human waste, and a host of substances that kill marine life and destroy the oceanic ecosystem. In addition to the dumping, "scientists are discovering that the growing ozone hole over Antarctica, caused chiefly by extensive use of chlorofluorocarbons in refrigeration and packaging, can reduce phytoplankton productivity.... This almost unnoticeable phytoplankton reduction could result in the demise of our ecosystem."[15]

Jacques Cousteau, the noted marine explorer, says that the greatest danger to the ocean is the dumping of nuclear waste and nuclear accidents in these waters because these hazardous materials require hundreds of years to disintegrate, if ever. His warnings are beginning to reach the public. And, in Maine, George Whidden, a retired fisherman, has launched a grass roots group called the Coalition to Cease Ocean Dumping, because "the EPA and enforcement are inadequate, city politics has a heavy hand in all of this and that. There's no time to wait for pending bills in congress. The ocean's been good to us.... It gives and gives; it's like a garden down there. Those bums don't know what they're doing to it. I can't see leaving a cesspool to my grandchildren or anyone else's."[16] These thoughts and actions are essential for the movement to blossom. It will in the 1990s.

*  *  *

When the American political and economic system fails to serve a segment of the citizenry or the nation as a whole, a grass roots constituency can emerge to counter the influence of corporate lobbyists, political action committees, political contributions, or vested interests. Many people believe that congress and the administration have become increasingly unable to legislate and enforce for the public good because of their own entanglements and compromises with powerful forces within the business and labor elite. They have come to share an assumption that, if a grievance is to be addressed, they must act in concert to confront a political and economic system that favors the rich and powerful. Most of the results achieved by grass roots organizations would not have been gained through routine government or corporate decisions, and these very failures have mobilized people to force change through legitimate channels once closed to them.

Grass roots activism has emerged as a powerful force during the past two decades, and with it has come a new energy for millions of Americans—many who would not have acted on their own or others' behalf even a few years ago. That they care about situations that distress them and that they feel empowered to confront the monolith (government, corporations, university, and the media) bode well for the future of the United States.

# APPENDIX A

Additional Excerpts from American Medical
Association Memo Dated June 1989

"Political movements in general, and the animal activist movement in particular, consist of layers of support and layers of supporters. At the center are the hardcore activists. Members of the Animal Liberation Front and Animal Rights Militia as well the leadership or organizations such as People for the Ethical Treatment of Animals (PETA) comprise this hardcore group. They believe most intensely in the movement and its goals and their role in the movement defines virtually every aspect of their lives and self-images. Hardcore activists often work full-time or nearly so for the movement, define their social lives around the movement and often make significant sacrifices to continue their work. However, the goals of the hardcore activists: a) abolition of use of animals in medical research; b) abolition of commercial animal agriculture and c) abolition of commercial and sport hunting and trapping, are extreme and not necessarily fully shared by those less fully committed to the movement. Finally, hardcore activists are generally prepared to resort to violent tactics to advance their agenda.

"Less intensely committed, but still dedicated strongly to the movement are the activists who may participate in demonstrations in their spare time. These are the 'foot-soldiers' of the movement who carry the greatest burden of political effort. They share most of the goals of the hardcore activists but are divided on the efficacy of violence.

"Still less intense in their support than the activists are the sympathizers. These are people who have an emotional commitment to the movement, may contribute money, may belong to one or more organizations and/or follow developments with interest. Sympathizers may write letters or simply discuss the issue with friends but generally will not participate in demonstrations or will do so only occasionally. Sympathizers do not necessarily embrace all the goals of the hardcore activists. Moreover, sympathizers are generally less willing to condone violent tactics. Nevertheless such people are vital to the success of the movement both financially and politically and are a key link between the activists and the broader public. The movement has succeeded in turning many children into sympathizers and the recruitment of children remains a primary goal of most animal activists.

"Beyond the sympathizers are [sic] the general public. They are generally uncommitted and may be won over or alienated depending on how successful the hardcore activists are in getting their message out and how successful the opposition is. The success of any movement depends on transforming members of the general public into sympathizers or at least neutralizing them so that they do not become unsympathetic. If the animal rights movement is to continue to be successful in the political arena, it must continue to mobilize activists and sympathizers. However, most of the public do not agree with all the extreme goals of the hardcore activists. The general public primarily wants to insure that animals are treated humanely and are not prepared to give up meat, leather shoes, or wool coats as demanded by the extremists. Moreover, the general public is not willing to condone violence.

"Animal activists have been successful in generating Congressional support for bills that would impede the use of animals in research or make research significantly more costly. They have already obtained strict regulations, unsubstantiated as to specific benefit to the animals—such as cage size or requirements to maintain the psychological well-being of primates. They have succeeded in getting 'pound laws' passed in many communities. Animal activists have been successful because those of us who know better, those of us who know the importance of biomedical research, those of us who are either involved in it or dependent upon it for our medical practice have not taken these groups seriously enough. We have been reluctant to step into the arena because we wanted to avoid being targeted by their efforts. We wanted to avoid threats to our research facilities and workers. We wanted to avoid placing institutional administrators in jeopardy. We wanted to avoid threats of bodily harm to ourselves, our families, or our animals. We wanted to avoid invasion and defacement of laboratories, personal property, and of research records, and we wanted to prevent the abduction of laboratory animals.

"Controversy surrounding the use of animals in biomedical research and education is not new; for over one hundred years antivivisectionists have been urging the cessation of animal use in research. In recent years however, the animal activist movement has become more radical with the emergence of animal rights groups who are dedicated to the elimination of the use of animals in biomedical and other scientific research. Activists use conventional political tactics such as propaganda, public relations campaigns, public protests, picketing, lobbying, organizing proxy fights at shareholder meetings, filing environmental impact challenges at new research facilities and litigation. In addition, the more radical elements of these groups are engaging in illegal activities such as breaking into and vandalizing research laboratories, stealing laboratory animals, and threatening and harassing individual scientists and their families."

# APPENDIX B

DEPARTMENT OF HEALTH & HUMAN SERVICES

*Memorandum*

*Date: September 29, 1987*

*From: Director of Intramural Research, NIMH*

*Subject: Reflections Following the 9/28/87 Meeting on the Animal Rights' Movement*

1. *The stakes are enormous. The animal rights' movement threatens the very core of what the Public Health Service is all about.*

2. *The "bunker" strategy is no longer tenable.*

3. *The health research community must participate with patient groups of health professions. Wherever feasible, the research institutions should leave the "out front" activists to the other groups. The PHS and its agencies should find some acceptable way to provide funding for some of these efforts and technical support for others.*

4. *Although it is important that we continue to work toward "having our house in order," we must realize that by making this our major focus, we tacitly accept the premise of the animal rights' movement and play into their hands.*

5. *The pro-active posture should focus in two directions:*

   *a) Contemporary examples of health advances directly dependent upon animal research. Here we should draw liberally from those areas that already enjoy wide public and congressional support, i.e. AIDS, dementia schizophrenia, various childhood disorders, etc. We should draw up a list of such illnesses and the research upon which treatment is dependent keeping in mind the existence of various specialized groups such as Danny Thomas and so forth. The example of the Juvenile Diabetes Association should be instructive.*

   *b) A pro-active stance should include a vigorous focus on the fundamental philosophical underpinnings of the animal rights movement, namely the moral equivalence between human beings and animals. This could be highlighted by some of the more outrageous quotes from Elizabeth Newkirk and Alex Pacheco, that dramatize how the movement's philosophy is based on a degradation of the concept of human nature.*

6. *The research institutions need to have effective spokespeople available, but they should not generally be the researchers themselves. A scientist whose laboratory has been raided is the least likely person to be effective as a spokesperson. The NIMH Intramural Program has developed four clinical investigators who have been trained in the arguments of the animal rights' people and who have had media training.*

7. *The PHS and the DHHS need a more concerted legislative strategy. All budget presentations should include a discussion of overly stringent animal regulations and their impact on the cost of research. Answers to questions from Congress con-*

*cerning what we are doing (or why we are not doing more) in a given area should include reference to the difficulties imposed by restrictive regulations and by the activities of animal activists.*

8. *The PBS should prepare a list of Senators and Congressman [sic] who have a special interest in health research on a particular disease. Even though many of these members do not sit on the same committees considering some of the animals rights' legislation, they should all be made aware of the existence of this legislation and their support should be enlisted just as it is for budgetary matters. Indeed, this is a kind of legislative agenda that should not cause difficulties for the Department, since it is consistent with the Administration's wishes to contain costs and restrain excessive regulation.*

9. *The PBS and/or its agencies should pull together groups to think of more creative ways to counter the long-term threat posed by the animal rights' movement. For example, it might be possible to fund special fellowships in research advocacy for investigators who may wish to include a year or two of such activity in their career. Although most investigators are not interested in such advocacy and are not skillful at it, there are a few who would be interested if there were financial incentives. A corollary would be the creation of research advocacy awards that could convey some of the prestige available for traditional research awards.*

10. *The Department of Education should be contacted concerning infiltration of high schools by the animal rights' people. PHS should sponsor counter-educational efforts, in collaboration with the voluntary health organizations and the grass roots health provider organizations such as the AMA.*

11. *The Department should fund a contract to provide assistance to the agencies in conducting and coordinating the myriad tasks associated with these efforts. This would include the collection and preparation of materials, the analysis of data on the cost of animal rights' destruction, and the cost of regulations. Brief packets of material could be prepared for direct use and for integration into budget testimony and into speeches, talks and articles prepared by our political and scientific leaders, as well as individual scientists.*

12. *In marshalling these various near term and long-range efforts, we should not lose sight of the fact that the NIH-NIMH Intramural Programs are facing a demonstration on November 9, probably to be preceded by a break-in. It is critical that contingency plans be worked out in advance, and that all levels of the Department approve them promptly.*

13. *Every year the Department sends hundreds of thousands of mailings on health issues to various publics. Why not include a brochure on the importance of animals in research to the appropriate audiences? In addition, all Departmental material relating to health and health research should be considered for possible inclusion of references to animal research.*

14. *In summary, I am suggesting a strategy at the other end of the spectrum from the "bunker strategy": we must consistently, aggressively, and unashamedly portray the importance of animals in research in every way that we possibly can. Although initially this may heighten opposition, it is far better in the long run because it is intellectually honest and, therefore, more credible. Our caution will signal*

*lack of conviction and resolve. Without these, we
cannot expect others to help up.*

Frederick K. Goodwin, M.D.

cc: James Wyngaarden, M.D.
Ms. Frankie Trull (FBMR)
Salvatore Canci, Ph.D.

# APPENDIX C

June 9, 1989
Retention Limit: 7/90

Mr. G.S. Gandall

Subject *INDUSTRY COALITION ON ANIMAL TESTING*

*This proposes that we proceed with establishing an industry coalition to augment current trade association efforts to address the growing issue of animal testing. Specifically, with Mr. Smale's agreement, we propose that he send out invitations for an initial organizational meeting which would include the CEO's of key companies concerned about this issue. We would like to hold this meeting by mid-July.*

*A statement describing the proposed mission, role and membership, developed by Ms. Linda Ulreay, is provided in Exhibit I. Briefly, we see the mission as follows:*

> *To sustain a public and legislative environment which supports the judicious use of animal testing as a necessary part of a corporation's responsibility to manufacture and market safe and effective products.*

*The key role of the coalition would be to direct public relations and legislative activities to support this mission. In addition, it would provide a forum for sharing learnings about activist activities. We see this coalition as a supplement to current trade association and Company efforts. It is not intended to replace or usurp current responsibilities.*

*Our proposed organization approach is to form an independent coalition, but primarily work through the Foundation for Biomedical Research (FBR), a non-profit public education group which has been supporting the use of animals for medical research and product safety testing for many years. They are highly experienced with this issue and well-regarded for their effectiveness, as is their Federal legislative lobbying sister organization, the National Association for Biomedical Research (NABR). A fact-sheet on these organizations is provided in Exhibit II, and we have additional materials available. We would coordinate public education and legislative efforts closely with CTFA, SDA and other trade associations.*

*The advantage of this approach is that programs, contacts and spokes-persons, such as Dr. Michael Debakey and Nobel Laureate, Dr. David Hubel, are already established. In addition, the Foundation will provide access to academic and medical leaders with interest in the issue. The Foundation's primary need is financial resources to broaden their reach.*

*The alternative is to work independently starting from scratch. We believe the required start-up time would needlessly delay the implementation of meaningful programs. We have done preliminary sensing with Johnson & Johnson, Bristol-Myers, and Merck concerning the proposed approach, and they are supportive.*

*The Coalition would be directed by the an Executive Committee. This group would also serve as the Product Safety Advisory Committee for PBR to provide direction for programs. In addition, the Coalition would be repre-*

sented on the board of Directors and Executive Board of
FBR. Prior to the initial meeting, we plan to establish a
small organizing committee to work logistics. Further
details of governance would be addressed by the
organizing committee following the initial meeting.

We have developed a prototype three-year educational
and legislative plan (see Exhibit III). Key elements
include a broad-based public relations and advertising
program, legislative education and lobbying efforts
focused on key states and development of a school
education program.Our initial cost estimate is roughly
$5MM per year, with an additional $2.5MM start-up
expenses in Year I to develop materials, etc.

Programs would be funded by membership contributions. We expect to establish two or more classes of
membership with dues based on company size. For the
largest companies, the year I contribution would be up
to $35M, with contribution of up to $250M in years II
and III. In the initial meeting, we would seek agree-
ments to commit up to the maximum level, but specific
amounts and timing of commitments would not be
finalized until programs are more specifically defined.
Details of the dues structure would be developed by the
organizing committee for approval by the Executive
Committee.

An agenda for the initial meeting is attached in Exhibit
IV. We see the objectives of this meeting as follows:

—Secure CEO agreement to the organization's mission
  statement and to commit financial and staff
  resources.
—Secure CEO input on fundamental points of the policy
  that the organization will adopt and operate on.
—Establishing a Steering Committee to finalize organizational details, establish working committees, and
  draft policy.

—Establish a process for inviting other member companies.

We have drafted a sample invitation letter, which is also attached. In addition to the CEO, we suggest a senior Public Affairs and technical representative from each Company be invited. Further, we suggest Mr. Smale consider issuing the invitation jointly with at least one other CEO.

We would welcome Mr. Smale's input on the mission statement, proposed membership and any expectations he may have on how this organization will operate. In addition, we would appreciate Mr. Smale's selection of a meeting date (no later than mid-July) and location (we recommend New York), so we can proceed with arrangements. We look forward to moving ahead quickly with this vital organization.

C. R. Otto

*EXHIBIT I*

## INDUSTRY ANIMAL TESTING COALITION

MISSION:

— Sustain a public and legislative environment which supports the judicious use of animal testing as a necessary part of a corporation's responsibility to manufacture and market safe and effective products.

ROLE:

— Develop industry policy on use of animals for product efficacy and safety testing.
— Provide on-going strategic and executional direction for a national public relations program.
— Provide on-going strategic and executional direction for influencing legislation, including

*coordination or activities with other interested parties (e.g., trade associations, lobbyists).*

— *Provide a forum for sharing learnings about activist activities.*

— *Provide a forum for discussion of consistent standards of humane care and use of animals and use of alternative methods.*

## MEMBERSHIP CRITERIA:

— *Demonstrated commitment to product safety as a key concern in the product development process.*

— *Strong reputation for science and research.*

— *Vested interest in improving understanding of the animal testing issue among key publics (e.g., consumers, legislators, etc.).*

— *Significant resources, both financial and personnel, are available to devote to coordination of coalition activities.*

## PROPOSED MEMBERSHIP:

*Bristol-Myers\*, Eastman Kodak, IBM, Johnson & Johnson\*, Merck\*, Monsanto, Syntex\*, 3-M, Colgate-Palmolive, Lever Bros., Gillette, and P&G with others to be invited following initial organizational meetings.*

*\*Have already indicated interest.*

## ORGANIZATION STRUCTURE OPTIONS:

— *Work with an existing organization (e.g., Foundation for Biomedical Research) with similar objectives—build upon the preexisting reputation and resources of the group to quickly gain credibility among target groups.*

— *Create new, independent operated organization directed by a full-time staff.*

*LLU2186*
*6/9/89*

*EXHIBIT III*

## *PROTOTYPE ANIMAL TESTING*
## *EDUCATION & LEGISLATIVE PLAN*

### *OBJECTIVES*

— *Educate legislators and consumers on how and why laboratory animals are used in product safety testing.*

— *Educate legislators and consumers that non-animal methodologies are not yet sufficiently advanced to replace the use of animal in testing.*

— *Block attempts to legislate prohibitions on product safety testing Using animals*

### *YEAR I*

*Media Relations/Education Plan*      *$ 2.0MM*

    *—Media Information Kit (print and broadcast).*

    *—Top 24 market annual media tour.*

— *Crisis response package for immediate implementation to address opposed activity.*

— *Media coverage tracking.*

*Consumer Advertising/Program*
*(Test and initial expansion)*      *$ 2.0MM*

*Consumer Education Plan*      *$ .5MM*

— *Education brochure and film*

— *Presentation kit for use with community groups.*

— *National Speaker's Bureau*

*School Program*      *$ 1.0MM*

— *Teacher's Presentation Kit and materials for K-6, Junior High, Senior High.*

— *Model curriculum program.*

*Legislative Program (in conjunction with Trade*

*Associations and National Association for Biomedical Research)*

— *Legislative Information Kit.*
— *Legislative briefings in "Bell Weather" states.*
— *Legislative Association briefings/ presentations.*
— *Coalition building with key interested groups (e.g., Consumer Federation of America, Consumers Union, National Grocers Association, American Bar Association, American Association of Poison Control Centers).*
— *Legislative defense package for impediment activation when objectionable legislation is introduced.*
— *Crisis Response Fund.*

*$ 7.5MM*

<u>*YEARS II & III*</u> *(per year)*

*Updated Information on Kits.*                    *$  .5MM*
*Continuation of media advertising, consumer and legislative of school program.*              *$ 3.5MM*
*Expansion of school program.*                    *$ 1.0MM*
                                                  *$ 5.0MM*

*CRO/VIR:coalition-3(7) 6/989  em  RL: 7/90*

# APPENDIX D

## THE
## PROCTER & GAMBLE
## COMPANY

GEOFFREY PLACE
VICE PRESIDENT–RESEARCH
AND DEVELOPMENT

P.O. BOX 599
CINCINNATI, OHIO 45201-0599

May 1990

Mrs. Jack Earle
P.O. Box 18114
S. Lake Tahoe, CA 95706

Dear Mrs. Earle:

Our Chairman and Chief Executive, Ed Artzt, received
your postcard, sent at the request of In Defense of
Animals, and he has asked me to respond to you. We
are gravely concerned about their blatant lies and
misrepresentations of Procter & Gamble.

Our Company remains committed—as it has been for
years—to reducing animal use. We have made
significant progress in this area. Over the past five
years, P&G's use of animals for personal care and
household product safety testing is down over 80%
worldwide.

Further, we are committed to eliminating animal
research wherever science allows, through the

development of alternate test methodologies. For the three year period 1986-89, we spent over $10 million developing alternatives. In March, we announced the first recipients of grants from the University Animal Alternatives Research Program we sponsor. When the program reaches full operation in two years, this will represent $450,000 in new additional funds annually for in vitro research.

Beyond this, let me share some other facts that In Defense of Animals' letter neglected to mention:

— Promising developments are continuing to unfold in the relatively new field of alternative test methodologies. But, new methods aren't all that's needed—the methods must be validated as predictive and useful, and then they must be accepted by the scientific, government and regulatory community alike.

P&G has been a leader in all of these arenas. Since 1987, P&G has published or presented over 70 papers on alternatives, helping to advance scientific and regulatory acceptance of alternative methods. Also, we have met with regulatory agencies to discuss acceptance of these new methods. P&G no longer uses the Draize or LD50 tests. Instead, we use alternatives developed by P&G which use fewer animals and are less distressful.

— We met with In Defense of Animals' representative, Michael Budkie, on 8/8/89, and discussed P&G's progress and leadership on alternative test methods. We shared information about exciting new non-animal eye safety tests which we are validating.

Mr. Budkie was also specifically briefed on the proposal to form an industry group to sponsor an educational program which is referenced in In Defense of Animals' mailing. He was advised that if any effort proceeds, it will be focused on helping people understand what is and isn't currently possible related to the use of alternative methods, and the progress being made on the three R's of alternatives—reduction, refinement and replacement. We believe,it is important that the public know about this progress.

It is worth noting that Mr. Budkie had an opportunity for further dialogue with our scientists at the conclusion of our 1989 annual shareholders meeting, but he left when the media departed. This certainly left us feeling that Mr. Budkie's primary agenda is with seeking publicity, not with working toward real solutions to this issue.

We're glad to know you care about animal welfare. To be certain that your funds are directed toward truly helping animals, check with the Council of Better Business Bureaus' Philanthropic Advisory Service. This clearinghouse exists only to help prospective donors learn more about philanthropic programs, fund-raising and finances. To date, In Defense of Animals has refused to provide information to this service. Perhaps In Defense of Animals is embarrassed to reveal how your funds are being used. To the best of our knowledge, none of it has gone for direct aid to animals.

We hope this helps you to better understand the real situation. P&G is very committed to further progress

and results. If you want more information on this
important issue, please contact us.

Sincerely,

Geoffrey Place
Vice President
Research and Development

11u2368/5-6

# APPENDIX E

IN DEFENSE OF ANIMALS
816 West Francisco Blvd.
San Rafael, California 94901
(415) 453-9984

*"We share [IDA's] goal of trying to eliminate the need for animals in product testing."*
Procter & Gamble Spokeswoman, Linda Ulrey

Dear Friend of Animals,

Procter & Gamble's concept of humaneness is literally enough to make you sick.

A trusting dog, is strapped into an unyielding steel restraining device. Then a lab technician forces a hose down the helpless dog's resisting throat and pours a caustic brew of harsh cleaning fluid into the trembling animal's stomach. The frightened dog whines in pain and terror as the chemicals sear and burn.

In response to In Defense of Animals' protests P&G spokesperson, Linda Ulrey, in a carefully prepared statement, assures the press that P&G animals are treated "humanely". With apparent sincerity, she goes on to say, "We share their goal of trying to eliminate the need for animals in product testing."

What outrageous misrepresentations—in light of the fact that a leaked memo revealed that P&G executives were contacting other giant corporations in an effort to create a $17.5 million campaign to perpetuate the agony of product testing on animals.

The multi-million dollar campaign was designed to convince our legislators, our friends, even our children,

319

that the purposeful blinding, poisoning, and burning of innocent animals by P&G "scientists" is both necessary and humane. Imagine it, millions of P&G dollars being spent to block our legislative efforts to end the cruelties of product testing on animals.

When the California legislature recently considered a bill that would ban the infamous Draize test, P&G was there, lobbying tirelessly to defeat the bill. I know, for I spent countless hours trying to counter their rhetoric. Their efforts to defeat the bill shocked many people who had received P&G's assurances that they really cared.

Dr. Martin Stevens, Laboratory Animal Director of the Humane Society of the United States had this to say:

"I wrote to P&G to express my surprise and disappointment that a P&G representative testified against California Bill AB 2461. P&G's action invites public criticism and has led to doubts about the sincerity of the company's commitment to alternative development."

Despite P&G's slick brochures and sophisticated rhetoric about the "millions" they are spending to develop alternatives, there can be no doubt that this giant multi-billion dollar corporation is acting in an outrageously cruel, hypocritical and two-faced manner.

You and I are being lied to by corporate America when they tell us all this cruelty is "necessary." We are being fed this lie by the same people who make their living tormenting animals... by the people, in short, who have a vested interest in keeping a $7 billion-a-year animal research and testing business just the way it is.

From the moment I heard of the horrid pain and suffering occurring in our nation's laboratories, I vowed I would do everything in my power to end these tragedies. That is why I am writing you today.

As a veterinarian, I've been trained to help animals and heal their wounds. I have been taught not to stand by or turn my back while animals suffer and die.

To put my concerns into action, six years ago I founded In Defense of Animals. With the help of thousands of caring people like yourself, I have used my veterinary training to end the terrible agony and suffering perpetrated on innocent, defenseless animals. The work is fraught with frustration, but it has been effective. What follows are but a few of our successes.

—In 1984, IDA filed a lawsuit to force the United States Department of Agriculture to end years of negligence and abuse at the University of California. The USDA responded by filing charges against the University, fining it a precedent setting $12,000 for over five years of animal cruelty and abuse. 1986 saw a successful IDA campaign end pound seizure in Stockton County, California.

—Since 1983, IDA has been at the forefront of the fight to stop construction of new animal research facilities. This past year, in a dramatic show of courage, activists occupied a crane high over the construction site of a proposed animal torture chamber. One month later the California Appellate (sic) Court ruled in our favor, challenging the necessity for the proposed underground facility.

—For the past four years IDA has acted as the national coordinator for World Laboratory Animal Liberation Day (WLALW)—an annual event that continues to put ever-increasing pressure on the animal abusers. This year thousands participated, protesting at over 70 research centers. Our concerns have been telecast to millions on the McNeil Leher Report, Nightline and CNN news.

—In 1988 IDA' Midwest coordinator, Michael Budkie, led a successful fight that ended the University of Cincinnati's cruel and infamous head injury experiments on cats.

—1989 saw IDA gain the dramatic release of nineteen greyhounds only days before they were to have their legs surgically broken by the U.S. Army.

—Earlier this year, we successfully sued the UC Davis campus to obtain the release of 21 illegally acquired greyhounds, most of whom were already in the midst of painful research. I am happy to report that they are all doing fine, having been placed in loving homes.

What started out for me as an effort on one campus has turned into a national drive to end animal cruelty wherever it exists. Protecting and advocating for animals has become my life's work.

This past year, with the help of thousands of people like yourself, IDA has been protesting P&G's cruelty with demonstration and direct actions in hundreds of cities across the country. We have generated thousands of letters, telegrams, and phone calls decrying the terrible pain and suffering. And we have initiated a boycott of P&G products.

Deciding to boycott a multi-billion dollar corporation like P&G was not an easy decision. We knew of their power to discredit and hurt us, but earlier attempts for change—like pleas from physicians and shareholders resolutions, had proven useless.

I urge you not to sit by and allow a corporate giant like P&G to use their millions to kill legislation that would end the agonies of animal testing. I ask you not to remain silent as P&G representatives talk out of both sides of their mouths—describing animal cruelty and torture as "humane"—giving the impression that they really care.

And so I ask you to act today.

With your participation and support we shall wage a determined and successful campaign, an effort that will ultimately convince P&G to join companies like Amway, Revlon, Avon and Benetton who have already ended their animal torture.

To this end we have designed a series of posters, stamps, brochures and postcards. Materials that will educate, motivate and eventually terminate P&G product testing on animals once and for all.

Here is what you can do today:

* Sign and send the accompanying postcard to P&G's Chief Executive Officer, Edwin Artzt. Call P&G's toll free number 1-800-543-0485, protesting their hypocrisy and cruelty. Punch out the accompanying P&G product card, and carry it with you. Boycott everything P&G makes!

* Spread the word. You can multiply your effectiveness by urging your friends, co-workers and neighbors to join the P&G boycott. Call or write for additional P&G Boycott Kits.

* And please, send as large a tax-deductible donation to In Defense of Animals, as you possibly can. Whatever you can send, your donation of $25, $50, $100 or more, will make an immense contribution towards ending the terrible mutilations and death.

I would like to propose that you help end animal suffering by letting me become "your" veterinarian. Not in the traditional sense, since I no longer practice with an office and patients. My practice now is with animals I am never allowed to see or touch—those gentle, frightened animals locked away in our nation's research laboratories—fellow beings I am determined to help.

I am asking you to become a key sponsor in the success of our efforts. It will cost tens of thousand of dollars to wage this fight effectively...but we really have no alternative. P&G's efforts to turn back the clock, to brainwash our children, and intimidate our legislators must be fought tooth and nail...at the stores that sell their products...at their annual shareholders meetings.

I have never held back in my efforts to win this fight. I now ask you not to hold back either. Your participation and support is essential if we are to reach our goal of creating the immense public pressure required to end the torture, the maiming, the killing.

Please, write letters, tell your friends, and contribute generously. Today. Nothing less will free the animals from torture in our nation's laboratories.

The animals have no voice to thank you with. But I do, and so on their behalf...thank you in advance for helping.

Sincerely,

Elliot M. Katz, D.V.M.<br>President

P.S. I urge you to take an active role in our P&G boycott. If we are to save 50,000 animals a year from being tortured to death, we must send Procter and Gamble a message it can't possible ignore!

P.P.S. I do hope you will respond quickly. As a donor to IDA, you will receive our quarterly newsletter along with regular reports on how we've put your money to work. Thank you for your very special sensitivity and caring.

# APPENDIX F

INTERDEPARTMENTAL CORRESPONDENCE

From:     FRSO          Date:   October 12, 1990

To:       All FR Employees

Subject:  RESPONDING TO "IN DEFENSE OF
          ANIMALS" 10/9/90 PROTESTS

Attached please find a packet of information to be used to educate yourself and your employees about the recent IN DEFENSE OF ANIMALS (IDA) protests. You will find included the following:

- A public P&G statement of the 10/9/90 protests.
- Information which can be used with external contacts (customers, media, etc.).
- A copy of the Company brochure "Human health and Safety Assurance."

Additionally, you are being provided a "Question and Answer" packet relating to animal research. THIS IS FOR INTERNAL USE ONLY AND SHOULD NOT BE COPIED OR DISTRIBUTED!

Please review all material carefully. As always, non-P&Gers with questions can be given our hotline number for additional information (1/800/262-1637).

Should you have any questions please contact your Manager or this office.

Richard L. Postler

RLP:alf
Attachments
c:/mm/doc/protests

TO:      Plant Sales and Technical Locations

ADVISORY: RESPONDING TO IN DEFENSE OF ANI-
         MALS 10/9/90 PROTESTS

Situation:   In Defense of Animals (IDA) is recruiting
             nationwide support from a variety of na-
             tional and local organizations for their up-
             coming demonstrations which will coincide
             with the Company's annual shareholders'
             meeting on Tuesday, October 9, 1990. Their
             literature talks about having demonstra-
             tions in 200 cities, but given their previous
             track record which has always fallen far
             short of claims, we do not expect a signifi-
             cant response for [t]his activity. Beyond Cin-
             cinnati, we know protesters will be
             returning to the San Francisco sales office
             and the Oxnard plant. We have no specifics
             about other possible protest sites, but all
             locations should be prepared to respond.

Objective:   Have all Company locations prepared to re-
             spond to local inquiries from the media,
             customers or consumers about "boycott
             P&G" demonstrations.

Strategy:    A responsive approach is recommended: re-
             ply to questions about activities and Com-
             pany position as they arise, rather than

proactively raising this issue in advance. It's important to answer questions, but there is no reason to draw additional interest/attention to this matter which could potentially end up publicizing the activitists' agenda even further. It appears that some of the media are tired of being "used" by the activists' tactics which are aimed solely at publicity. Therefore, responding in a factual, courteous manner rather than using a critical or "strike back" approach, which could fuel media interest, will minimize further publicity potential.

What To Expect:   Demonstrators to date have been orderly and courteous overall. Recently some have stated they will do whatever it takes to get their point across, including civil disobedience. It's important to use the minimum force required to maintain control. While willful destruction or disorderly conduct will not be permitted, maximum tolerance of the activists is suggested—arrests would only result in publicity for the activists.

In Defense of Animals is making available graphic brochures, picket signs and even printed tee shirts with boycott P&G slogans. During previous demonstrations, some locations have received stuffed animals covered with symbolic blood and products left with refund requests. (For your information, the Company is not honoring these requests—we provide refunds for dissatisfaction with product performance only.)

Materials Available for Handling Inquiries:

For external and internal use:

— A public statement for use on October 9, 1990.

— A packet of information materials (blue folder) on animal research for use with any external contacts ranging from the media to our customers (These materials may be photocopied, except for the Reader's Digest reprint).

— Copies of the Company's brochure, "Human Health and Safety Assurance." (Additional copies may be ordered by mailing or faxing a request to Joyce Sullivan (ADSB) P&G Cincinnati, or FAX #513-983-2466. Sales reps may order by STORS. Request form #038-5866 entitled, "Human Health & Safety Assurance—A Progress Report: Animal Research & The Search for Alternatives.")

For internal use only:

— Questions and Answers about animal research—for use in verbally responding to employee, customer or other questions, but do not photocopy or distribute.

— Recent IDA correspondence outlining some of their planned activities and examples of some of their brochures/signs.

For further information or assistance, contact Issues Management:

Linda L. Ulrey (513) 983-5796
William F. Dobson (513) 983-9546

Please advise Issues Management about any locations where demonstrations occur. A brief hand written note summarizing the activity and copies of any resulting media coverage would be appreciated.

MEDIA STATEMENT: *OCTOBER 9, 1990 ANIMAL AC-*
*TIVIST DEMONSTRATIONS TAR-*
*GETING THE PROCTER &*
*GAMBLE COMPANY*

(The Procter & Gamble Company is the target of animal activist demonstrators again. The following is the Company reaction to such publicity events.)

We are disappointed these groups are here. They are targeting the wrong company—Procter & Gamble is committed to reducing the use of animals in non-drug research as rapidly as possible. However, we will not expose the users of our products to risk to achieve this goal.

Our commitment is a real one as evidenced by the fact that we use only 10% of the animals used just six years ago for establishing the safety of our personal care and household cleaning products. Procter & Gamble does not do animal research when the necessary safety information is already available and we do not routinely retest established products.

While we've made great progress in reductions, it's a scientific fact today that alternative test methods are not sufficiently developed to completely replace the use of animals in establishing the safety of new materials. To ensure continued progress, we have ongoing research programs to develop and validate alternatives. To our knowledge, P&G has invested more money and assigned more top scientists to develop alternative methods than any other corporation in the U.S. Since 1986, the Company has spent nearly $14.5 million.

The development of alternative test methods should be a priority for everyone who has a stake in this issue.

Procter & Gamble will continue to devote the effort and commitment needed to achieve further progress. We invite others and scientific resources to foster further advances. This is the way real progress will be made.

ANIMAL RIGHTS DEMONSTRATIONS—*19/9/90*

NOTE:

The following statement may be used as either a written statement for distribution or as the basis for a recorded statement, depending on the situation at your location. Your on-site assessment of the situation is important for determining the appropriate way to respond.

When you are dealing with the media, please keep the following in mind:

1. Your location does not conduct animal testing, so there is no reason for you to be the media's expert. Stick to the scripted statement. Should you be pressed for details, remind them that your location does not conduct testing and ask them to contact Cincinnati for additional details. You are not obligated to respond to a question just because someone asks it.

   Refer inquiries for further information to:
   Linda L. Ulrey, (513) 983-5796
   William F. Dobson (513) 983-9546

2. Avoid specific mentions of the demonstrators. That is, do not mention the groups by name because that is exactly what they are seeking—further recognition and publicity for themselves.

3. Avoid activist bashing. Do not refer to their campaign or efforts in any way that could be construed as derogatory. Communicate facts that will allow listeners and readers to make intelligent, informed deci-

sions. Bashing reduces our credibility and has potential to create a backlash.

STRICTLY CONFIDENTIAL

1990 ANIMAL TESTING QUESTIONS & ANSWERS

1Q. If companies like Avon/Revlon/Dial/Amway can eliminate animal testing, why can't P&G?

1A. Any company that is concerned about the safety of its products must rely heavily on safety information based on animal research. Some companies use only a limited range of the materials that have been previously safety tested on animals. Others require the material supplier to conduct the testing for them. We do these things as well.

However, these companies are not like P&G—they are not the innovators in solving consumer problems, they do not formulate entirely new materials to respond to changing consumer needs. Certainly, use of material[s] that already have established safety information requires no further animal research. But, when we develop new materials whether for drugs or consumer products, we have the ultimate responsibility for assuring the new material is safe for consumer use. It's a scientific fact that non-animal alternatives are not available yet to adequately assure product safety. We will use the most appropriate methods to assure safety even if it involves some animal research.

2Q. If P&G was really concerned about reducing animal use, it would not have opposed the California legislation which would have banned any animal eye and skin tests including the Draize eye test.

2A.  When we see ill advised legislation being proposed,
we will oppose it, and the California legislation was
clearly in this category. Reducing the use of animals
in research requires scientific solutions not legislative ones.

We were not alone in our belief that this legislation
was ill advised. At least 70 other organizations and
corporations opposed the bill including the U.S.
Food and Drug Administration, the California Department of Health Services, California Poison Control Centers, California Medical Association,
Johnson & Johnson, Mary Kay cosmetics, ARCO
and Chevron. Ultimately, the Governor did not sign
the bill saying, "There is not consensus in the
scientific community that non-animal testing could
adequately protect the health of consumers for all
products covered by the bill. Thus it is inappropriate
to criminalize the performance of these tests...."

3Q.  Why doesn't P&G disclose its animal use numbers to
the public?

3A.  Such emphasis and focus on numbers exercises
serves no practical purpose in reducing animal use.
Comparisons of specific numbers from one year to
the next offers no meaningful measure of the Company's commitment to the development and use of
alternatives. In fact, it is a disservice because it
takes attention away from the science of alternatives
where real progress can be made.

For example, the search for alternatives itself can
cause the number of animals to be inflated. Just last
year almost half of the animals we used testing
personal care and household cleaning products were
devoted to alternative test development. Animals are
required to confirm that new alternative methods
are productive and useful. If P&G had not invested

heavily in alternatives research and new product innovation, our use of animals for the past several years would have been even further reduced.

Finally,we have seen the numbers released by companies misrepresented or selectively used to support the views of those presenting them. This has not clarified the issue whatsoever. Instead, it has lead (sic) to further misunderstanding and criticism.

4Q. Aren't P&G's plans to form an animal testing coalition inconsistent with the message it usually conveys about moving away from use of animals?

4A. No. The primary goal for the coalition concept is education. We regularly hear from consumers who have questions about animal testing and many have some misunderstandings. An education program is a natural outgrowth of these information requests. Industry, in general, needs to provide more information about its use of animal and non-animal studies to ensure human health and safety. Our interest in an education program in no way changes our commitment to developing alternative testing techniques.

5Q. Recent coalition publicity indicated you will be spending $17.5 million on a national education program. Why don't you spend that money on alternatives research?

5A. First, P&G never had plans to spend $17.5 million—that preliminary number was a total 3-year budget projection supported by all coalition members. Any other representation is false and misleading.

Secondly, P&G's commitment to alternatives development—in terms of time, money and effort—is and will continue to be very substantial. Over the past four years, we have devoted $14.5 million to alternatives development and nearly $4.5 million in the last fiscal year alone. In June, 1989, a new university grant research program was announced which provides additional funding of up to $450,000 annually for alternative methods development.

6Q. Why does P&G perform tests on animals for product safety when not required by law?

6A. P&G has a moral and legal responsibility for ensuring that all its products are safe for intended use and foreseeable accidental misuse. We need to know if a product can harm a child and thus not be marketed, and we need to know the appropriate first aid procedure if a product is accidentally ingested or spilled.

The federal government has direct and indirect requirements for product safety and efficacy testing. In order for many new products to receive approval for marketing, data must be available demonstrating the product's safety and efficacy. In a majority of the cases, animal testing is needed to meet those requirements. To date no regulatory agency, state or federal, has confirmed the use of alternative test methods.

Here is an excerpt from a 6/13/90 letter James S. Benson, Acting Commissioner of the Food and Drug Administration sent to California just prior to the Governor's veto of legislation that would have made the conduct of an animal test (Draize eye test) a crime:

> "The use of animal tests by industry to establish the safety of regulated products is necessary to minimize the risks from such products to humans."

7Q. Does P&G use the Draize rabbit eye test?

7A. No. Instead, when it is necessary to obtain eye data, we use a low volume alternative developed by P&G scientists. The test uses one-tenth the amount of test substance required in the Draize method. Importantly, the low volume test simulates more closely what happens when humans accidentally get product into their eye. These changes result in significantly less stress in the test animal and predict more accurately the eye irritation responses humans might experience.

P&G also actively supports in-house and outside research efforts to identify *in vitro* alternatives to eye irritation tests. At this time, there is no validated *in vitro* test systems which alone can provide the information needed to judge potential hazard to human eyes.

8Q. Does P&G obtain animals from pounds or from sources who could have stolen them.

8A. No. P&G does not use pound or stolen animals in research. (P&G uses animals specifically bred for research and testing unless they are animals such as farm animals which are not specifically bred for research purposes. This applies to all P&G research and testing conducted in-house or at contract labs.)

9Q. Do animals get pain killers if the experiment causes pain?

9A. Animals are anesthetized or given pain-relieving drugs when possible. Only in those tests where the painkilling drugs will interfere with getting meaningful results from the study, and research continues into drugs and treatments to help alleviate the effects of arthritis, headaches, etc.

# APPENDIX G

## HOW TO REACH GRASS ROOTS ORGANIZATIONS

*ART UPDATE*
Americans for Responsible
  Television
Box 627
Bloomfield Hills, Michigan
  48303

EDF Letter
Environmental Defense
  Fund
257 Park Ave. South
New York, New York 10010

*Earth First!*
P.O. Box 83
Canyon, California 94716

*Extra!*
Fairness & Accuracy in
  Reporting
130 W. 25th St.
New York, New York 10001

*Greenpeace*
P.O. Box 3720
Washington, D.C.
  20077-7880

*AARP Bulletin*
3200 E. Carson St.
Lakewood, California
  90712

*Everyone's Backyard*
Citizens' Clearinghouse for
  Hazardous Wastes
Box 926
Arlington, Virginia 22216

*Global Pesticide Monitor*
Pesticide Action Network
965 Mission St.
San Francisco, California
  94103

*Sea Shepherd*
Box 7000-S
Redondo Beach, California
  90277

*World Rivers Review*
301 Broadway, Suite B
San Francisco, California
  94133

*In House*
Newsletter for Center for
  Investigative Reporting
530 Howard St., 2nd Floor
San Francisco, California
  94105

*International Barometer*
1025 Connecticut Ave.,
  N.W.
Suite 707
Washington, D.C. 20036

*Newsletter*
Hand Gun Control Inc.
1235 Eye Street, N.W.
  Suite 1100
Washington, D.C. 20005

*PETA News*
People for Ethical
  Treatment of Animals
Box 42516
Washington, D.C. 20015

*World Rainforest Report*
301 Broadway, Suite A
San Francisco, California
  94133

*Newsline*
Natural Resources Defense
  Council
40 West 20th St.
New York, New York 10011

*Perspective*
In Defense of Animals
21 Tamal Vista Blvd.
Corte Madera, California
  94925

*MADD in Action*
669 Airport Freeway
Suite 310
Hurst, Texas 76053

*RID-USA, Inc. National
  Newsletter*
Box 520
Schenectady, New York
  12301

# NOTES

## Introduction

[1]Alexis de Tocqueville, *Democracy in America*, Edited by J.P. Mayer, vol. I (Garden City: Anchor Books, 1969), p. 411.

[2]Rachel Carson, *Silent Spring* (Boston: Houghton Mifflin, 1979).

[3]Frank Graham, Jr., *Since Silent Spring* (Boston: Houghton Mifflin, 1970).

[4]"Hunting Bears" (editorial), *San Francisco Chronicle*, August 20, 1989.

[5]Natural Resources Defense Council, *Annual Report*, Washington D.C., 1986–87.

[6]Gregg Easterbrook, "Cleaning Up Our Mess," *Newsweek*, July 24, 1989, pp. 38–40.

[7]Howard and Marion Higman, interview with author, July 24–25, 1989.

[8]Noam Chomsky, *Necessary Illusions* (Boston: South End Press, 1989), p. 136.

## Chapter 1:   The Beginnings

[1]Lois Marie Gibbs, *Love Canal: My Story* (Albany: State University of New York Press, 1982); Marsha Manatt, *Parents, Peers and Pot* (Washington, D.C.: U.S. Department of Health, Education and Welfare, 1979); "A Mother's Crusade," *Organic Gardening*, April 1989, pp. 32–37; Larry Kramer, *Report from the Holocaust* (New York: St. Martin's Press, 1989).

[2]Lois M. Gibbs, interview with author, September 12, 1989.

[3]Ibid.

[4]Marsha Manatt, *Parents, Peers, and Pot*, pp. 23–4.

[5]The national membership organization was the National Federation of Parents for Drug Free Youth (NFP). The national resource organization is Parent Resource Institute for Drug Education (PRIDE).

[6]Larry Kramer, *Reports from the Holocaust*, pp. 162–63.

[7]David Leavitt, "The Way I Live Now," *New York Times Magazine*, July 1989, p. 28.

[8]Larry Kramer, *Reports from the Holocaust*, pp. 141–43.

[9]Larry Kramer, interview with author, August 15, 1989.

[10]Randy Shilts, interview with author, August 21, 1989.

[11]Paula Spann, "Getting Militant About AIDS," *Washington Post*, March 28, 1989, p. 1 (Style).

[12]Randy Shilts, interview with author, August 21, 1989.

[13]Philip J. Hilts, "Wave of Protests Developing on Profits From AIDS Drug," *New York Times*, September 15, 1989, p. 8.

[14]"Avoid ACT UP, Sullivan Tells Health Department," *San Francisco Chronicle*, June 17, 1990, p. 1.

[15]Ibid.

[16]Anne W. Garland, *For Our Kids' Sake* (Washington, D.C.: Natural Resources Defense Council, 1989).

[17]"Mothers and Others Support Legislation," *Newsline*, Natural Resources Defense Council, New York, vol. 7, no. 2, May/June 1989 p. 1.

[18]Joseph H. Highland, et al., *Malignant Neglect* (New York: Alfred A. Knopf, 1979).

[19]Ibid. p. 207.

[20]James McCullagh, "A Mother's Crusade," *Organic Gardening*, April 1989, pp. 32–37.

[21]Ibid., p. 36.

[22]Anne W. Garland, *For Our Kids' Sake.*

[23]Paul Allen, interview with author, August 17, 1989.

[24]"Yeutter Defends Aid for Apple Industry," *San Francisco Chronicle*, May 24, 1989.

[25]"Alar Banned Immediately in Some Foods," *San Francisco Chronicle*, March 20, 1989, p. 8.

[26]Elliot Diringer, "New Cancer Cluster in Farm Town," *San Francisco Chronicle*, September 14, 1989, p. 1.

[27]Sally Ann Cornell, "And the Children Keep on Dying," *San Francisco Chronicle*, June 10, 1990, p. 4.

[28]Ibid.

[29]James McCullagh, "A Mother's Crusade," *Organic Gardening*, April 1989, p. 35.

[30]Keith Schneider, "Weaning Chemical Use: Seeds of Revolt on Farms," *New York Times*, September 10, 1989, p. 1.

## Chapter 2:  Grass Roots Tactics

[1]Charles A. Madison, *Critics and Crusaders* (New York: Henry Holt and Company, 1947–48), p. 181.

[2]Tom Regan, *The Struggle for Animal Rights* (Clark's Summit, Pa.: International Society for Animal Rights, 1987), p. 176.

[3]Robert L. Taylor, *Vessel of Wrath* (New York: New American Library, 1966), p. 325.

[4]"Perspective," Memorandum from Committee for Protection of Animal Subjects (Berkeley: University of California), October 31, 1986.

[5]"Activists Set New Heights for Animal Rights," *Perspective*, vol. 4, no. 1, Corte Madera, Ca.: In Defense of Animals, pp. 8–9.

[6]Dr. Elliot Katz, interview with author, July 5, 1989.

[7]Sam Howe Verhouck, "Nuclear Dump Plan Ignites Protests," *New York Times*, September 20, 1989, p. 9.

[8]"Anti-Abortion Group Fined $110,000 for Clinic Blocking," *San Francisco Chronicle*, May 1, 1989, p. 1.

[9]Sue Hutchinson and James Baker, "The Right to Life Shock Troops," *Newsweek*, May 1, 1989, p. 32.

[10]"High Court Upholds Sharp State Limits on Abortions," *New York Times,* July 3, 1989, p. 1.

[11]"A Squawk Over Logging," *San Francisco Chronicle,* May 3, 1989, p. 4.

[12]Dick Russell, "The Monkeywrenchers," *Crossroads: Environmental Priorities For the Future,* ed. Peter Borrelli (Washington: Island Press, 1988), p. 27.

[13]Jim Robbins, "Saboteurs for a Better Environment," *New York Times,* June 3, 1989, p. 10.

[14]Dick Russell, "The Monkeywrenchers."

[15]"Earth First Co-Founder Quitting to Start New Group," *San Francisco Chronicle,* August 16, 1990, p. A24.

[16]Jayne Garrison, "Compound Q Tests Serve as a Challenge to FDA," *San Francisco Examiner,* July 2, 1989, p. 1.

[17]"How Compound Q Trials Went Private in S.F.," *San Francisco Chronicle,* June 28, 1989, p. A8.

[18]Gina Kolata, "Critics Fault Secret Effort to Test AIDS Drug," *New York Times,* July 2, 1989, p. B7.

[19]Marsha Manatt, *Parents, Peers, and Pot II* (Washington, D.C.: Department of Health and Human Services, 1983), pp. 41–58.

[20]"Send It Back," *Action Bulletin* no. 22 (Arlington, Va.,: Citizen's Clearinghouse for Hazardous Wastes, April 1989), p. 2.

[21]Matthew L. Wald, "Rockwell Threatens to Close Nuclear Weapons Plan," *New York Times,* September 16, 1989, p. 10.

[22]Marsha Manatt, *Parents, Peers and Pot II,* pp. 84–102.

[23]Peter Singer, *Animal Liberation* (New York: Avon Books, 1975).

[24]Edward Abbey, *The Monkey Wrench Gang* (New York: Avon, 1975).

[25]Marsha Manatt, *Parents, Peers, and Pot.*

[26]Peter Borrelli et al., *Crossroads: Environmental Priorities for the Future* (Washington, D.C.: Island Press, 1988).

[27] Ibid., xiv.

[28] "Coming Full Circle," Workbook, Environmental Defense Fund, New York, 1988.

[29] Randy Hayes, interview with author, August 11, 1989.

[30] Ibid.

[31] "Boycott Ended! Burger King Follows Through," Press release, Rainforest Action Network, San Francisco, November 16, 1988.

[32] Ingrid Newkirk, interview with author, August 18, 1989.

[33] Douglas McGill, "Cosmetics Companies Quietly Ending Animal Tests," *New York Times*, August 1, 1989, p. 1.

[34] "Avon Stalling," *PETA News*, Washington, D.C., July/August 1989, p. 9.

[35] "International Benetton Boycott," *PETA News*, Washington, D.C., January/February 1989, pp. 8–9.

[36] "PETA History: Compassion in Action," Fact Sheet no. 2, People for the Ethical Treatment of Animals, Washington, D.C.

[37] Jerry Roberts and Susan Yoachum, "Some Say Initiative Process Is a Mess," *San Francisco Chronicle*, August 10, 1990, p. A8.

[38] "California Judge Rules Telephone Notice on Toxic Products Is Inadequate," *New York Times*, August 28, 1989, p. 9.

[39] Elliot Diringer, "800 Number For Toxic Facts Isn't Working Out, Judge Says," *San Francisco Chronicle*, August 28, 1989, p. A18.

[40] Tom Huntington, interview with author, June 28, 1989.

[41] John L. Thomas, *The Liberator* (Boston: Little, Brown & Co., 1963), pp. 222–23

[42] Annetta Miller, Mary Hager, Betsy Roberts, "The Elderly Duke It Out," *Newsweek*, September 11, 1989, pp. 42–43.

[43] Martin Tolchin, "How the New Medicare Law Fell on Hard Times in a Hurry," *New York Times*, October, 1989, p. 1.

[44] "Legal Limits Harsh," *San Francisco Chronicle*, September 15, 1989, p. A21.

[45]Susan Rich, interview with author, August 18, 1989.

[46]Ibid.

[47]Patricia Gallagher, "Firms Facing a Spreading Animals Rights Fight," *Cincinnati Enquirer*, October 23, 1988, p. 1.

[48]Ibid.

[49]Karen Tumulty and Martha Groves, "Exxon Stockholders Debate the Oil Spill," *Los Angeles Times* and *San Francisco Chronicle*, May 19, 1989, p. A6.

[50]Ibid.

[51]*New York Times*/CBS News Poll, *New York Times*, September 17, 1989.

[52]Tod Ensign, interview with author, August 14, 1989.

[53]Bobby Muller, interview with author, August 17, 1989.

[54]Norman Melnick, "Agent Orange Cases Ordered Re-Evaluated," *San Francisco Examiner*, May 9, 1989, p. 1.

[55]Ibid.

[56]Harriet Chiang, "Exxon Sued In Behalf of Alaskan Wildlife Caught in Oil Spill," *San Francisco Chronicle*, August 18, 1989, p. A16.

[57]Tom Huntington, interview with author, June 28, 1989.

[58]W.E.B. DuBois, *John Brown* (New York: International Publishers, 1909).

[59]Ibid.

[60]Charles A. Madison, *Critics and Crusaders* (New York: Henry Holt and Co., 1947–48), p. 48.

[61]W.E.B. DuBois, *John Brown*, p. 299.

[62]Ibid., p. 56.

[63]Robert Lewis Taylor, *Vessel of Wrath* (New York: New American Library, 1966).

[64]Ibid., p. 118.

[65]"ALF Oregon Raid," *PETA News*, Spring 1987, p. 8.

[66]Jim Robbins, "Saboteurs for a Better Environment," *New York Times*, June 16, 1990.

## Chapter 3:   The Opposition: Its Tactics

[1]"AMA Animal Research Action Plan," Xerox copy, June 1989.

[2]"Reflections Following the 9/28/87 Meeting on the Animal Rights' Movement," Memorandum, Department of Health and Human Services, September 29, 1987.

[3]"Article: 'The Secret of NIH's Comments,'" Letter, National Institute of Health, Washington, D.C., June 12, 1989.

[4]"The Corporate Hypocrisy Award," *News Briefs*, In Defense of Animals, Fall 1990, p. 16.

[5]Barry Commoner, "The Environment," *Crossroads: Environmental Priorities For the Future*, ed. Peter Borrelli (Washington: Island Press, 1988), p. 162.

[6]Will Collette, "The Polluters' Secret Plan," Citizen's Clearinghouse for Hazardous Wastes, Arlington, Va., June 1989, p. 4.

[7]Ibid., p. 14.

[8]Ibid., p. 19.

[9]Jerome Cramer, B. Russell Leavitt, J. Madeline Nash, "They Lied To Us," *Time*, October 31, 1988, pp. 60–65.

[10]Will Collette, "The Polluters' Secret Plan," pp. 21–23.

[11]Charles Hillinger and Mark Stein, "Vegetarian Terrorists Ride Herd on Ranchers," *Los Angeles Times*, November, 19, 1989, p. 1.

[12]Ibid., p. 32.

[13]"Archie McPuff: No Joke," Action Bulletin no. 23, Citizen's Clearinghouse for Hazardous Wastes, Arlington, Va., 1989, pp. 1–2.

[14]"McToxics Retrospective," *Everyone's Backyard*, Citizens's Clearinghouse for Hazardous Wastes, Arlington, Va., August 1990, pp. 4–6.

[15]Ibid., p. 4.

[16]John Holusha, "Packaging and Public Image: McDonald's Fills a Big Order," *New York Times*, November 2, 1990, p. A1.

[17]"Group Seeking Curbs on Disposable Diaper Use," *Colorado Daily*, Boulder, Colo., July 25–28, 1989, p. 1.

[18]Michael deCouray Hinds, "Buried Under a Ton of Diapers," *San Francisco Chronicle*, December 25, 1988, p. 3.

[19]Elliot Diringer, "Cloth Diaper Supply Drying Up," *San Francisco Chronicle*, May 22, 1989, p. A11.

[20]Jonathan Yardley, "On Diapers and Other Disposables," *Washington Post*, June 26, 1989, p. B2.

[21]"A Plan to Recycle Disposable Diapers," *San Francisco Chronicle*, October 3, 1979, p. 1.

[22]Marla Williams, "The Reincarnation of Disposable Diapers," *San Francisco Chronicle*, July 5, 1990, p. A6.

[23]"Plastic Industry Grasps for Straws," *Everyone's Backyard*, Citizen's Clearinghouse for Hazardous Wastes, Arlington, Va., vol. 8, no. 1, p. 6.

[24]Anne W. Garland, *For Our Kids' Sake*, Natural Resources Defense Council, Washington, D.C., 1989, pp. 21–25.

[25]Michael Weisskopf, "Five Chains to Phase Out Produce Treated With Carcinogenic Pesticides," *Washington Post*, September 12, 1989, p. A16.

[26]Robert Burns, "U.S. Knew in 1948 of A-Plant's Risks," *San Francisco Chronicle*, July 14, 1990, p. A2.

[27]Ibid., p. A2.

[28]Tom Bailie, "For a Nuclear Guinea Pig, the Unusual Was the Usual," *San Francisco Chronicle*, July 15, 1990, p. A16.

[29]For a complete review of these acts, see *Freedom of Information Guide*, Washington D.C., WANT Publishing Company, 1984.

[30]Natural Resources Defense Council, *Annual Report*, Washington, D.C., 1986–87.

[31]Randy Shilts, *And the Band Played On* (New York: St. Martin's Press, 1987).

[32]Ibid., p. 397.

[33]Randy Shilts, *And the Band Played On.*

[34]"Apple Growers Say They'll Stop Using Alar by Fall," *San Francisco Chronicle*, May 16, 1989, p. 1.

[35]"Rules for Lab Animals Spark Controversy," *Washington Post*, October 3, 1989, p. B6.

[36]"Program to Label Environmentally Safe Products," *San Francisco Chronicle*, April 3, 1990, p. A5.

## Chapter 4:   Media: The Trade-offs

[1]Martin A. Lee and Norman Solomon, *Unreliable Sources: A Guide to Detecting Bias in News Media* (New York: Lyle Stuart, 1990), p. 340.

[2]Gaye Tuchman, *The TV Establishment* (Englewood Cliffs, N.J.: Prentice-Hall, 1974), p. 11.

[3]Ibid., p. 341.

[4]Douglas C. McGill, "Cosmetics Companies Quietly Ending Animal Tests," *New York Times*, August 1, 1989, p. 1.

[5]Frederick P. Sutherland, "The Owl Is Not the Problem," *San Francisco Chronicle*, August 27, 1989, p. A17.

[6]John Holusha, "McDonald's Acts to Recycle Plastic," *New York Times*, October 16, 1989, p. C1.

[7]Elliot Diringer, "Loggers Say They're Endangered, Owl Isn't," *San Francisco Chronicle*, October 16, 1989, p. 1.

[8]Martin A. Lee and Norman Solomon, *Unreliable Sources*, p. 345.

[9]Lois Marie Gibbs, *Love Canal: My Story* (Albany: State University of New York Press, 1982), p. 87.

[10]Larry Kramer, *Reports from the Holocaust* (New York: St. Martin's Press, 1989), p. 145.

[11]Ibid.

[12]Martin A. Lee and Norman Solomon, *Unreliable Sources*, pp. 350–54.

[13]Sheldon Marcus, *Father Coughlin* (Boston: Little Brown, 1973), p. 37.

[14]David Bennett, *Demagogues in the Depression* (New Brunswick: Rutgers University Press, 1969), p. 60.

[15]George Gerbner, interview with author, August 15, 1989.

[16]Paula Spann, "The Woman Who Took on Trash," *Washington Post*, November 1, 1989, p. B1.

[17]Michael Dougan, " 'Married' to Viewers' Tastes," *San Francisco Examiner*, October 5, 1989, p. D3.

[18]Ibid.

[19]"Sponsor Boycotts—More Support Than the Professionals Expected," *ART Update*, (Bloomfield Hills, Michigan), Spring 1990.

[20]Todd Gitlin, *The Whole World Is Watching* (Berkeley and Los Angeles: University of California Press, 1980), p. 292.

## Chapter 5: Inside the Organization

[1]Marsha Manatt, *Parents, Peers, and Pot II*, (Washington, D.C.: Department of Health and Human Services, 1983), p. 38.

[2]Ibid., pp. 147–52.

[3]"National Youth Drug Education Programs," Office of Inspector General, Department of Health and Human Services, New York Region, 1988, p. 19.

[4]"Stopping Drugs: Part II," Frontline, WGBH-TV, Boston, Mass., February 1987.

[5]Matthew Wald, "Energy Department to Pay $73 Million to Settle Uranium Case in Ohio," *New York Times*, July 1, 1989, p. 1.

[6]Jerome Kramer, Russell Leavitt, Madeleine Nash, "They Lied to Us," *Time*, October 31, 1988, pp. 60–65.

[7]Anne Witte Garland, *For Our Kids' Sake* (Washington, D.C.: Natural Resources Defense Council, 1989).

[8]Lois Marie Gibbs, *Love Canal: My Story* (Albany: State University of New York Press, 1982), pp. 12–15.

[9]Bobby Muller, interview with author, August 17, 1989.

[10]Tom Regan, *The Struggle for Animal Rights* (Clark's Summit, Pa.: International Society for Animal Rights, 1987), p. 123.

[11]John L. Taylor, *The Liberator* (Boston: Little, Brown, 1963), pp. 93–96.

[12]Bobby Muller, interview with author, August 17, 1989.

[13]Dick Russell, "The Monkeywrenchers," *Crossroads: Environmental Priorities for the Future*, ed. Peter Borrelli (Washington, D.C.: Island Press, 1988), p. 46.

[14]"ACT UP Forms Coalition with Homeless Advocates," *San Francisco Chronicle*, August 16, 1990, p. 8.

[15]"Compassionate Living," People for the Ethical Treatment of Animals, Washington, D.C., 1988, pp. 12–13.

[16]George Snyder, "Report of Revolt and Defections Among MADD Volunteers," *San Francisco Chronicle*, March 17, 1990, p. A7.

[17]"Watchdog Watch," *Chronicle of Philanthropy* (Washington D.C.), May 15, 1990, p. 30.

[18]"Dissidents Question the Ties Between Fund Raising and the Charity 'Mothers Against Drunk Driving,'" *Chronicle of Charity*, May 2, 1989, pp. 21–23.

[19]"More State Chapters May Leave MADD," *Mobile Register*, May 2, 1989, p. 6.

[20]"MADD Troubles Continue in Alabama," *Mobile Press*, July 4, 1989, p. 9A.

[21]Ibid.

[22]Thomas Adams, Hank Resnick, Joan Brann, and Linda Wiltz, "Stop Drug Abuse Before It Starts," *The Just Say No Handbook*, Pacific Institute for Research and Evaluation, (Walnut Creek, CA., August 1985).

[23]David Bennett, *Demagogues in the Depression: American Radicals and the Union Party, 1932–36* (New Brunswick: Rutgers University Press, 1989), p. 66.

[24]Will Collette, "The Polluters' Secret Plan," Citizen's Clearinghouse For Hazardous Wastes, Arlington, Va., 1989, p. 30.

[25]Elizabeth Fernandez, "Abortion Activists Square Off," *San Francisco Examiner*, July 10, 1989, p. Al.

[26]Stephanie Salter, "A Spy Goes Inside Operation Rescue," *San Francisco Examiner*, July 17, 1989, p. A19.

## Chapter 6:  The Challenge and the Future

[1]Edward Abbey, *The Monkey Wrench Gang* (New York: Avon, 1975), p. 158.

[2]Marsha Manatt, interview with author, August 1977.

[3]Tom Wicker, "Power of the People," *New York Times*, July 18, 1984, Editorial page.

[4]Geoffrey Cowley, "An Electromagentic Storm," *Newsweek*, July 10, 1989, p. 77.

[5]Associated Press, "EPA Study Links Some Cancers, Magnetic Fields," *San Francisco Chronicle*, December 14, 1990, p. A16.

[6]Sidney Wolfe, "Worst Pills, Best Pills," Public Citizen Health Research Group, Washington, D.C., 1988.

[7]"Nursing Homes Need Kindly Hands," *Modern Maturity*, December 1989–January 1990, p. 100.

[8]Melinda Beck, "The Geezer Boom," *Newsweek*, Winter/Spring Special Edition, 1989, pp. 62–68.

[9]"Housing Fund Cuts Assailed," *San Francisco Chronicle*, July 16, 1989, p. A8.

[10]Peter Kilborn, "Workplace Injuries Rising, and the Computer Is Blamed," *New York Times*, November 16, 1989, p. A21.

[11]"New Jersey Approves Tough Assault Gun Law," *San Francisco Chronicle*, May 18, 1990, p. A6.

[12]Charles Wolfe, "Massacre Creates Gun Control Activists," *Los Angeles Times*, November 19, 1989, p. A30.

[13]"Brady's Gun Control Message," *San Francisco Chronicle*, November 1989, p. A4.

[14]Thor Heyerdahl, *The RA Expeditions*, (Garden City: Doubleday & Co., 1971), pp. 209–10.

[15]Maria Goodavage, "Murky Waters," *Modern Maturity*, August-September 1989, pp. 44–50.

[16]Jerry Howard, "The Lobster Man," *Modern Maturity*, August-September 1989, p. 50.

# SELECT BIBLIOGRAPHY

Abbey, Edward. *The Monkey Wrench Gang.* New York: Avon Books, 1975.

Bennett, David. *Demagogues in the Depression.* New Brunswick, N.J.: Rutgers University Press, 1969.

Borrelli, Peter, et al. *Crossroads: Environmental Priorities for the Future.* Washington, D.C.: Island Press, 1988.

Carson, Rachael. *Silent Spring.* Boston: Houghton-Mifflin, 1962.

Chomsky, Noam. *Necessary Illusions.* Boston: South End Press, 1989.

DuBois, W. E. B. *John Brown.* New York: International Publishers, 1909.

Garland, Anne W. *For Our Kids' Sake.* Washington, D.C.: Natural Resources Defense Fund, 1989.

Gibbs, Lois M. *Love Canal: My Story.* Albany: University of New York Press, 1982.

Gitlin, Todd. *The Whole World Is Watching.* Berkeley and Los Angeles: University of California Press, 1980.

Graham, Frank Jr. *Since Silent Spring.* Boston: Houghton-Mifflin, 1970.

351

Heyerdahl, Thor. *The RA Expedition.* Garden City: Doubleday, 1971.

Highland, Joseph, and Fine, Marcia. *Malignant Neglect.* New York: Knopf, 1979.

Kramer, Larry. *Reports from the Holocaust.* New York: St. Martin's Press, 1989.

Lee, Martin A., and Solomon, Norman. *Unreliable Sources: A Guide to Detecting Bias in News Media.* New York: Lyle Stuart, 1990.

Madison, Charles A. *Critics and Crusaders.* New York: Henry Holt, 1942-1948.

Manatt, Marsha. *Parents, Peers and Pot II.* Washington, D.C. Department of Health and Human Services, 1983.

Marcus, Sheldon. *Father Coughlin.* Boston: Little Brown, 1969.

Regan, Tom. *The Struggle for Animal Rights.* Clark's Summit, Pa.: International Society for Animal Rights, 1987.

Shilts, Randy. *And the Band Played On.* New York: St. Martin's Press, 1987.

Singer, Peter. *Animal Liberation.* New York: Avon Books, 1975.

Taylor, Robert L. *Vessels of Wrath.* New York: New American Library, 1966.

Tocqueville, Alexis de. *Democracy in America*, edited by J. P. Mayer. Garden City: Anchor Books, 1969.

Tuchman, Gaye. *The TV Establishment.* Englewood Cliffs, N.J.: Prentice-Hall, 1974.

Uhl, Michael, and Ensign, Tod. *G.I. Guinea Pigs.* New York: Playboy Press, 1980.

# Index

353